Excel Programming
Weekend Crash Course®

Peter G. Aitken

WILEY

Wiley Publishing, Inc.

Excel Programming Weekend Crash Course®

Published by
Wiley Publishing, Inc.
909 Third Avenue
New York, NY 10022
www.wiley.com

Copyright © 2003 by Wiley Publishing, Inc., Indianapolis, Indiana. All rights reserved.

Library of Congress Cataloging-in-Publication Data: 2003101920

ISBN: 0-7645-4062-9

Manufactured in the United States of America

10 9 8 7 6 5 4 3 2

10/RR/QY/QT/IN

Published by Wiley Publishing, Inc., Indianapolis, Indiana
Published simultaneously in Canada

About the Author

Peter G. Aitken has been writing about computers and programming for over 10 years, with some 30 books as well as hundreds of magazine and trade publication articles to his credit. His recent book titles include *Visual Basic .NET Programming with Peter Aitken, Office XP Development with VBA, XML the Microsoft Way, Windows Script Host,* and *Teach Yourself Visual Basic .NET Internet Programming in 21 Days.* For several years he was a Contributing Editor at *Visual Developer Magazine* where he wrote a popular Visual Basic column. He is a regular contributor to *Microsoft OfficePro* magazine and the DevX Web site. Peter is the proprietor of PGA Consulting, providing custom application and Internet development to business, academia, and government since 1994.

Credits

Acquisitions Editor
Jim Minatel

Project Editor
Mark Enochs

Technical Editor
Ken Slovak

Copy Editor
Susan Hobbs

Permissions Editor
Laura Moss

Media Development Specialist
Travis Silvers

Project Coordinator
Maridee Ennis

Graphics and Production Specialists
Beth Brooks, Sean Decker, Carrie Foster,
Lauren Goddard, LeAndra Hosier,
Kristin McMullan, Lynsey Osborn

Quality Control Technicians
Laura Albert, John Tyler Connoley,
John Greenough, Andy Hollandbeck,
Carl William Pierce, Dwight Ramsey,
Charles Spencer

Proofreading and Indexing
TECHBOOKS Production Services

Preface

Microsoft Excel is a powerful spreadsheet program; in fact, it's the most widely used spreadsheet program worldwide, but Excel is a lot more than just a spreadsheet program. Unknown to many users, Excel is also a sophisticated platform for development of custom applications. Lurking behind its mild-mannered spreadsheet disguise is a powerful and full-featured programming language called Visual Basic for Applications (VBA). If you have recorded and played back an Excel macro, you have used VBA — perhaps without being aware of it.

There's much more to VBA programming than recording macros, however. Nearly any user can write VBA programs to perform a wide variety of tasks in Excel, ranging from the simple, such as automating financial calculations, to the complex, such as creating a data entry system with custom forms and data validation. Unfortunately, many users shy away from taking advantage of Excel's programmability because it seems too complicated, and they cannot find a good source of information to guide them through the learning process. Excel programming can be somewhat complicated, which is unavoidable for such a powerful tool, but the truth is that almost any reasonably computer-literate person can learn how to program in Excel. That's where this book comes in handy.

Who Should Read This Book

This book is aimed at anyone who wants to use programming to improve his or her Excel skills. Perhaps you only want to write programs for your own use, or maybe you need to create Excel programs for use by your coworkers. In either situation, this book is aimed at you. The book was written specifically with the nonspecialist in mind. You do not need to have any programming knowledge or experience to use this book because everything from square one is explained. Of course, if you do have some programming experience, it will not hurt, but the important point is that such experience is not required.

Weekend Crash Course Layout and Features

This book contains 30 sessions, each of which is designed to be completed in about 30 minutes. Each session has a review section at the end and a list of questions so you can test your knowledge. The sessions are organized into six parts; the main purpose of each part is to provide a convenient breaking point to help you in pacing your progress. At the end of each part, you'll find additional questions related to that part's session topics. The answers for the part review questions are provided in Appendix A.

Part I: Friday Evening

The first session provides an introduction to programming with Excel, including an overview of many of the advantages. You'll also find some basic information about programming in this session.

The second session teaches you how to use the VBA Code Editor. This tool is part of the Excel installation, and you use it to create, test, and run your programs.

Session 3 deals with the Excel Object Model. This is the set of tools that the Excel application makes available for you to use in your programs.

Session 4 introduces you to the VBA language, your primary tool for writing programs.

Part II: Saturday Morning

Sessions 5 through 9 cover the VBA language. You need a good knowledge of the VBA language's elements and syntax to write programs. This includes learning about operators, control constructs, procedures, and modules, as well as how to work with dates, times, and text. The final session in this part, Session 10, shows you how to work with Excel's ranges and selections.

Part III: Saturday Afternoon

Sessions 11 through 14 cover the fundamentals of controlling Excel through VBA code. You'll learn how to work with columns, rows, and cells; how to program with custom formulas and built-in functions; and how to format a worksheet. The last two sessions deal with find and replace operations and creating custom toolbars.

Part IV: Saturday Evening

Sessions 17 and 18 show you how to use Excel's powerful charting capabilities in your programs. Then Sessions 19 and 20 present the basics of creating custom dialog boxes for your programs with Excel's user forms.

Part V: Sunday Morning

Sessions 21 and 22 finish the coverage of user forms, including a complete example. Sessions 23 through 26 deal with the topics of Excel events, security considerations, and debugging distributing an application, and creating custom classes.

Part VI: Sunday Afternoon

The remaining sessions deal with a variety of topics, including runtime errors, database tasks, add-ins, and online help.

I recommend that you work through the sessions in order. At the very least you should complete Sessions 1 through 9 before branching off to other topics.

The Companion Web Site

On the book's companion Web site, you'll find code listings of sample programs and a self-assessment test, which consists of over 80 multiple-choice and true or false questions. Just go to www.wiley.com/compbooks/aitken.

Features

As I have mentioned, each session is designed to take about 30 minutes. It's not a race, however, so don't worry if it takes you a bit longer. It's what you learn that's important. The following time-status icons let you know how much progress you've made throughout each session.

30 Min.
To Go

20 Min.
To Go

10 Min.
To Go

Done!

The following icons identify bits of information that are set apart from the text:

A note is an important bit of information that you should know about.

A tip is a suggestion for an easier or faster way to do something when programming Excel.

This icon warns you of something you should never do.

This icon points you to other sessions where related material can be found.

Menu selections are indicated using the ⇨ symbol. Thus, File ⇨ Save means to open the File menu and then select the Save command.

Code and VBA keywords in the text are indicated by a special font `like this`. Code listings that are separate from the text are also in this font. Italics are used to indicate placeholders in code. Here's an example:

```
SaveAs filename
```

When you enter this code, you do not actually type *filename*. Rather, you replace *filename* with a specific filename as explained in the text.

Acknowledgments

I appreciate the efforts of all the people at Wiley who have helped make this book happen, in particular Acquisitions Editor, Jim Minatel and Project Editor, Mark Enochs. My thanks also go to Technical Editor, Ken Slovak, and the Copy Editor, Susan Hobbs.

Contents at a Glance

Contents

Excel Programming
Weekend Crash Course®

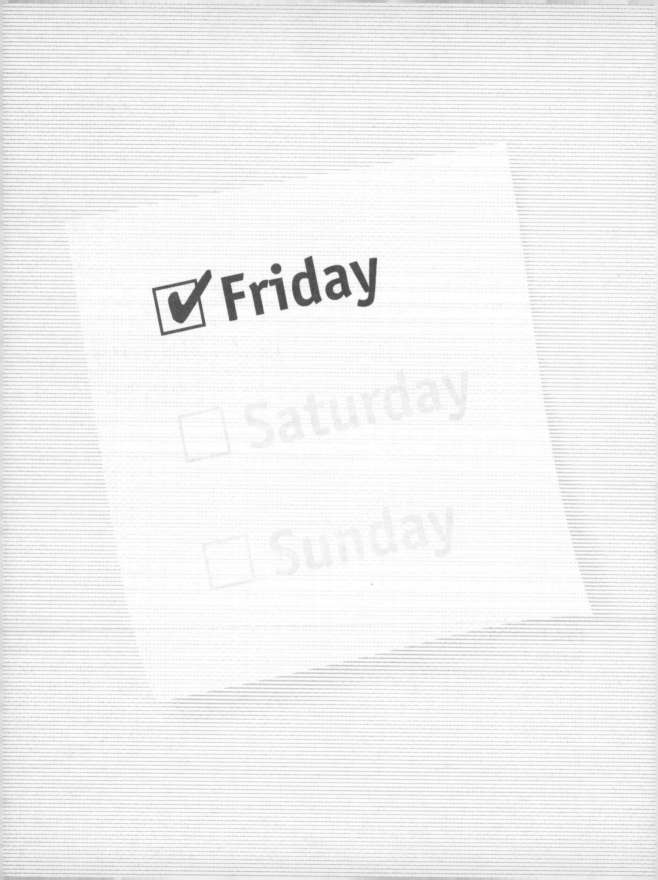

Part I — Friday Evening

PART

I

Friday Evening

Microsoft Excel Programming—Why and How

Session Checklist

✔ The advantages of Excel programming

✔ Fundamentals of programming

✔ The Excel object model

✔ Programming and macros

✔ Designing your custom application

✔ Your first Excel program

**30 Min.
To Go**

Most people think of Excel as merely a spreadsheet program, and with good reason — Excel *is* a spreadsheet program. As a spreadsheet program, Excel is a powerful application that provides a wide range of tools for the manipulation, analysis, and display of data. The majority of users never go beyond using Excel in this way — truth be told, many users have no need.

Under the surface, however, Excel is much more than an application program. It provides a sophisticated programming language that enables you to control any and all aspects of the program. Anything you can do with the keyboard and mouse you can also do with programming. For the power user, programming turns Excel into a flexible development tool for the creation of custom solutions to your data manipulation and analysis needs. This session takes a look at the advantages of Excel programming, and provides necessary background information on the technologies that are involved.

Advantages of Programming

Programming offers several important advantages to the Excel user. As mentioned earlier in this session, these advantages will not be relevant to all users, but they can apply to a surprisingly large percentage of situations.

Saving Time

Just about anything that a program can do in Excel can also be accomplished by a user with a keyboard and mouse. In a race, however, the program is always faster. Even if you are an expert user and do not need to spend any time figuring out how to perform the required tasks, a program will still beat you by a huge margin. What might take you half an hour to perform manually will be done in a few seconds by a program.

Reducing Errors

Even the most skilled typist hits the wrong key now and then, and every "mouse master" has been known to click the wrong button or command once in a while. In contrast, programs do not make mistakes — they are reliable servants, carrying out your commands over and over again with complete accuracy.

This is not to say that programs cannot contain errors. A program will do exactly what the programmer tells it to do; if your instructions are wrong or incomplete, the resulting program can cause errors. Dealing with program errors is an important topic, enough so that an entire session is devoted to it.

Enforcing Standards

In many organizations, adherence to data-processing standards is an important aspect of maximizing productivity. For example, each sales representative may be required to submit a weekly summary spreadsheet. If those spreadsheets all follow the same structure and format, it is fairly straightforward to automate the process of extracting data into a summary report. The slightest deviation from the proper format, however, is likely to throw a wrench into the gears. By using programming for the individual spreadsheets rather than manual data entry, you can ensure that there are no deviations from the correct spreadsheet format.

Integrating with Other Applications

Excel does not always work alone — it has the capability to share data and interact with other applications. These capabilities are most developed with, but not restricted to, other Microsoft Office applications. For example, an Excel program could use Outlook to create an e-mail message containing data from a spreadsheet and then send the message to a list of recipients. Programming is not required for Excel to interact with other programs, but it makes tasks possible that would be difficult or impractical to perform otherwise.

Programming Fundamentals

What exactly is programming? It's really not as mysterious as it may sound. Perhaps you already have some experience with computer programming of one sort of another. If not, this section gives you some background information about what programming is and how it works.

Creating Instructions

Programming is really nothing more than creating instructions that tell the computer what to do. In an office, for example, you might ask your assistant to make copies — that's an instruction. A computer program is the same — you tell the computer what to do. The primary difference is that computers are really dumb and can't figure out the fine points on their own, so you must tell them exactly what to do in excruciating detail. Explicit instructions are at the heart of any program.

Some instructions manipulate data. This can be as simple as adding two numbers, or as complex as creating a chart. Other instructions control the execution of the program itself. For example, a program could be designed to perform one task on weekdays and another task on weekends. Still other instructions control how the program interacts with the user, such as how it responds to the user's selections from a menu or dialog box.

Handling Data

Every computer program works with data. This data can come in many forms — text, numbers, and graphics — but for now you don't need to be concerned with these details. A fundamental part of programming consists of handling the data that the program uses. You need a specific place to keep the data, and you also need to be able to get at the data when necessary. From this perspective, data can be divided into two categories:

- **Data stored outside the program.** For the most part, this category comprises data that is stored in the cells of an Excel worksheet. Your program does not need to create storage for such data, although the program can read and write it.
- **Data stored within the program.** For data that is not stored elsewhere, a program needs to create a storage location. A program uses *variables* to store internal data. As you'll see in later sessions, Excel programming offers a wide range of internal data storage capabilities.

When you are programming with Excel, the data-handling capabilities available to you are quite impressive. They provide a variety of data types that are specialized for storing different kinds of data. You learn more about these data types in later sessions.

The VBA Language

You will use the VBA language to write Excel programs. VBA stands for Visual Basic for Applications, and it is one of the two essential parts of Excel programming. The name Visual Basic for Applications reflects the fact that VBA is based on Microsoft's Visual Basic programming language, and that it is designed for programming within applications — specifically, the applications that comprise the Microsoft Office suite (Excel, Word, Access, PowerPoint, and Outlook). VBA is relatively easy to learn, as programming languages go, but does not sacrifice power and flexibility.

The task of programming in VBA is simplified by the VBA Editor, which is part of your Excel installation. You can open the VBA Editor by pressing Alt+F11 when in Excel, or by selecting Tools ⇨ Macro ⇨ Visual Basic Editor from the menu. The VBA Editor is shown in Figure 1-1. The blank window is where you enter your program's VBA code. Other elements in the Editor provide tools for organizing, running, and debugging your programs. Later sessions cover these features.

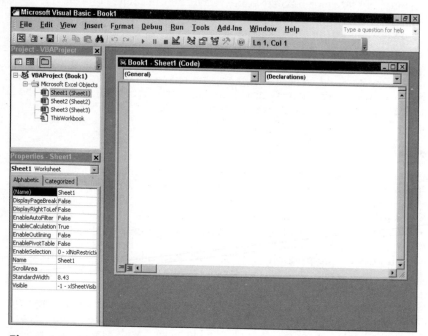

Figure 1-1   *The VBA Editor*

The Excel Object Model

20 Min.
To Go

The other essential component of Excel programming is the Excel object model. To understand the object model, it helps to have some background information about the inner workings of programs such as Excel.

Objects

As computer programming evolved over the years, programs have gotten more powerful and, unavoidably, more complicated. With increasing complexity came an increased possibility of errors, and programmers found themselves spending more and more time tracking down and fixing the causes of these errors. It soon became apparent that many, if not most, program errors were caused by unexpected and unintended interactions between various parts of a program. If a programmer could reduce or eliminate these interactions, errors would be drastically curtailed.

At the same time, programmers found themselves writing the same program functionality over and over again. Most Windows programs have a menu, for example, and programmers

Objects and Classes

You'll see the words *object* and *class* used in discussions of object-oriented programming, often interchangeably. Technically, they have different meanings. A class is a plan or definition, where an object is an implementation of that plan (sometimes called an *instance*). To use an analogy, the blueprints for a car would be the class, while an actual car built from those plans would be an object. You can create multiple objects from the same class.

would have to write the code for a menu from scratch for each new program. It would be much better if the code for a menu could be written once and then reused as needed in new programs.

These (and other) factors were the impetus behind the development of a programming technique called *object-oriented programming*, or OOP. With OOP, a program is viewed as a collection of related sections, or modules, that have different functions. Some of these modules are part of the program's interface, such as menus, toolbars, and dialog boxes. Other modules relate to the data with which the program works, such as (for Excel) workbooks, worksheets, and cells. Each of these modules is an object; see the "Objects and Classes" sidebar for more information on nomenclature.

OOP offers numerous advantages compared with older traditional methods of programming. These include:

- **Reduced errors.** By design, objects are self-contained units that are isolated from each other as much as possible. An object's interactions with the rest of the program are tightly controlled, and unintended interactions (and the resulting errors) are eliminated.
- **Code reuse.** An object — or more accurately, a class — is by its very nature reusable, not only in the same program, but in other programs as well.

Excel, as well as the other Office programs, was created using OOP techniques. Under the skin, therefore, Excel consists of a large collection of objects that work together to provide the program's functionality. You'll see how this relates to programming Excel in the next section.

Components and Automation

The objects that are part of the Excel application are written so that they are available to other programs. In computer talk, the objects are said to be *exposed*. This is part of the Component Object Model (COM) technology that is central to the Windows operating system itself as well as to most applications that run on Windows. The term *component* or *COM component* is used to refer to objects that are exposed in this manner; therefore, the objects that are exposed by Excel are sometimes referred to as components. Note that a single component may expose more than one class.

How does a programmer make use of exposed components? The answer is another COM technology called *automation* (called OLE — object linking and embedding — automation in the past). Automation permits an external program to access and control exposed components. Automation also permits components to interact with each other — for example, you could embed an Excel spreadsheet in a Word document. For the present purposes, automation permits a VBA program to use the Excel components. Other programming languages, such as C++ or Java, can use automation too, but that is not relevant here.

The COM components that your VBA programs can use exist as files on your hard disk and were installed as part of the Office or Excel installation. A component can operate in two ways:

- An automation client controls and makes use of classes exposed by other components.
- An automation server exposes classes for use by other components.

An automation component can act in one or both of these roles. For programming Excel, VBA is acting as a client, and the Excel components are acting as servers. Some Excel components act as clients to manipulate other components.

The result of this arrangement is that an Excel programmer has VBA, a powerful programming language, as well as access to all of the components that comprise the Excel application. This is an extremely powerful combination — Excel is your well-trained and capable servant, and VBA is the means you use to tell it what to do. The sum of all the components exposed by Excel is referred to as the Excel object model.

The Excel object model is covered in detail later in the book, primarily in Session 3.

Macros and Programming

If you have ever used Excel's macro feature, you have already done some Excel programming. A macro is a sequence of user actions that is recorded and can be played back later to duplicate the original actions. This saves time because you don't have to manually redo the steps each time. To record a macro, select Macro from Excel's Tools menu and then select Record New Macro. As you perform actions in Excel, they are translated into the corresponding VBA commands. When you stop the recording, the resulting VBA is saved and can be played back as needed. Recording macros can be a useful tool for the Excel programmer.

Recording macros is covered in more detail in Session 2.

Designing Your Custom Application

When creating a custom Excel program, as with all programming, it is important to do some planning before you start writing code. The importance of planning cannot be overemphasized. For a simple project it may take only a few minutes; for a large, complex project, it may take days. In either case it is going to save you time and hassles down the road.

Before you begin, make certain that you know what is needed. A lot of problems can arise when there is a misunderstanding between the client and the programmer. You may write a great program, but if it is not what the customer needs you have wasted your time! Don't assume that you know what is wanted — make sure, in detail.

After you know your goal, start planning the details of the program. For simple programs this step may be trivial because there is only one way to accomplish the desired ends. With more complex programs, you have choices to make. How many worksheets and workbooks will be needed? Will any user forms be required? How will the functionality be divided up? Should you define any classes for the project? Of course, plans that you make at this stage are not set in stone — you can always modify them later as circumstances dictate. Even so, having some plan at the outset, even if it is an incomplete plan, is a real help.

Your First Excel Program

10 Min.
To Go

To give you a taste for Excel programming, this section presents a short program that illustrates some of the basic principles. You are not expected to understand all the details of the program at this point, but working through the required procedures will help in understanding the material in the following sessions.

This program does not do anything complicated. The desired goal is to create a program that does the following:

1. Starts with a blank worksheet.
2. Enables the user to enter a series of numbers in specified cells.
3. Calculates the sum of the numbers.
4. Saves the workbook to disk.

The following sections guide you through the process of creating and running this program.

Creating and Naming the Program

These first steps create the basic program structure and assign a name to it.

1. Start Excel. As usual, it starts with three blank workbooks displayed.
2. Press Alt+F11 to open the VBA Editor.
3. At the top left of the VBA Editor, there is a window labeled "Project - VBAProject" that lists the currently open worksheets: Sheet1, Sheet2, and Sheet3, as shown in Figure 1-2. Double-click the Sheet1 entry, and a code-editing window opens.

4. Select Procedure from the Insert menu. The Add Procedure dialog box displays. Enter a name for your program, such as MyFirstProgram. You can use letters and numbers, but no spaces (some programmers use an underscore in place of spaces to separate words).
5. Click OK. The VBA Editor inserts the first and last lines of the procedure (program) in the code-editing window (see Figure 1-3).

At this point, you have created the empty "skeleton" of your program. Next, you add the code that provides its functionality.

Programs and Procedures

Is a program the same thing as a procedure? Not really. Some simple programs such as this one are contained in a single procedure. More complex programs contain multiple procedures.

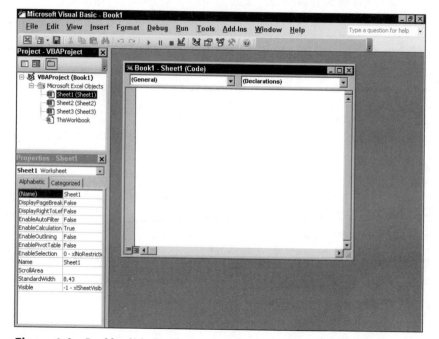

Figure 1-2 *Double-click the Sheet1 entry to open a code-editing window.*

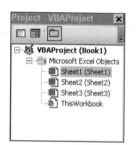

Figure 1-3 *The VBA Editor inserts the first and last lines of the program.*

Writing the Code

The tasks that the program's code needs to perform are as follows:

1. Move the cursor to cell B2.
2. Accept a number from the user, and enter it in the cell.
3. Move to cell B3.
4. Repeat until numbers have been entered in five cells: B2 through B6.
5. Enter a formula in cell B7 to add the column of numbers.
6. Save the workbook to disk.

The code uses several elements of VBA and the Excel object model. Before entering the code, you should have some idea of how it works:

```
Range("B2").Select
```

This code uses the Range object to move the Excel cursor to the indicated cell — in this case, cell B2.

```
ActiveCell.Value = InputBox("Enter Value")
```

This code has two parts. The InputBox function displays a dialog box on the screen and prompts the user to enter data, using the supplied text "Enter Value" as the prompt text. The ActiveCell object is then used to take the value entered by the user and insert it into the currently active worksheet cell (the cell that the cursor is on).

The above two code elements repeat five times to enter values in cells B2 through B6. After moving the cursor to the cell B7, the following code executes:

```
ActiveCell.Formula = "=Sum(B2..B6")
```

Here, the ActiveCell object is used again, this time to enter a formula into the active worksheet cell. The formula uses Excel's built-in Sum function to calculate the sum of the values in cells B2 through B6.

```
ActiveWorkbook.SaveAs Filename:="MyFirstProgram.xls"
```

This final line of code uses the ActiveWorkbook object to save the workbook to disk under the specified filename.

With an understanding of how the code works, you can now enter it into the VBA Code Editor. The full program is shown in the following listing. Remember that the Code Editor already entered the first and last lines — you need to enter only the remainder of the code. Try to be accurate because even a minor spelling error will prevent the program from running.

```
Public Sub MyFirstProgram()

Range("B2").Select
ActiveCell.Value = InputBox("Enter value")
Range("B3").Select
ActiveCell.Value = InputBox("Enter value")
Range("B4").Select
ActiveCell.Value = InputBox("Enter value")
Range("B5").Select
ActiveCell.Value = InputBox("Enter value")
Range("B6").Select
ActiveCell.Value = InputBox("Enter value")
Range("B7").Select
ActiveCell.Formula = "=Sum(B2..B6)"
ActiveWorkbook.SaveAs Filename:="MyFirstProgram.xls"

End Sub
```

Running the Program

After the code has been entered, you can run the program and see how it works. Here are the steps required:

1. Use the Windows taskbar to activate Excel.

2. Press Alt+F8 to open the Macros dialog box, shown in Figure 1-4. (You can also display this dialog box by selecting Tools ⇨ Macro ⇨ Macros from the Excel menu.)

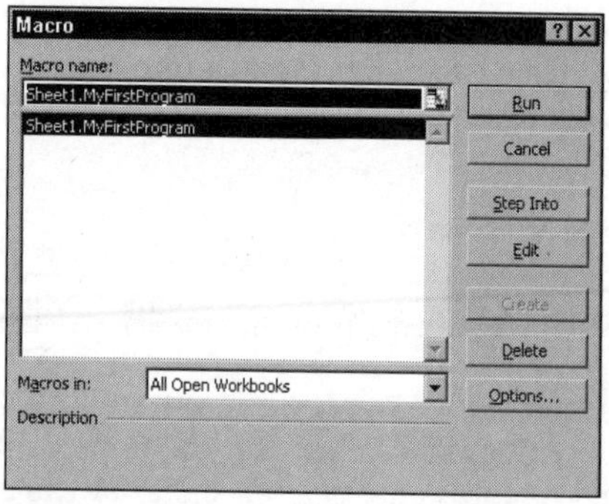

Figure 1-4 *Selecting the program to run*

3. In the Macros dialog box, select Sheet1.MyFirstProgram (this name indicates that the program is stored in Sheet1); then click the Run button.

4. The program prompts you to enter a value, repeating this action five times.

When the program finishes, your worksheet should look like Figure 1-5 (although you entered different numbers, of course).

Even though this is a simple program, it illustrates some of the advantages of Excel programming as related to accuracy and consistency. Specifically, it ensures that:

- Data is entered into the proper worksheet cells.
- The correct formula is used.
- The workbook is saved under the correct name.

With the fundamentals under your belt, you are ready to move on to the next session and start learning the details of Excel programming.

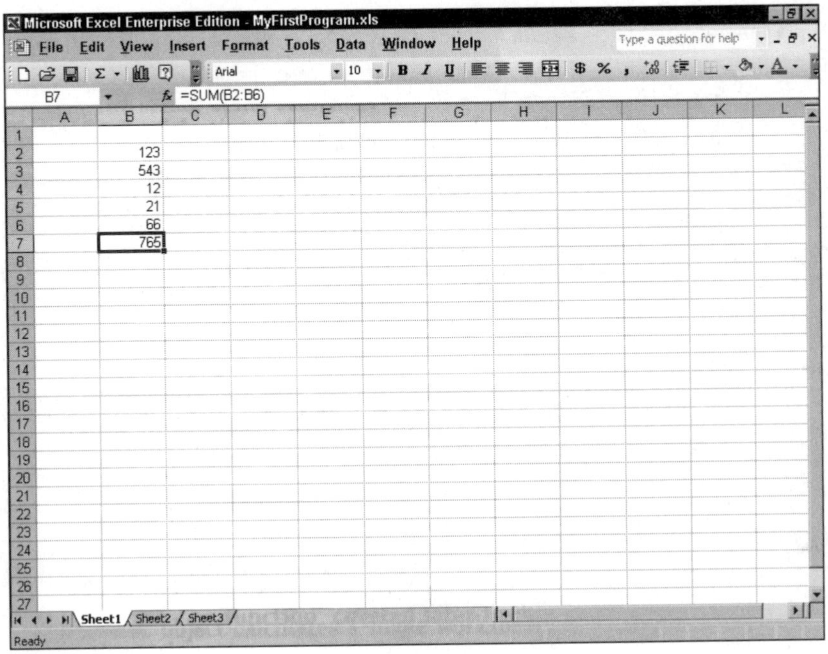

Figure 1-5   The worksheet after the program runs

REVIEW

Done!

In this session you learned some of the fundamentals and background of Excel programming, including:

- There are several advantages of programming Excel.
- You use the VBA language to write Excel programs.
- Excels makes its functionality available to VBA as components.
- The components that Excel exposes are collectively called the Excel object model.
- Excel macros are a simple form of programming.
- Planning ahead is important when designing a program.

Quiz Yourself

1. Name three advantages of programming with Excel. (See the "Advantages of Programming" section.)

2. What are the two main parts of a program? (See the "Programming Fundamentals" section.)

3. What's the distinction between a class and an object? (See the "The Excel Object Model" section.)

4. How does a program access Excel's functionality? (See the "The Excel Object Model" section.)

5. What is a macro? (See the "Macros and Programming" section.)

6. What should a programmer do before starting to write code? (See the "Designing Your Custom Application" section.)

The VBA Code Editor

Session Checklist

✔ How VBA projects are organized

✔ Using the Project Explorer

✔ Sharing code between projects

✔ Using the editing tools

✔ Working in the Property Window

✔ Using macros in programming

✔ Using online help

**30 Min.
To Go**

The VBA Editor is the tool you use to create and edit your VBA programs, but it is much more than a simple editor. It also enables you to run and debug your programs, keep your code organized, deal with code security, design user input forms, and view online help information.

Some functions of the Editor are covered in other sessions, specifically security (Session 24), debugging (Session 25), and user forms (Sessions 19 through 21).

Code and Project Organization

At the lowest level, VBA code is organized into units called *procedures* (or sometimes *sub procedures*). A procedure contains the following:

- An opening line that consists of the keyword Sub followed by the procedure name and parentheses.
- A closing line that is always End Sub.
- Between the opening and closing lines, one or more lines of code.

You learn more about procedures in Session 7. For now it is enough to understand that procedures are used to organize VBA code.

When you record a macro (as described later in this session), it is saved as a procedure. The procedure name is the same name you assigned to the macro.

VBA procedures are stored in workbooks. The code in a single workbook comprises a VBA *project*. Within a project, the code is organized in a manner that may seem confusing at first glance, but after you understand it, provides a lot of flexibility.

Each project is subdivided into a number of components, as follows:

- A set of Microsoft Excel objects comprising an object for each worksheet that the project workbook contains plus the special object named ThisWorkbook. These components are always present in a project.
- One or more modules.
- One or more forms.
- One or more class modules.

The last three items — modules, forms, and class modules — are present only if you explicitly add them to the project (as you learn later in the book).

Each of these components can contain code. When you are writing VBA code, you face the question of where to place the code. Class modules and user forms are used for special purposes. Your choices are:

- **A worksheet.** Place code in a worksheet if you want the code associated with that specific worksheet.
- **ThisWorkbook.** Place code in ThisWorkbook if you want the code associated with the entire project (workbook).
- **A module.** Place code in a module if there is no specific reason to place it elsewhere.

Class modules, user forms, and their special purposes are covered in Sessions 26 and 19 through 21.

Where you place your code is not all that critical because the system is designed so that code is available for use regardless of its location. In addition, it is an easy matter to move code from one location to another should the need arise. When in doubt, create a module (explained later in this session) and place the code there.

The Project Explorer

The Project Explorer, displayed in the top left corner of the VBA Editor screen, displays the organization of the currently open VBA projects, as shown in Figure 2-1. The information is displayed hierarchically. There is a top-level node for each open project (workbook). Under that node are child nodes for Excel objects and — if any have been added to the project — modules, class modules, and forms. To open the code-editing window for a component, double-click it. To add a new module, select Insert ⇨ Module. Modules are assigned default names in the form of Module1, Module2, and so on.

Figure 2-1 *Project components are listed in the Project Explorer.*

There are three buttons at the top of the Project Explorer, just below its title bar. From left to right they are:

- **View Code.** Displays the code for the current object.
- **View Object.** Displays the visual designer for the current object. This is applicable only for user forms.
- **Toggle Folders.** Toggles the Project Explorer between its regular view and folders view. The functionality is the same either way.

Many elements on the VBA Editor screen have an associated context menu. Right-click the element, and this menu displays a list of commands that are available for the object.

Importing and Exporting Modules

As has been mentioned previously in this session, each VBA project is stored in a single file along with its associated workbook. Individual modules, therefore, are not stored as separate files. You can, however, export a module to a separate file and then import that file into another VBA project. This works for modules, class modules, user forms, and Microsoft Excel objects. This capability enables you to share code between projects and even with other programmers. Why write the same code more than once? If you have written the VBA code for performing certain tasks — specific financial calculations, for example — you can reuse it in as many projects as needed.

To export a module, do the following:

1. Right-click the module in the Project Explorer, and select Export File from the pop-up menu. The Export File dialog box is displayed (see Figure 2-2).

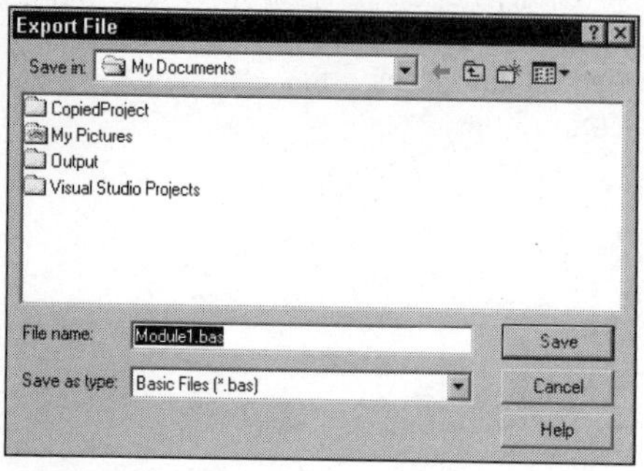

Export File   ? X

Save in: My Documents

- CopiedProject
- My Pictures
- Output
- Visual Studio Projects

File name: Module1.bas   Save

Save as type: Basic Files (*.bas)   Cancel

    Help

Figure 2-2   *Exporting a module*

2. Use the dialog box to select the folder for the exported file to be saved in.
3. Accept the default filename, or enter one of your own. The file extension is specified by Excel based on the type of element being exported: .CLS for Microsoft Excel objects and class modules, .BAS for regular modules, and .FRM for user forms.
4. Click Save.

To import a module:

1. Right-click the project name in the Project Explorer, and select Import File from the pop-up menu. The Import File dialog box is displayed.
2. Select the desired .BAS, .FRM, or .CLS file.
3. Click Open.

Editing Tools

**20 Min.
To Go**

Within an editing window, the Code Editor works like any other text editor in most respects. With it, you can move the cursor; enter and delete text; copy, cut, and paste; and so on. There are, however, some special editing features provided by the VBA Code Editor that are designed specifically to ease the task of writing VBA code. They are:

- **Auto Syntax Check.** When you complete a line of code, the Editor checks its syntax and notifies you if there is a problem; otherwise, syntax errors are caught only when the code is executed.
- **Auto List Member.** This feature displays a list of items that could logically complete the code statement you are typing. You can select from the list or continue typing something else.

- **Auto Quick Info.** When you enter the name of the VBA function, the Editor displays information about the function and its parameters.
- **Auto Indent.** This feature automatically indents each new line of VBA code to align with the previous line. Use Tab to indent more or Shift+Tab to indent less.

These features are all optional, and can be turned on or off according to your personal preferences. To select which features are active:

1. Select Tools ➪ Options to display the Options dialog box.
2. Select the Editor tab (see Figure 2-3).

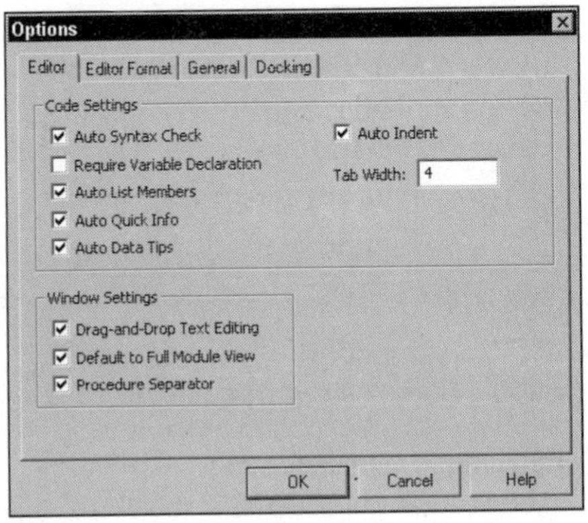

Figure 2-3 Setting VBA Editor options

3. Put a check mark next to the options you want to use, and remove the check mark from those you do not want to use.
4. Click OK.

Another useful feature of the Editor is its capability to display different types of text using different colors and/or fonts. For example, VBA keywords can be displayed in a different color than normal text, such as variable names. These options are set on the Editor Format tab of the Options dialog box.

> **Note** VBA Code Editor options have no effect on how your code runs or how the final program operates. They are for the programmer's convenience only.

You learned earlier in this session that procedures are a basic unit of VBA code organization. When an editing window contains two or more procedures, there are two ways they can be displayed:

- **Full module view.** All procedures display at once (although you may need to scroll down the window to view some of them) with a horizontal line between the end of each procedure and the beginning of the next.

- **Procedure view.** A single procedure displays at a time; when the cursor is at the end or beginning of the displayed procedure, press PgDn or PgUp to view the previous or next procedure.

To toggle between these two modes, use the Full Module View and Procedure View buttons at the bottom of the editing window (see Figure 2-4).

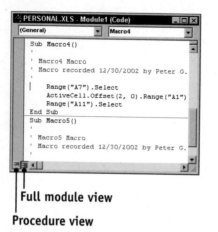

Full module view

Procedure view

Figure 2-4   *Switching between Full Module View and Procedure View*

Use the drop-down list at the top right of the editing window to immediately view any procedure in the module.

The Property Window

The Property Window is located by default in the lower left corner of the VBA Editor screen. This window displays the properties of the object that is current, or active, in the Editor. A *property* is an attribute of an object that controls some aspect of the object's appearance or behavior. For example, a Worksheet object has a Name property that specifies the worksheet's name and also (among many others) a Visible property that determines whether the worksheet is visible onscreen. Some objects have very few properties. A module, for example, has only the Name property. Figure 2-5 shows the Property Window when a worksheet is selected in the Project Explorer.

The Immediate Window

The Immediate Window is used to display output from the Debug.Print statement when the program is running. To display or hide this window, select View ➪ Immediate Window or press Ctrl+G. You'll see how Debug.Print is used in later sessions.

Figure 2-5   The Property Window showing the properties of a worksheet

The Properties Window has two tabs that enable you to view the object's properties listed either alphabetically (as in the figure) or grouped by category. The left column displays the property names, and the right column displays the value. Select a property name to change it. Properties fall into four categories:

- **Boolean properties that are either True or False.** Select from the drop-down list or double-click the property name to toggle its value.
- **Enumerated properties that must be one of a defined set of values.** Select from the drop-down list.
- **Properties that are set using a dialog box.** Click the ellipses in the value column to display the corresponding dialog box.
- **Unrestricted properties that can take any value.** Click in the value column and edit the property value.

The VBA Editor Menus

The VBA Editor has a fairly involved menu system (see Table 2-1). Many of these menu commands are mentioned as needed throughout the book — for example, the Debug menu commands are covered in the Session 25. A few commands are for rarely used advanced features that are beyond the scope of this book. Others, such as the commands on the Window menu, should be familiar to anyone who has used Windows programs before and therefore are not covered here.

Table 2-1 *Selected VBA Editor Menu Commands*

Menu	Command	Action
File	Save	Saves the current project (workbook)
File	Close and Return . . .	Closes the Editor and returns to Excel
File	Remove . . .	Removes the specified object from the project
Edit	Undo	Reverses the most recent editing action
Edit	Redo	Reverses the most recent Undo action
View	Microsoft Excel	Displays Excel without closing the Editor
View	Toolbars	Enables you to display, hide, or customize toolbars
Insert	Procedure	Inserts a procedure into the current module
Insert	UserForm	Inserts a new user form into the current project
Insert	Module	Inserts a new module into the current project
Insert	Class Module	Inserts a new class module into the current project
Tools	Options	Enables you to set VBA Editor options
Tools	. . . Properties	Enables you to set project properties

The Editor provides toolbar buttons and keyboard shortcuts for many menu commands.

Using Macros in Programming

As mentioned in Session 1, a macro is a form of programming. A macro is a record of actions carried out in Excel and can include any action that the user might take — entering data, selecting menu commands, creating charts, printing, and so on. While a macro is being recorded, the user actions are translated into VBA code. After the macro has been recorded, it can be played back whenever needed to recreate the same actions.

Strictly speaking, recording a macro is not programming because you are simply recording actions and not actually writing a program from scratch. Even so, macro recording can be useful to the VBA programmer in two ways:

- You can record a macro for certain actions, and examine the resulting macro to get a feel for the VBA code that is required; then write your own code as needed.

- You can record a macro and use the resulting VBA code as-is or with modifications in your own program.

Because of these potential uses for macros, it's worthwhile to understand how they work.

Recording a Macro

Follow these steps to record a macro.

1. From the Excel menu, select Tools ⇨ Macro ⇨ Record New Macro. Excel displays the Record Macro dialog box, shown in Figure 2-6.

Record Macro ☒

Macro name:

Macro1

Shortcut key: Store macro in:

Ctrl+☐   This Workbook   ▾

Description:

Macro recorded 12/30/2002 by Peter G. Aitken

OK   Cancel

Figure 2-6   *The Record Macro dialog box*

A macro name must begin with a letter. Subsequent characters can be letters, numbers, or the underscore character. Spaces and other characters are not allowed.

2. In the Macro Name field, enter a descriptive name for the macro.

3. If you want to run this macro using a keyboard shortcut, enter the key in the Shortcut Key field. For example, if you enter **M**, you'll be able to run the macro by pressing Ctrl+M. Otherwise leave this box blank.

4. Select the macro storage location from the drop-down list. Your options are:

   - **This Workbook.** The macro is stored in the current workbook.

   - **New Workbook.** The macro is stored in a new workbook. You are prompted to name and save this new workbook when you exit Excel.

   - **Personal Macro Workbook.** The macro is stored in a personal macro workbook. Choose this option if you want the macro available whenever you run Excel.

5. If desired, edit the text in the Description box. This text is included as a comment (an explanatory note) in the macro code.

6. Click OK. Excel displays a small toolbar and begins recording your actions

7. Perform the actions that you want recorded in the macro.

8. When finished, click the Stop Recording button on the toolbar.

Please refer to the section "Code and Project Organization" earlier in this session for more details on how and where VBA code is stored.

Cell References in Macros

The small toolbar that is displayed while a macro is recording contains one other button in addition to the Stop button. This is the Relative Reference button. To use this feature, you need to know something about how Excel refers to worksheet cells.

In a macro — or in any VBA code for that matter — it is often necessary to refer to specific cells in the worksheet. There are two ways this can be done. The first is by *absolute reference,* which identifies a specific cell by its absolute row and column position. An absolute reference to cell A2, for example, always refers to that cell and never to any other cell.

The second type of reference is a *relative reference* that identifies a cell by its position relative to the currently active cell (the cell with the thick black border). For example, "one cell down" is a relative reference, as is "two cells down and three cells to the right." Clearly, the specific cell referred to by a relative reference depends on the location of the active cell.

Cell references are covered in more detail in Session 11.

Excel defaults to recording macros using absolute references. Suppose, for example, you started with cell A1 active and recorded a macro that consisted of pressing the down arrow key four times. The resulting macro would contain the VBA equivalents of the following commands:

    Go to cell A2
    Go to cell A3
    Go to cell A4
    Go to cell A5

If, during macro recording, you click the Relative Reference button, Excel switches to using relative references (click the button again to return to absolute reference recording). With relative references, the same macro would be recorded as the VBA equivalents of these commands:

    Go down one cell
    Go down one cell
    Go down one cell
    Go down one cell

Whether you decide to use absolute or relative references, or a combination of the two, depends on the needs of your program.

VBA and the Excel object model often provide more than one way to perform a task. Just because a recorded macro codes a task in a certain way does not mean you have to do it exactly that way in your programs.

Viewing and Running Macros

**10 Min.
To Go**

To run a macro, you can press the associated hot key if one was assigned to the macro. You can also select Tools ⇨ Macro ⇨ Macros, or press Alt+F8 to display the Macro dialog box (see Figure 2-7).

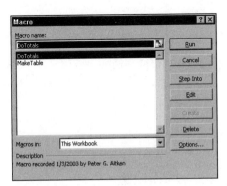

Figure 2-7 *You can select a macro to run in the Macro dialog box.*

This dialog box enables you to run a macro as well as perform other actions. Select the desired macro and then:

- Use the Macros In list to select which macros will be displayed in the list.
- Click Run to run the selected macro.
- Click Step Into to debug the macro (see Session 25 for more information on debugging).
- Click Edit to open the macro in the VBA Editor for viewing and editing.
- Click Delete to delete the macro.
- Click Options to change the shortcut key assigned to the macro and/or change the macro description.

If you select the Edit option, you can copy code from the macro and then paste it into your own programs.

Online Help

The VBA Editor provides an excellent online help system that contains detailed information about the VBA language, the Excel object model, and the Editor itself. There are several ways to access this information.

One method is context-sensitive help, accessed by pressing F1. The Editor keeps track of what you are doing, and when you press F1, it displays help information that is relevant to the task at hand. For example, if you have selected an item in the Project Explorer, pressing

F1 displays help about using the Project Explorer. If the Editor cannot figure out what you are doing at the moment, a message to that effect is displayed.

Another method is help for dialog boxes. Most of the dialog boxes in the Editor include a Help button. Clicking that button displays help information about the dialog box settings.

The final and perhaps most flexible method is to search for relevant information. Selecting the menu command Help ⇨ Visual Basic Help displays the Search and Table of Contents pane for the Help system, as shown in Figure 2-8.

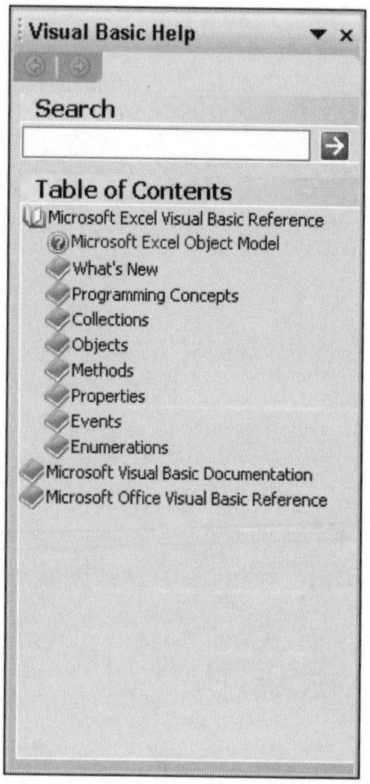

Figure 2-8 *The Search and Table of Contents pane for online help*

To use the Table of Contents, select the relevant topic to view related subtopics and then "burrow down" as needed to find the specific information you need. Use the Back button to retrace your steps.

To search, enter the search term or phrase in the field; then press Enter, or click the Start Searching button. Help displays a list of relevant help topics, as shown in Figure 2-9 for a search on the term "array." Click a specific topic heading to view the details.

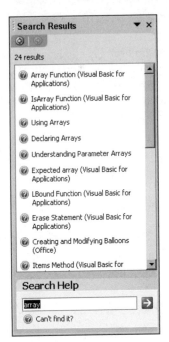

Figure 2-9   *Displaying the results of a Help search*

You can quickly search Help by entering the search phrase in the box at the right end of the editor's menu bar and pressing Enter.

Most individual help topics use hyperlinks to provide additional information. Some links are displayed at the top of a topic; the specific links available vary from topic to topic. For example, many topics have a See Also link, for related information, and an Example link, to display a code example. Links within the body of a topic provide links to term definitions. Buttons at the top of the topic window are for the following tasks:

- **AutoTile/Untile.** Toggles between the Topic window overlapping the Editor window and the two windows being tiled so they do not overlap.
- **Back.** Moves to the previous topic.
- **Forward.** Moves to the next topic.
- **Print.** Prints the current topic.

Done!

REVIEW

The VBA Editor provides you with a powerful "command center" for developing your Excel projects. More than just a code editor, it also has tools for organizing the components of your project and setting object properties. Some of the Editor's more specialized capabilities are covered in subsequent sessions. Some important things you learned in this session are:

- VBA code is organized in procedures, which are located in modules.
- The Project Explorer enables you to view the contents of your project and add new modules.
- You can reuse code by exporting a module from one project and then importing it into another.
- The Editor has several convenience features that improve the speed and accuracy of code editing.
- You use the Property Window to view and set an object's properties.
- Excel macros are recorded as VBA code and can be helpful aids in programming.
- The VBA Editor has an online help system that provides information on the VBA language, the Excel object model, and the Editor itself.

QUIZ YOURSELF

1. Where does the VBA Editor store your code? (See the "Code and Project Organization" section.)

2. What are the three choices for locating code in a VBA project? Which of these three should generally be used? (See the "Code and Project Organization" section.)

3. How can you share code between projects? (See the "Importing and Exporting Modules" section.)

4. The VBA Editor offers several optional features, such as Auto Syntax Check, that can assist with your code editing. How do you turn these options on and off? (See the "Editing Tools" section.)

5. In the Property Window, how do you set an enumerated property? (See the "The Property Window" section.)

6. How do absolute cell references differ from relative references? (See the "Cell References in Macros" section.)

The Excel Object Model

Session Checklist

✔ Using properties and methods

✔ Working with collections

✔ The object hierarchy

✔ The Workbook object

✔ The Worksheet object

**30 Min.
To Go**

The Excel object model is one of the two pillars of Excel programming (the other being the VBA language). As you saw in Session 1, the Excel application is made up of objects that provide the program's functionality. Because these objects are "exposed" — that is, available to manipulation from the outside — they can be controlled by VBA code to create custom programs. The collection of objects exposed by Excel is called the Excel object model, and this session gives you an overview of the model and some of its most fundamental components.

Understanding Properties and Methods

When discussing objects, it is essential to have an understanding of object properties and methods, collectively called *members*. In one sense an object is its properties and methods because these are the only aspects of an object that are exposed to the outside world (that is, to your program). When you use an object, you are working with its properties and methods.

A *property* is a piece of information that is associated with an object. A property might provide some information about the object or specify some aspect of the object's appearance (for objects that have a display component) or behavior. Using a car as an example, its properties would include its color, the station to which the radio is set, and the amount of gas in the tank. Some object properties are *read-only*, meaning that you can determine their value but not change it (for example, the number of doors). Others are *read-write* and can be read as well as changed, such as the radio station.

In contrast, a *method* is something that the object can do, such as an action it can perform. Continuing with the car analogy, its methods would include "speed up," "turn," and "stop." Many methods take arguments, information that specifies exactly how the method should work. The "turn" method, for example, might have a "direction" argument that could be either "right" or "left."

Notation for properties and methods follows the standard *ObjectName.MemberName* format. When a method takes arguments, there are three ways you can do it. The first is to include the arguments, in parentheses and in the correct order, following the method name:

```
ObjectName.MethodName(argument1, argument2, ...)
```

In the rare case of a property that takes arguments, you must also use this syntax. The arguments must be in the precise order defined by the method definition.

Another way of including arguments in a method call is essentially the same, but omits the parentheses:

```
ObjectName.MethodName argument1, argument2, ...
```

Again, the arguments must be in the correct order.

The final way to include arguments is called *named arguments* and is perhaps the easiest and clearest. It makes use of the argument name, as provided in the method definition, and the := operator, followed by the argument value. Thus:

```
ObjectName.MethodName argument1name:=argument1value, _
argument2name:=argument2value
```

Here's a real example:

```
MyWorkbook.SaveAs Filename:="AnnualSales.wks"
```

There are two advantages to using named arguments. One is having clarity in your code. Each argument's name is a description of its purpose and therefore helps you or others understand code that was written earlier. The other is simplicity. Many methods have lots of optional arguments, and you may want to call the method with most of the arguments left at their default values. Without named arguments, the method can identify an argument only by its position in the argument list, so you have to include placeholders (commas) for all optional arguments that you are omitting (and using the default value). In other words, a placeholder is a comma followed by another comma — the omitted argument would go between the commas if it were included. With named arguments, this is not necessary — include only those optional arguments that you want to change from the default.

The Importance of Object References

To work with an object, you need a reference to it. This is nothing more than a name used in code to refer to the object. Sometimes the object already exists, and all your code needs to do is obtain a reference to it. An example is when your program opens a workbook and needs to work with one of its existing worksheets. At other times the object does not exist, and your program must create it as well as obtain a reference — for example, when you add a new worksheet to a workbook. Both of these techniques are explained throughout the book for the various Excel objects with which you'll be working.

Working with Collections

The Excel object model makes frequent use of *collections*. This is a special class (the Collection class) that is designed specifically for keeping track of multiple instances of other objects. Whenever there is the potential for more than one copy of an object to exist, Excel almost always uses a collection.

Here's an example. An Excel workbook can contain multiple worksheets. This is handled as follows:

- The workbook is represented by a Workbook object.
- The Workbook object has a Sheets collection.
- The Sheets collection contains one Sheet object for each sheet in the workbook.

 Why is the collection containing worksheets called Sheets **instead of** Worksheets? **This is because Excel has both worksheets, which contain rows and columns of data as well as embedded charts, and chart sheets, which contain only a single chart. Thus, the** Sheets **collection contains** Sheet **objects, which come in two types: worksheets and chart sheets. If you want to obtain only worksheets or only chart sheets, use the** Worksheets **or** Charts **properties (as described later in this session).**

This example illustrates the convention used for naming collections as the plural of the object contained — the Sheets collection contains Sheet objects, the Windows collection contains Window objects, and so on. There are very few exceptions to this rule, which will be pointed out throughout the book.

A Collection object has the Count property, Count that gives the number of objects in the collection. This is a read-only property — you can read but not change its value.

There are two ways to refer to an object in a collection. One is by its numerical position within the collection; the other is by the object's unique *key*. The key for a collection depends on the object it contains and is usually the piece of information that identifies an object. In the Sheets collection, for example, the unique key is the sheet's name. Thus,

```
Sheets(1)
```

references the first sheet in the current workbook, while

```
Sheets("SalesData")
```

references the sheet named "SalesData." This latter method is more useful because you usually do not know the position of an object in a collection.

When you reference a collection member, you can use the reference in two ways. One is directly, as in the following line of code that causes the specific worksheet to recalculate all of its formulas.

```
Sheets("SalesData").Calculate
```

You can also assign the reference to a variable and then use the variable to refer to the object. For example:

```
Set MyWorksheet = Sheets("SalesData")
```

This assumes that the variable MyWorksheet has been created as a type of variable that can hold a sheet reference You learn about this in Session 4. Note the use of the Set keyword, which is required whenever assigning object references. The result is that MyWorksheet refers to the worksheet "SalesData" and could be used as follows:

```
MyWorksheet.Calculate
```

 Even when there are two or more references to an object, there is still only one object.

Most collections provide methods to add new objects to the collection and also to delete objects. Adding an object uses the Add method. The syntax is:

```
CollectionName.Add(arguments)
```

Arguments provides details on how the object is to be created and differ depending on the specific collection in use. The Add method returns a reference to the newly created object, which you can ignore if you do not need it. To delete an object, use the Delete method.

A particularly useful tool when working with collections is the For Each In statement. This statement sets up a code loop that repeats once for each item in a collection. The syntax is as follows:

```
For Each Item In Collection
...
Next
```

Item is a variable that has been declared as the correct data type to refer to the contents of the collection. *Collection* is a reference to the collection. *Item* is set to reference the first element in the collection, and the code in the loop (indicated by the ...) is executed. When the Next statement is reached, execution loops back to the For Each statement, *Item* is set to refer to the next element in the collection, and the process repeats until all elements in the collection have been processed. If the collection is empty to begin with, execution simply skips over the loop. An example of using this loop is presented in the section on the Workbook object later in this session.

This has been a quick introduction to collections. You'll learn more of the details where specific collections are covered throughout the book.

The Object Hierarchy

**20 Min.
To Go**

The Excel object model is organized in a hierarchy. At the top of this hierarchy is the Application object that represents the Excel application itself. All other objects in the Excel object model are subsidiary to Application. The Application object is always available to your code.

> **If you were writing VBA code in another Office program, such as Word, and needed to program Excel, you would need to explicitly create the Excel Application object. That, however, is beyond the scope of this book. When you are programming within Excel, the Application object is always available as an implicit reference.**

The Workbook object has several immediate children, the most important of which is the Workbooks collection. This collection contains one Workbook object for each open workbook. Each Workbook object has a Sheets collection, which contains one Sheet object for each worksheet or chart sheet that the workbook contains. Figure 3-1 illustrates the structure of the object model as described so far.

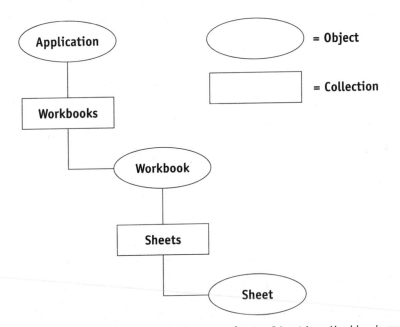

Figure 3-1 *The relationships between the* Application, Workbook, *and* Sheet *objects*

Needless to say, the Excel object model is much more complicated than this diagram might suggest. There are many other objects and collections not shown here that are covered in later sessions.

The Workbook Object

Each open workbook in Excel is represented by a Workbook object, which is maintained in the Workbooks collection of the Application object. This section shows you how to perform various important tasks with a Workbook object.

Creating and Opening Workbooks

You use the Workbooks collection's Add method to create a new workbook. The syntax is:

```
Workbooks.Add(Template)
```

Because the Workbooks **collection is a child of the** Application **object, the full syntax for this would be:**

```
Application.Workbooks.Add(Template)
```

When programming within Excel, however, Application **is always available as an implicit reference, so it does not need to be specified although it can be.**

Template is an optional argument specifying the name of an existing workbook file (on disk). If the argument is included, a new workbook is created based on the existing workbook. If the argument is omitted, a new workbook is created containing three empty workbooks. The method returns a reference to the newly created workbook, which can be used or ignored. For example:

```
Dim MyWB As Workbook
Set MyWB = Workbooks.Add
```

As always, the Set keyword is used because the statement assigns an object reference. The variable MyWB refers to the new workbook, and can be used to manipulate it. A reference to the workbook also exists in the Workbooks collection.

To open an existing workbook from disk, use the Open method:

```
Workbooks.Open(Filename)
```

The *Filename* argument is the name of the workbook file to open, including the full path if necessary. This method opens the specified workbook, adds it to the Workbooks collection, and returns a reference to the workbook. Here's an example:

```
Dim MyWB As Workbook
Set MyWB = Workbooks.Open("c:\data\sales.xls")
```

If the specified file does not exist or cannot be opened for any other reason (such as a sharing violation), a runtime error occurs.

For more about dealing with this and other kinds of errors, see Session 27.

Your code should always take possible errors into account, particularly when working with files. Sample code in this session and others usually omits the error-handling code for the sake of clarity, but that does not mean you can do the same!

Saving and Closing Workbooks

To save a workbook under its existing name, use the Save method. A workbook's name is either the name you assign using the SaveAs method (described later in this session) or the default name (Book1, Book2, and so on) that Excel assigns when a new workbook is created. The Save method takes no arguments.

To save a workbook under a new name, use the SaveAs method:

`WB.SaveAs(Filename)`

WB is a reference to the workbook, and *filename* is the name under which to save it. The name can include the .XLS extension or not; if this is omitted, Excel automatically adds it. The name can also include drive and/or path information if you do not want the workbook saved in Excel's default data folder. For example:

`MyWB.SaveAs("g:\data\sales\march.xls")`

The SaveAs method has some additional, optional arguments that are used to assign a password to a workbook, specify the backup mode, and set other save options. Please refer to VBA's online help for the details.

Another method, SaveCopyAs, enables you to save a copy of a workbook under a new name without changing the name of the open workbook. The syntax is:

`WB.SaveCopyAs(Filename)`

To close an open workbook, use the Close method, as shown in the following syntax:

`WB.Close(SaveChanges, Filename, RouteWorkbook)`

Here's what each of these optional arguments do:

- SaveChanges. Set this argument to True to save changes made since the workbook was last saved, or False to discard such changes. If omitted, the user is prompted to save changes.
- Filename. This argument designates the name to save the workbook under. If omitted, the current workbook name is used. If the workbook has not been assigned a name (it's still using the default name Book1, Book2, and so on) and this argument is omitted, the user is prompted for a name.
- RouteWorkbook. This argument is relevant only if a routing slip is attached to the workbook and it has not already been routed. Set to True to route the workbook, or False to not route it. If this argument is omitted and a routing slip is attached, the user is prompted.

The following code example shows how to use a For Next In loop to close all open workbooks, saving any changes.

```
Dim WB As Workbook
For Each WB in Workbooks
    WB.Close SaveChanges:=True
Next
```

Referencing Workbooks

To manipulate a workbook in code, you must have a reference to it. There are several ways to do this, and the one you use depends on your specific situation.

One method is to assign a reference when you either create or open the workbook with the Add or Open methods, respectively. Thus:

```
Dim MyNewWB As Workbook
Dim MyOpenedWB As Workbook
Set MyNewWB = Workbooks.Add
Set MyOpenedWB = Workbooks.Open("expenses.xls")
```

Note that a variable used for an object reference must be created with the proper type.

 For details on creating an object reference variable with the proper type, turn to Session 4.

If the workbook already has been created or opened — in other words, if it already exists in the Workbooks collection — you can reference it directly from the collection. Thus, the code

```
Workbooks(Name)
```

returns a reference to the workbook with the specified name. Note that the name must include the extension: sales.xls and not just sales. If the specified workbook does not exist, an error occurs.

Finally, VBA provides a couple of special keywords that can be used to refer to workbooks:

- ActiveWorkbook. This references the active workbook.
- ThisWorkbook. This references the workbook in which the code is running.

The concept of the active workbook is easy to understand: It represents the workbook that is active and on-screen. The ActiveWorkbook keyword can be extremely useful.

The need for ThisWorkbook, however, may not be clear. In many situations, the VBA code that is executing is located in the same workbook that's being manipulated by the code, and there is no need for ThisWorkbook. At times, however, code that is located in one workbook is manipulating data in another workbook. When such code needs to refer to the workbook it is in rather than to the workbook that is being manipulated, it uses the ThisWorkbook keyword. This situation arises most often when you are programming add-ins; then use the `ThisWorkbook` keyword to ensure that a reference applies to the workbook the code is in and not to the active workbook.

The `ThisWorkbook` keyword is not the same as the ThisWorkbook element that is listed in the Project Explorer.

Printing Workbooks

10 Min. To Go

You use the `PrintOut` method to print all or part of a workbook. The syntax for this method is:

```
WB.PrintOut(From, To, Copies, Preview, ActivePrinter, PrintToFile,
Collate, PrToFileName)
```

All of the arguments to this method are optional:

- `From`, `To`. The first and last pages of the workbook to print. The default is to print the entire workbook.
- `Copies`. The number of copies to print. The default is 1.
- `Preview`. If set to True, the Excel Print Preview window opens for the user to view. The default is False.
- `ActivePrinter`. The name of the printer to use. The default is the Windows default printer.
- `PrintToFile`. If True, the output is sent to a disk file rather than to the printer. The default is False.
- `Collate`. If True and multiple copies are being printed, the output is collated. The default is False.
- `PrToFileName`. The name of the file for output (relevant only when `PrintToFile` is True).

The `PrintOut` method is available with several other Excel objects, including `Chart`, `Range`, `Window`, and `Worksheet`.

E-Mailing a Workbook

The `Workbook` object's `SendMail` method enables you to e-mail a workbook to one or more recipients. The workbook is sent as an attachment to an e-mail message using whatever e-mail system is installed on the system. The syntax is:

```
WB.SendMail(Recipients, Subject, ReturnReceipt)
```

Here's what each of these arguments do:

- `Recipients`. A required argument listing one or more recipients for the message (see the text for details).

- Subject. Optional argument specifying the message subject. If omitted, the name of the workbook is used as the message subject.
- ReturnReceipt. If True, a return receipt is requested. Optional; the default is False.

A message recipient can be specified either as an explicit e-mail address, or as the name of an entry in the address book. If there is only one message recipient, pass the recipient's name or the address itself as the argument:

```
WB.SendMail recipients:="George Bush"
```

For more than one recipient, create an array containing one entry for each recipient; then pass the array as the method argument:

```
Dim recip As Variant
recip = Array("George Bush", "someone@somewhere.com", "Bill Gates")
WB.SendMail recipients:=recip
```

Other Workbook Methods and Properties

The Workbook object has a large number of properties and methods — too many to cover in this book. Many of these members are rarely used, but in any case you can use the online documentation to find the details. A few of these members are needed on a regular basis, and are summarized in Table 3-1. Refer to online help for more details on how to use these.

Table 3-1 *Additional Members of the Workbook Object*

Name	Property or Method	Description
ActiveSheet	Property	Returns a reference to the active sheet
Charts	Property	Returns a Sheets collection containing a Sheet object for every chart sheet in the workbook
CreateBackup	Property	If True, a backup is created when the workbook is saved.
FullName	Property	The full name (path and filename) of the workbook
HasPassword	Property	True if the workbook is password-protected
HasRoutingSlip	Property	True if there is a routing slip attached to the workbook
Path	Property	The path of the workbook file

Name	Property or Method	Description
ReadOnly	Property	True if the workbook has been opened as read-only
Saved	Property	True if the workbook has been saved since the last change
Sheets	Property	Returns a Sheets collection, containing a Sheet object for every worksheet and chart sheet in the workbook
Worksheets	Property	Returns a Sheets collection, containing a Sheet object for every worksheet in the workbook
Activate	Method	Makes the workbook active
AddToFavorites	Method	Creates (in the Favorites folder) a shortcut to the workbook
NewWindow	Method	Creates a new window
Post	Method	Posts the workbook to a public folder on a Microsoft Exchange Server
PrintPreview	Method	Displays the workbook in the Print Preview window
WebPagePreview	Method	Previews the workbook as it would appear if saved as a Web page

The Worksheet Object

As mentioned earlier in this session, a worksheet is one of two types of sheets that a workbook can contain (the other being a chart sheet). This section provides important information on working with Worksheet objects.

 Chart sheets are covered in Sessions 17 and 18.

Adding and Deleting Worksheets

To add a new, blank worksheet to a workbook, use the Worksheets collection's Add method. The syntax is:

```
WB.Add(Before, After, Count)
```

The arguments are all optional:

- Before. This is a reference to the existing worksheet before which the new sheet is to be added.
- After. This is a reference to the existing worksheet after which the new sheet is to be added.
- Count. This argument designates the number of new worksheets to add. The default is 1.

Clearly, you would not use the Before and After arguments at the same time. If neither of these arguments is included, the new sheet is inserted before the currently active worksheet. Note that the Add method returns a reference to the newly added sheet. If Count is more than 1, the reference is to the last added worksheet.

You can also add a new worksheet by calling the Sheets **collection's** Add **method, but there is no advantage to doing so.**

After creating a new worksheet, it is a good idea to set its Name property to something other than the default Sheet1 and Sheet2 names assigned by Excel. This name is displayed on the worksheet's tab on the Excel screen and can also be used to retrieve a reference from the Worksheets or Sheets collection.

```
Dim MyNewWorksheet As Worksheet
Set MyNewWorksheet = ActiveWorkbook.Add
MyNewWorksheet.Name = "Sales Totals"
```

A worksheet that you add in code is by default hidden. If you need to make it visible so the user can work with it, set its Visible **property to True.**

To delete a worksheet, call the Worksheet object's Delete method:

```
SomeWorksheet.Delete
```

Remember that you can also get a reference to a worksheet from the Worksheets collection:

```
SomeWorkbook.Worksheets(SheetName).Delete
```

When code tries to delete a worksheet, Excel normally displays a prompt to the user asking him or her to confirm the delete action. If you want to delete a worksheet without this prompt being displayed, you must set the Application object's DisplayAlerts property to False:

```
DisplayAlerts = False
SomeWorksheet.Delete
DisplayAlerts = True
```

Be sure to set the `DisplayAlerts` **property back to True after the** `Delete` **method is called, as in the previous example.**

Referencing Worksheets

You have already seen a couple of ways to reference a specific worksheet in a workbook, using the reference returned when the worksheet is created or obtaining the reference from the `Worksheets` collection. Another useful way to obtain a reference is with the `ActiveSheet` property of the `Workbook` object. This property returns a reference to the active sheet (worksheet or chart sheet) that is on top, or active, in the specified workbook. If there is no active sheet, the property returns the special value `Nothing` (see the sidebar, "The Usefulness of Nothing.").

For more on `If` **statements, see Session 6.**

The Usefulness of Nothing

There are situations where an object variable does not refer to any object: It refers to nothing, and VBA has the special keyword `Nothing` to represent this. An object variable contains `Nothing` when it has been declared but not yet initialized (has not been assigned an object reference). Thus:

```
Dim MyWB As Workbook
' At this point MyWB contains Nothing
Set MyWB = Workbooks.Add

' Now that it has been initialized, MyWB no longer contains Nothing
```

The value `Nothing` is also returned by some object properties under certain conditions, such as the `ActiveSheet` property when there is no active sheet. You can test for an object reference containing `Nothing` using the `Is Nothing` clause in an `If...Then` statement:

```
If SomeObjectReference Is Nothing Then
    ...
End If
```

Finally, you can (and should) explicitly set an object reference to `Nothing` when you are finished using the object:

```
Set SomeObjectReference = Nothing
```

When the last reference to an object is destroyed in this way, the memory occupied by the object is freed up for other purposes.

Copying and Moving Worksheets

An entire worksheet can be copied or moved to a new location within the original workbook or to a different workbook. The syntax for copying is as follows (use the Move method for moving a worksheet; the syntax is the same as Copy):

```
Sheet.Copy(Before, After)
```

Sheet is a reference to the worksheet to be copied. If you want to copy to a location in the original workbook, use the Before or After argument (but not both) to specify the existing worksheet that the copied worksheet is to be placed before or after. For example, this code copies Sheet1 and places it after Sheet3.

```
Worksheets("Sheet1").Copy After:=Worksheets("Sheet3")
```

When copying within a workbook, the copy is given the name of the original worksheet with an index, such as "Sheet1 (2)."

To copy a worksheet to another workbook, omit the After and Before arguments. Excel creates a new workbook and then copies the worksheet to it.

There is no way to directly copy or move a worksheet to an existing workbook. To do so, you must use the Range object to copy the data to the Windows Clipboard and then paste the data to the new location. See Session 10 for details.

Done!

REVIEW

Any VBA program that you write will depend on the Excel object model. This session introduced you to this object model and covered some important background material. Among the things you learned in this session are:

- You work with objects through their properties and methods.
- Excel uses collections to keep track of multiple object copies.
- The object model is organized as a hierarchy with the Application object at the top.
- Excel workbooks are represented by Workbook objects in the Workbooks collection. Methods are provided for creating new and opening existing workbooks, saving and closing workbooks, and other required tasks.
- Worksheets are represented by Sheet objects in the Sheets collection. You can add, delete, copy, and move worksheets as needed.

QUIZ YOURSELF

1. What is the main difference between a property and a method? (See the "Understanding Properties and Methods" section.)

2. How do you add a new object to a collection? (See the "Working with Collections" section.)

3. What is the general rule for naming collections? (See the "Working with Collections" section.)

4. What object is at the top of the Excel object hierarchy? (See the "The Object Hierarchy" section.)

5. How do you assign a name to a newly created workbook? (See the "Saving and Closing Workbooks" section.)

6. How do you reference the currently active worksheet? (See the "Referencing Workbooks" section.)

Syntax and Data in VBA

Session Checklist

✔ The basics of VBA syntax

✔ How to use constants

✔ How to declare program variables

✔ The different variable types available for number, text, and other types of data

✔ Early versus late binding

✔ Using static and dynamic arrays

✔ Defining user-defined types and enumeration

✔ Understanding variable scope

**30 Min.
To Go**

E very Excel program works with data of one kind or another, and the VBA language provides a powerful set of tools for maintaining data. This session explains how to maintain different types of data in your VBA programs, specifically how to store data in the program while it is running. First, however, you need to understand the fundamentals of VBA syntax.

VBA Syntax Fundamentals

Syntax in a programming language is similar in concept to syntax in the English (or any other) language. It provides rules as to how the language elements are to be used and organized. Ending sentences with a period is an example of an English syntax rule. Before you start writing your own VBA code, you need to understand these fundamentals.

A VBA program is composed of statements. There is usually a single statement per line of code. There are two exceptions to this:

- Multiple statements can be separated by a colon and placed on the same line.
- A single statement can be broken over two or more lines with the line continuation character (a space followed by an underscore).

Using the first technique to place multiple statements per line is not recommended because it provides no real advantage and can make the code more difficult to read and understand.

On the other hand, use of the line continuation character can be a real help. Some lines of VBA code are quite long and will extend past the right edge of the editing window, making viewing and editing the code difficult. To break a line, type a space and then an underscore, and press Enter. The only place you cannot use the line continuation character is within a quoted string. I recommend indenting each continuation line with respect to the first line. VBA does not care about this, but it makes it more obvious to anyone reading the code that these are continuation lines and not independent lines.

Comments

A *comment* is text in a VBA program that is ignored and has no effect on the program operation. You can (and should) use comments to document how the code works, provide details about procedure arguments, and add reminders to yourself or another programmer.

One way to create a comment is with the apostrophe (single quote) character. Anything following an apostrophe, to the end of the line, is considered a comment. The apostrophe can be at the start of the line, or in the middle:

```
' This is a comment.
' Dim MyWB As Workbook 'This is a comment too.
```

You can also use the REM keyword (standing for "remark") to mark a comment. Note that REM must be at the start of a line:

```
REM This is a comment.
Dim MyWB As Workbook REM This is not permitted
```

You'll see that the VBA Editor displays comments in a different color — green by default.

You can use the apostrophe to "comment out" code. This can be useful during development when you want to see how a program runs without one or more existing lines of code. Rather than deleting the lines, you can convert them to comments. You can easily uncomment the code later if you decide to keep it.

Source Code Formatting

So-called *white space* in your code — spaces, tabs, and blank lines — is ignored by VBA, but it can be used to format the code for readability, a practice I strongly recommend. This can include using blank lines to separate sections of code that are functionally distinct and indenting statements more or less depending on their logical relationship with other statements. (As you learn more about VBA statements, in this session and also in Session 6, this suggestion will make more sense to you.)

Employing Constants

A *constant* represents data that does not change during program execution. The data value is constant, hence the name. There are two types of constants in VBA, literal and symbolic.

A *literal constant* is typed directly into the code and can be either a number or a string (text); string constants must be enclosed in double quotes. Here are two examples:

```
MyString = "four"
MyNumber = 4
```

Here, the "four" and the 4 are literal constants. For numbers, VBA also recognizes scientific notation and, using the &H prefix, hexadecimal notation:

```
1.2E5       ' 1.2 times 10 to the 5th power, or 120000
&HFE        ' Equivalent to decimal 254
```

 Hexadecimal notation is based on powers of 16, in contrast to the commonly used decimal system that uses powers of 10. Hex notation uses the digits 0–9 in the usual way plus the letters A–F to represent the values 10 through 15.

A *symbolic constant* is one that has been assigned a name. You then use that name anywhere in your program that you need the constant value. The Const keyword is used to define a symbolic constant:

```
Const ConstantName = ConstantValue
```

ContantName is any valid VBA name (see the "VBA Naming Rules" sidebar). ConstantValue is a literal constant defining the constant's value, which can be either numeric or string. Here are two examples:

```
Const MYNAME = "Joe"
Const MYBIRTHYEAR = 1961
```

Symbolic constants offer two advantages. The constant name can (and should) be descriptive, which helps with code readability. Most important, should you need to change the constant's value, you only have to do so in one location, where the constant is defined, and not in every location where it is used in the code.

VBA Naming Rules

VBA's naming rules apply to symbolic constants, variables, properties, and just about anything else you can assign a name to in code. A VBA name:

- Must start with a letter
- Can be up to 255 characters in length
- Cannot be a VBA keyword
- Cannot contain a period, space, or the characters: !, @, #, &, %, or $

It's a good idea to create descriptive names that provide some idea of what the variable or other named element does. Because you cannot use spaces, multi-word names can be made clearer using a combination of upper- and lowercase (for example, InterestRate) or by using the underscore in place of spaces (for example, Total_2001). Case does not matter; thus, Total, total, and TOTAL are considered the same name in VBA.

I have found it useful to use all uppercase for constant names, and a combination of upper- and lowercase for other elements such as variables. For example, INTEREST_RATE would be a constant while InterestRate would be a variable. This is certainly not required by VBA, but it does make it easy to distinguish constants from variables in code.

Declaring and Using Variables

As the name suggests, a variable holds data that can change during program execution. In VBA, a variable has a *type* that determines what kind of data the variable can hold. When you create or declare a variable, you specify its type according to the needs of the program. In its simplest form, the syntax for declaring a variable is a single statement containing:

1. The Dim keyword.
2. The variable name.
3. The As keyword.
4. The name of the variable type.

Thus the code would look like:

```
Dim varname As type
```

You can also declare two or more variables on the same line as follows:

```
Dim varname1 As type1, varname2 As type2, ...
```

Variable names follow the same naming rules that were presented earlier in this session. A variable name must be unique within its scope. You learn about scope later in the session.

Variable Declaration and Option Explicit

One of VBA's weaknesses is that it lets programmers get away without declaring variables. In fact, this is its default behavior — just use variables in code without worrying about declarations or Dim statements. This sounds pretty easy, so why do I call it a weakness?

Working without variable declarations is an invitation to errors and bugs. The reason is because if you misspell a variable name, VBA just treats the misspelling as a new variable name. This can lead to all sorts of problems. In addition, if a variable is not declared, it is automatically created as type Variant, which is a real hog when it comes to processor time and memory resources.

If variable declaration is required, VBA automatically catches a misspelled variable as "undeclared," preventing the kind of errors mentioned above. Also, because you must explicitly declare each variable, you can use the data type that is best suited to the data.

To require variable declaration, include the Option Explicit statement in each module, at the beginning before any procedures. You can also turn this setting on for all modules (highly recommended!) by selecting Tools ➪ Options to display the Options dialog box; then, on the Editor tab, select the Require Variable Declaration option.

Numeric Variables

20 Min. To Go

VBA's numeric types fall into two categories:

- **Integers.** Numbers with no fractional part. For example, -5, 1, and 1,234.
- **Floating point.** Numbers with a fractional part. For example, 1.01 and -0.06.

Within each of these two categories, there are three different types that differ in the range of values they can hold, and, for the floating-point types, their accuracy (or precision). These are summarized in Table 4-1. When declaring a variable, choosing between an integer type and a floating-point type is usually easy, and you should use an integer type whenever possible because they take less memory and are faster in calculations — although, to be honest, with today's computers the difference is not likely to be noticeable. Within each category, you must select a specific type based on the nature of the data that the variable will hold. Note that the Currency type is specialized for holding money values.

Table 4-1 *VBA's Numeric Data Types*

Name	Type	Range	Precision
Byte	Integer	0 to 255	N/A
Integer	Integer	-32,768 to 32,767	N/A

Continued

Table 4-1 *Continued*

Name	Type	Range	Precision
Long	Integer	-2,147,483,648 to 2,147,483,647	N/A
Single	Floating point	-3.4×10^{38} to 3.4×10^{38} *	6 digits
Double	Floating point	-1.79×10^{308} to 1.79×10^{308} *	14 digits
Currency	Floating point	-9.22×10^{11} to 9.22×10^{11} *	4 digits

* *Approximate values.*

When you declare a numeric variable, it is assigned the initial value 0.

String Variables

String variables are used to hold text data. A *variable-length string* can hold any length of text you put in it, up to some huge maximum of about two billion characters. You don't need to worry about the string size because it automatically adjusts to fit its data. The keyword for declaring this type of variable is `String`:

```
Dim Name As String
```

The other type of string in VBA is a *fixed-length string*. You set the string's length when you declare it, and this remains its maximum capacity. A fixed-length string can be declared to contain anywhere from 1 to about 64,000 characters. To declare a fixed-length string, use the `String` keyword followed by the * (asterisk) symbol and the desired size:

```
Dim MyFixedLengthString As String * 12
```

If you assign a string that's too long to a fixed-length string variable — that is, longer that the variable's declared length — the excess characters are lost. For example:

```
Dim str As String * 5
str = "New York"
```

The variable now contains "New Y" (remember, spaces count as characters, too).

Some strings, such as "1234," look like numbers. To VBA, however, it is just a string and cannot be used in numeric calculations. For example, ZIP codes are usually stored as strings, such as "01345" to ensure that the leading 0 displays.

VBA has some tools for converting strings to numbers; these are covered in Session 10.

Date Variables

In VBA, the term *date* is used to refer to both dates and times. Dates are represented numerically as floating-point numbers. The integer part of the number represents the date as the number of days since December 30, 1899 (with negative numbers for prior dates), and the fractional part of the number represents the time of day as a fraction of the 24-hour day. Fortunately, you never need to deal with these numeric date representations directly because VBA has a powerful set of tools for working with dates in more conventional formats. These are covered in Session 8.

The Date data type is designed specifically to hold date information. To set a date value, you can use any of the commonly accepted formats placed between # (pound) symbols, as shown here:

```
Dim day1 As Date, day2 As Date, day3 As Date
day1 = #March 7, 2003#
day2 = #1/1/2003#
day3 = #July 4, 2003#
```

Object Variables

The Object data type can hold a reference to any object. It is rarely used, however, because it is preferred to declare variables as the specific type they will hold. Thus:

```
Dim GenericObject As Object
Dim SpecificObject As Worksheet
```

The variable GenericObject can hold a reference to any kind of object, while the variable SpecificObject can reference only a Worksheet object. It might seem that use of the Object data type is better because it provides more flexibility, but this is not the case. Here's why.

Use of the Object data type is called *late binding*. The program does not know what object type the variable will refer to until the program runs and a reference is actually assigned to the variable. This slows things down a bit, although not significantly. More important, it makes the editor's Auto List feature unavailable.

When you declare a variable as a specific object type, it is called *early binding*. VBA "knows" what type the variable is and, while you are editing, can use Auto List to display the object's properties and methods. This can be a real convenience.

> **To enable the Auto List feature, select Tools ⇨ Options, select the Editor tab, and put a check next to the Auto List Members option. With Auto List, when you type the name of an object variable followed by a period, the Editor displays a list of that type's properties and methods, from which you can select.**

Declaring a variable as a specific object type is not the same as initializing it. Here's an example:

```
Dim ws As Worksheet
```

After this code, the variable ws exists and is of type Worksheet, but it does not reference anything — it contains the value Nothing. To initialize the variable it must be assigned a specific reference, for example:

```
Set ws = Worksheets.Add
```

Now, the variable ws refers to the new worksheet that was created by the Add method.

The Set keyword must be used whenever you are assigning an object reference.

In most cases, you get your object references from collections, either as an existing collection member or by using the Add method. In some situations, however, there is no relevant collection, and you must create the object using the New keyword. The syntax is:

```
Set ObjectVariable = New ObjectName
```

You can also combine the declaration and initialization in one statement:

```
Dim ObjectVariable As New ObjectName
```

Boolean Variables

A Boolean variable can hold a True/False value. Boolean variables (and properties) are used frequently in VBA programming to hold data that can be on/off, yes/no, and so on. When you declare a Boolean variable, it is automatically initialized to False. VBA provides the keywords True and False to use for Boolean values:

```
Dim UpToDate As Boolean
UpToDate = True
```

The Variant Type

Variant is VBA's most flexible data type as well as the default type. This means that if you declare a variable without specifying a type, it is created as type Variant:

```
Dim x          ' X is type variant
```

You can also explicitly specify the type:

```
Dim x As Variant
```

The Variant data type can hold almost any type of data, the exceptions being fixed-length strings and user-defined types. Thus, a given Variant variable can hold an integer, a floating-point value, a string, or an object reference. A Variant can even hold an entire array. The downside is that Variant data requires more memory to store, and more computer power to process, than other data types. This means that you should not use Variant variables simply as a convenience to avoid having to decide which of the more specific data types to use. Rather, restrict use of this data type to situations where its flexibility is really needed. This includes:

- For data that must be treated as a number or as a string depending on the circumstances.
- For procedure arguments that can take different kinds of data.
- For retrieving data from worksheet cells when you do not know what kind of data the cell contains.

Working with procedure arguments is covered is Session 7, and retrieving data from worksheet cells is covered in Session 10.

Using Arrays

10 Min. To Go

An array lets you store multiple data items in one place. The array has a name, and the individual items are identified by a numeric index. When you create an array, you specify one of VBA's data types, and all the elements in the array are of that type. Arrays are useful for storing related data together in one location. For example, suppose your program needs to work with sales figures for the 12 months of the year. You could create an array with 12 elements and store January's figure in element 1, February's in element 2, and so on. Using an array for data often makes your code simpler and easier to write. VBA has two types of arrays — static and dynamic.

Static Arrays

A *static array* has a fixed size or number of elements. You specify the array size when you declare it, and the size cannot change during program execution. The declaration syntax is:

```
Dim ArrayName(n) As Type
```

ArrayName must follow the usual VBA naming rules, and type can be any of VBA's data types. The size of the array is specified by n. Actually, the size will be one more than n because VBA array indexes start by default at 0; therefore, the declaration

```
Dim MyArray(50) As Integer
```

actually results in an array with 51 members, at indexes 0 through 50. Array elements are referenced using the array name and an index in parentheses:

```
MyArray(0) = 1
MyArray(25) = 72
```

You can use an integer variable or constant as the index:

```
Dim idx As Integer
idx = 12
MyArray(idx) = 44    ' Same as MyArray(12)
```

If you do not want to use 0 as the lower array index, you have two choices. One choice is to include the Option Base 1 statement at the start of a module, outside of any procedures. This results in all arrays in the module having a lower bound of 1 instead of 0. The other choice provides more flexibility, using the To keyword in the array declaration:

```
Dim ArrayName(lowerbound To upperbound) As Type
```

Lowerbound must be smaller than upperbound, and both must be integers. Here's an example:

```
Dim MyArray(20 To 40) As Long
```

Arrays with a single index are called *one-dimensional* arrays. You can also create arrays with two or more indexes by specifying the additional indexes in the Dim statement.

```
Dim TwoDimensions(10, 10) As Single
```

This array has 121 elements, references as TwoDimensions(0, 0) through TwoDimensions(10, 10). The first dimension has 11 elements numbered 0 through 10. The second dimension also has 11 elements. The total number of elements is the product of 11 times 11. You can use the To keyword in multidimensional arrays:

```
Dim ChessBoard(1 To 8, 1 To 8) As String
```

VBA does not impose any specific limits on the number of elements in an array, or the number of dimensions. Available system memory and disk space, however, impose practical limits, but these limits are not likely to pose a problem. In the situation where a system is running low on both free memory and disk space, you might encounter problems, but this is very unlikely to happen.

 If your program tries to use an array element that does not exist, a runtime error occurs. For example, if you create an array with the statement Dim MyArray(20) As Integer, **then you'll get an error if you try to use** MyArray(21), MyArray(30), **and so on.**

Dynamic Arrays

A *dynamic array* does not have a fixed size. It can be enlarged or shrunk as needed by code during program execution. A dynamic array is declared by using empty parentheses in the Dim statement:

```
Dim MyDynamicArray() As type
```

Before using the array, you must set its size using the ReDim statement:

```
ReDim MyDynamicArray(size)
```

The size argument specifies the number of array dimensions and the number of elements in each dimension, just as for static arrays. Here are some examples:

```
Dim Dynamic1() As String
Dim Dynamic2() As Integer
Dim Dynamic3() As Object
...
ReDim Dynamic1(100)        ' 1 dimension, 101 elements 0 through 100
ReDim Dynamic2(-5 To 5)    ' 1 dimension, 11 elements -5 through 5
ReDim Dynamic3(5, 5, 5)    ' 3 dimensions, 216 total elements
```

You cannot change the type of a dynamic array with a ReDim statement, but you can change its size as many times as needed. When you use ReDim, any data in the array is normally lost. You can preserve existing array data (with some limitations) by including the Preserve keyword in the ReDim statement:

```
ReDim Preserve Dynamic1(100)
```

The limitations on preserving data with Preserve are:

- If you make an array smaller, data in the trimmed elements is lost.
- For multidimensional arrays, you can change the size of only the last dimension.
- You cannot change the number of dimensions.

The program shown in Listing 4-1 demonstrates the use of a dynamic array. To use this program, place the cursor at the top of a column of numbers in any worksheet and then run the program. The program goes down the column, copying the number from each cell and placing it in the array. For each cell, ReDim is used to add another element to the array. When an empty cell is found, the program then goes through the array and calculates the total of all the values. This result is placed in the cell at the bottom of the column.

In case you need a little review, here are the steps required to create and run this program.

1. In Excel, place a column of numbers in a worksheet.
2. Press Alt+F11 to open the VBA Editor.
3. In the Project Explorer, double-click the name of the worksheet in which you placed the numbers. A code-editing window opens.
4. Place the code from Listing 4-1 into the editing window.
5. Switch back to the Excel screen, and make sure the Excel cursor is at the top cell in the column of numbers.
6. Press Alt+F8 to open the Macros dialog box.
7. Select the macro named SumColumn and then click Run.

The program uses some VBA elements with which you are not yet familiar. You may be able to figure them out, but if not, you should not be concerned. The point here is to demonstrate a dynamic array.

Listing 4-1 *Demonstrating the use of a dynamic array*

```
Public Sub SumColumn()

Dim data() As Single
Dim total As Single
Dim count As Integer
Dim i As Integer
Dim finished As Boolean
count = 0

Do
    count = count + 1
    ReDim Preserve data(count)
    data(count) = ActiveCell.Value
    ActiveCell.Offset(1, 0).Activate
    If ActiveCell.Value = "" Then finished = True
Loop Until finished

For i = 1 To UBound(data)
    total = total + data(i)
Next

ActiveCell.Value = total

End Sub
```

Determining Array Size

VBA provides two functions that enable you to determine the size of an array. Specifically, you can determine the largest and smallest legal index for an array. The functions are:

```
UBound(arrayname, dimension)
LBound(arrayname, dimension)
```

UBound returns the largest, and LBound the smallest, legal index for the specified array. The dimension argument is optional and specifies the dimension of the array. The default is 1. For example:

```
Dim MyArray(1 To 5, 10 To 25)
x = LBound(MyArray)       ' Returns 1
x = UBound(MyArray, 2)    ' Returns 25
```

User-Defined Types

A user-defined type (UDT) allows the programmer to define custom data elements that are specifically suited for the data at hand. A UDT can contain two or more elements, each element being a variable or array. UDTs are defined with the Type...End Type statement:

```
Type TypeName
      Element1Name As Type
      Element2Name As Type
      ...
End Type
```

Each element follows the same rule as regular VBA variables. You can mix data types in a UDT as dictated by the needs of your program, and you can use any available type. An element can be an array as well as another UDT. Here's an example of a UDT designed to hold employee information:

```
Type EmployeeInfo
      FirstName As String
      LastName As String
      SSNum As String * 10
      HireDate As Date
      HealthPlan As Boolean
      Salary As Currency
End Type
```

It may be useful to see exactly what the lines of this code do:

- The first line begins the definition of a UDT named "EmployeeInfo."
- The second line declares a variable in the UDT named "FirstName" of type String.
- The third line declares a variable in the UDT named "LastName" of type String.
- Remaining lines declare other variables within the UDT.
- The last line marks the end of the UDT definition.

The definition of a UDT must be placed in a module, outside of any procedures. After a UDT is defined, you can use it in variable declarations such as VBA's built-in data types. Here are some examples:

```
Dim SomeEmployee As EmployeeInfo
Dim AllEmployees(100) As EmployeeInfo
```

To access the elements of a UDT, use the *name.element* syntax. Thus:

```
SomeEmployee.FirstName = "Jane"
SomeEmployee.LastName = "Jones"
AllEmployees(1).FirstName = "Sam"
```

Enumerations

An enumeration is a defined data type that contains a set of symbolic constants as specified by the programmer. When a variable is declared as an enumeration type, it can take only these predefined values. Enumerations are useful when a variable's data can take only certain values, such as a variable to hold the name of the month. By using an enumeration that contains the 12 month names, you ensure that a variable of that type never can hold erroneous data.

You use the Enum...End Enum statement to define an enumeration:

```
Enum EnumName
     Member1
     Member2
     . . .
End Enum
```

Here's an example:

```
Enum Flavor
     Vanilla
     Chocolate
     Strawberry
     Coffee
End Enum
```

Each constant in an Enum statement is assigned a numeric value. If you do not specify the values, they are assigned in order starting with 0. In the previous example, Vanilla has the value 0, Chocolate has the value 1, and so on. If desired, you can specify the values explicitly:

```
Enum Flavors
     Vanilla = 1
     Chocolate = 4
     Strawberry = 7
     Coffee = 16
End Enum
```

An Enum statement must be defined at the module level, outside of any procedure (similar to a UDT). It then becomes available as a data type that you can use in your variable declarations:

```
Dim MyIceCream As Flavor
Dim MenuItems(50) As Flavor
```

When working with an Enum variable, VBA's Auto List feature displays a list of the Enum statement's defined constants, which is a real convenience because you can simply select from the list rather than type the data in manually.

Understanding Variable Scope

A variable that is declared in a VBA program is available only in certain parts of the program. This is referred to as the variable's *scope*, and a variable can be used only within its scope. In other parts of the program, it effectively does not exist. In fact, you can have two variables of the same name with different scopes, and they are completely independent of each other.

VBA offers three levels of scope:

- **Procedure level.** Scope limited to a single VBA procedure.
- **Module level.** Scope limited to a single module (all procedures in the module).
- **Project level.** Scope extends throughout the project.

To create a variable with procedure-level scope, declare it using a Dim statement inside a procedure. You should always use procedure-level scope unless there is a specific reason to use a wider scope. Most variables in your program will have this scope.

To create a variable with module-level scope, declare it using a Dim statement at the module level (outside any procedures). Use module-level scope when multiple procedures in the module need access to a variable, as is the case with property procedures (which are covered in Session 26). In this context, you can use Private in place of Dim, but it has the same effect:

```
Private Total As Integer
```

Project-level scope can take two forms. If you declare a variable at the module level using the Public keyword, its scope extends throughout all modules in the current project as well as any other open VBA projects. If you include the statement Option Private Module at the start of the module, variables declared with Public have scope throughout the current project only.

 When two variables with the same name have overlapping scopes, the variable with the more restrictive scope takes precedence.

When deciding what scope to use for a variable, the rule is to use the most restrictive scope possible. Most variables in a program have procedure-level scope. By isolating variables within procedures, you remove the possibility of unintended changes and interactions and the resulting program bugs and errors. Information that must be shared between two or more procedures can be passed back and forth by means of procedure arguments and return values. Variables with wider scope should be used sparingly, and only when it is unavoidable.

Done!

REVIEW

Almost any Excel program needs to work with data, and VBA provides a lot of flexibility in this regard. Numerous data types provide storage for all kinds of data, including numbers, text, dates, and object references. Among the things you learned in this session are:

- The fundamental syntax of VBA, including the use of comments.
- How to use literal and symbolic constants.
- VBA's naming rules.
- How to declare variables.
- Types of numeric, string, and object variables.
- About variable scope.
- How to create and use static and dynamic arrays.
- Defining user-defined types and enumerations.

QUIZ YOURSELF

1. How do you split a VBA statement over two or more lines? (See the "VBA Syntax Fundamentals" section.)
2. What are the two ways to create a comment? (See the "Comments" section.)
3. Name two advantages of symbolic constants. (See the "Employing Constants" section.)
4. Should you use the Option Explicit statement in your programs? Why? (See the "Variable Declaration and Option Explicit" sidebar.)
5. What data type is designed to hold money values? (See the "Numeric Variables" section.)
6. What statement is used to create a user-defined type? (See the "User-Defined Types" section.)
7. When should you use the Object data type? (See the "Object Variables" section.)
8. What does the term *variable scope* refer to? (See the "Understanding Variable Scope" section.)

PART

I

Friday Evening
Part Review

1. What is a program?
2. How do you start the VBA Editor from Excel?
3. How do you insert a new code module in a VBA project?
4. What's the easiest way to copy code from one VBA project to another?
5. What is a property?
6. How do you create an absolute cell reference?
7. How do object properties and methods differ?
8. Must a method call always include arguments in the precise order as defined for the method?
9. Which VBA statement is used to loop through all the members of a collection?
10. In a VBA program running in Excel, when is it necessary to use the `Application` keyword?
11. How would you save a copy of a workbook under a new name without changing the original workbook's name?
12. What method is used to print the current workbook?
13. How do you obtain a reference to the active worksheet in a workbook?
14. How do you change a worksheet's name in code (the name that displays on the worksheet's tab)?
15. How can you prevent Excel from displaying its confirmation dialog box when you delete a worksheet in code?
16. What is the `Nothing` keyword used for?
17. How can your VBA code determine how many worksheets are present in a workbook?
18. What is the function of the `Workbook.CreateBackup` property?
19. How would you obtain the full path and filename of a workbook?

20. Suppose more than one workbook is open in Excel. How would you activate a specific workbook?

21. How can you tell if a workbook has been saved since the last time it was changed?

22. What restrictions, if any, are there on using the line continuation character in VBA code?

23. What are VBA's rules for indenting code?

24. How does VBA store dates internally?

25. You declare a VBA array as follows: `Dim Data(100) As Integer`. How many elements does the array contain?

26. How can a program determine the size of an array?

27. What does *variable scope* refer to?

28. How would you declare a variable to be available throughout the entire project?

PART

II

Saturday Morning

Operators

Session Checklist

✔ The assignment operator

✔ Numerical and string operators

✔ Logical operators

✔ Comparison operators

✔ Operator precedence

**30 Min.
To Go**

A n *operator* is a symbol that instructs your program to carry out a specific action with data, such as adding two numbers. Operators are essential for many programs, including programs that perform numerical calculations and comparisons. VBA has several categories of operators that are used for different types of data and different kinds of operations.

The Assignment Operator

In VBA, the equal symbol (=) is the assignment operator, and is used to assign a value to a variable or property. For example,

```
x = 5
```

This line of code assigns the value 5 to the variable x. Note that this is a different meaning than the equal symbol usually has in mathematics, which is to state that the two items are, in fact, equal.

The rules for using the assignment operator are:

- The item on the left side of the assignment operator must be some element that can be assigned a value — that is, a variable, property or, in a Const statement, a constant.

- When assigning an object reference, the line must begin with the Set keyword.

- The item on the right side of the assignment operator must be an expression — anything that evaluates to a value.

The term *expression* means any VBA code that can be reduced, or evaluated, to a single numerical or string value. Thus, 5+2-1 is an expression because it can be evaluated to the single value 6. Likewise "Micro" & "soft" is an expression because it evaluates to the single value "Microsoft."

There are some restrictions regarding the data types of the two elements in an assignment statement.

- If you assign a string value to a numeric variable, any value other than True or False to a Boolean variable, or any nonobject value to an object variable, an error occurs.

- If you assign a value to a numeric variable that is out of the range for that type, an error occurs.

- If you assign a number value to a string variable, the number is converted to the text equivalent.

- If you assign a floating-point value to an integer variable, the value is rounded to the nearest integer.

The = symbol is also used by VBA as a comparison operator, as explained later in this session. It is always clear from the context whether this symbol is being used for assignment or comparison.

The concept of an expression is important in programming. An expression is anything that can be evaluated to a value. It can be a numeric value, a string, an object reference, or a logical (True/False) value.

Numerical Operators

The *numerical operators*, sometimes called the mathematical operators, perform operations with numbers. The familiar operations of addition, subtraction, multiplication, and division are represented by the symbols +, -, *, and / respectively. There are three less commonly used operations:

- **Integer division (\\).** Performs a division, and returns the integer part of the answer; therefore, 11\\3 evaluates to 3.

- **Exponentiation (^).** Raises a number to a power. In VBA, 4^2 means "four to the second power" or 4^2, and evaluates to 16.

- **Modulus (mod).** Performs a division and returns the remainder. For example, 18 mod 5 evaluates to 3. Floating-point numbers are rounded to integers when used with mod.

20 Min. To Go

String Operators

There is a single *string operator*, the concatenation operator represented by the symbol &. Concatenation means simply putting two strings together. Here's an example:

```
Dim s1 As String, s2 As String, s3 As String
s1 = "Micro"
s2 = "soft"
s3 = s1 & s2
```

The first string, s1, contains the text "Micro," and the second string, s2, contains the text "soft." When you concatenate, or combine, them, the result is that s3 contains "Microsoft."

Sometimes the + symbol is used for concatenation. This is a holdover from earlier versions of VBA and should not be used in your programs. It works fine, but it is better to use the & symbol to make your code as clear as possible.

Even though it has only one string operator, VBA has extremely powerful text-handling capabilities.

VBA's text-handling capabilities are covered in Session 10.

Logical Operators

Logical operators work with logical (True/False) values. With one exception, these operators combine two logical values into a single True/False value. You see examples of this on a regular basis in daily life. For example, suppose you are shopping for a TV set and have the following criteria:

- At least 36-inch screen
- Stereo sound
- Costs less than $500

Your decision whether to buy a particular model could be phrased logically as follows:

```
Buy TV = (36" screen?) and (stereo sound?) and (less than $500?)
```

Here, you are using the And operator to say, in essence, that you will buy the TV if and only if all the conditions are True.

VBA has six logical operators, as summarized in Table 5-1.

Table 5-1 *VBA's Logical Operators*

Operator	Example	True if	False if
And	A And B	A and B are both True	A, B, or both are False
Or	A Or B	Either A or B is True	A and B are both False
XOr (Exclusive Or)	A Xor B	If A and B are different	If A and B are the same
Eqv (equivalence)	A Eqv B	If A and B are the same	If A and B are different
Imp (Implication)	A Imp B	If A is False and B is True or False	If A is True and B is False
Not	Not A	A is False	A is True

Comparison Operators

The comparison operators are used to perform comparisons between expressions. A comparison expression is actually a logical expression, evaluating to True or False depending on the data and operator used. For example, the equal sign is the comparison operator that asks "are these two expressions equal?" Therefore, the expression

    10 = 5

evaluates to False. This and the other comparison operators that are used with numbers are listed here:

- = Equal to
- > Greater than
- < Less than
- >= Greater than or equal to
- <= Less than or equal to
- <> Not equal to

These comparison operators can be used with strings (text) as well. When comparing strings, the concepts of "greater than" and "less than" are based on the ASCII values of the characters in the strings being compared. Because of the way ASCII codes are assigned, this corresponds (for the letters) to alphabetical order, so "apple" is considered to be less than "banana."

 Computers use numbers internally to represent characters of the alphabet, punctuation marks, and so on. ASCII (American Standard Code for Information Interchange) is the universally accepted code that specifies which number corresponds to which character. Search for "character set" in VBA's online help for a chart of ASCII codes.

There's a twist, however, in that upper- and lowercase letters have different ASCII codes, with the uppercase codes all being less than the lowercase codes. VBA's default, therefore, is to consider "Apple" to be unequal to, and less than, "apple." In most cases, this type of text comparison is not wanted, and you have two ways around it.

One approach is to include the statement `Option Compare Text` at the start of the module, outside of any procedure. This instructs VBA to perform text comparisons with upper- and lowercase letters being equivalent, so that "Apple" does equal "apple." This applies to all text comparisons within the module.

The other approach is to use VBA's `UCase` or `LCase` function to convert a string to all upper- or lowercase, and then perform the comparison:

```
UCase(string1) = UCase(string2)
```

These functions do not change the original strings but only make temporary uppercase copies for the comparison.

The final string comparison operator is `Like`, which determines if a string matches a pattern. It is used as follows:

```
string Like pattern
```

`Pattern` is itself a string composed of the elements described in Table 5-2. The elements you use, and their order, depend on what you want to match. Table 5-3 shows some examples of patterns, and what they match and do not match.

Table 5-2 *Elements Used in the Pattern for the* `Like` *Operator*

Element	Matches
A single character	The character itself
*	Any sequence of 0 or more characters
?	Any single character
#	Any digit
[list]	Any character in list
[!list]	Any character not in list

Table 5-3 *Pattern Examples for the* `Like` *Operator*

Pattern	Matches	Does Not Match
b[ae]t	bat, bet	but, bit
[a-d]??	ace, bad, cat, dig	fix, apple, coast, vice

Continued

Table 5-3   *Continued*

Pattern	Matches	Does Not Match
c?d	cad, cod, cud, c!d	cook, dad, cd
#####-####	Any "ZIP plus 4" ZIP code	Anything else
[!5]####	Any five-digit number not starting with 5	Anything else

The final comparison operator is used to compare object references. The Is operator returns True if two references refer to the same object:

```
ObjectRef1 Is ObjectRef2
```

You can also use Is to determine if an object reference does not reference anything (contains the value Nothing):

```
ObjectRef Is Nothing
```

Operator Precedence

**10 Min.
To Go**

With some expressions, there is no doubt as to how it will be evaluated. Other more complex expressions, however, can be ambiguous. Look at this expression:

```
12 * 3 + 5
```

If the multiplication is done first, you have 36 + 5 resulting in 41. If the addition is performed first, you have 12 * 8 resulting in 96. VBA's rules of operator precedence resolve this sort of situation by specifying the order in which operations are carried out. In highest to lowest precedence order, they are:

- Exponentiation (^)
- Multiplication (*) and division (/)
- Integer division (\)
- Modulus (mod)
- Addition (+) and subtraction (-)
- String concatenation (&)

In the previous example 12 * 3 + 5, the multiplication is performed first and the result is 41.

When the order of execution is not modified by operator precedence or parentheses, it always proceeds from left to right in the expression.

You can modify the order of execution in an expression by using parentheses. Anything within parentheses is evaluated first, regardless of operator precedence. Thus,

```
12 * (3 + 5)
```

evaluates to 96 because the addition is performed first. You can nest parentheses as needed, in which case execution starts with the innermost set and then works outward. Parentheses must always come in left-right pairs.

Done!

REVIEW

The VBA language provides a full set of operators for use in your programs. Operators are instructions that perform various kinds of manipulations, or operations, on data. This session showed:

- The assignment operator is used to assign values to variables.
- Numerical (or mathematical) operators perform common operations with numerical values.
- The concatenation operator combines two strings.
- You use the logical operators to work with True/False values.
- The comparison operators enable you to perform comparisons between data items.
- VBA's operator precedence rules determine the order in which operations occur within an expression.

QUIZ YOURSELF

1. What does "assignment" mean in VBA? (See the "The Assignment Operator" section.)
2. How do you determine the remainder of a division? (See the "Numerical Operators" section.)
3. The expression A Xor B is true under what conditions? (See the "Logical Operators" section.)
4. When performing string comparisons, is "yes" always equal to "YES?" Explain. (See the "Comparison Operators" section.)
5. Do the expressions A + B / C and (A + B) / C evaluate the same? Explain. (See the "Operator Precedence" section.)

Control Constructs

**30 Min.
To Go**

The VBA language includes several elements that are used to control the flow of execution in the program. Called *control constructs*, these elements fall, for the most part, into the following two categories:

- Conditional statements that execute sections of code, or not, depending on program conditions. These are the `If...Then` and the `Select Case` statements.

- Loop statements that execute sections of code zero, one, or more times, depending on program conditions. These are the `Do...Loop`, `For...Next`, and `For Each...Next` statements.

A good understanding of these control constructs is an essential element of VBA programming.

With...End With

The With...End With construct cannot be called a control statement because it does not modify code execution. It does, however, provide a handy short-hand that simplifies writing code in certain situations. Recall that for using an object property or an object method, the syntax is:

```
ObjectName.PropertyName
```

If you need to access a lot of properties or methods of the same object it can require writing the object name over and over again many times. With...End With lets you simplify the code as follows:

```
With ObjectName
    .Property1 = Value1
    .Property2 = Value2
    .Method1
    .Method2
End With
```

The above is exactly equivalent to the following:

```
ObjectName.Property1 = Value1
ObjectName.Property2 = Value2
ObjectName.Method1

ObjectName.Method2
```

With...End With is just a convenience, but it can save a lot of typing.

The If...Then Statement

The If...Then statement, or If statement for short, is used in a program to execute a block of code if a specified logical condition is True. Optionally, it can also execute another block only if the condition is False. In its simplest form, the If statement looks similar to:

```
If condition Then
    block1
End If
```

If condition is True, the statements in the block (indicated by *block1*) are executed. If condition is False, they are not executed. The block of statements can contain one or more VBA statements, with no real length restriction (although it is good practice to keep things short).

If there is only one statement to be executed, the End If can be omitted and the entire If construct placed on one line:

```
If condition Then statement
```

In another variant, there is an Else clause and two blocks of statements:

```
If condition Then
     block1
Else
     block2
End If
```

If condition is True, the statements in *block1* are executed. If it is False, *block2* is executed. One of the two blocks is always executed.

The final variant of the If statement lets you check multiple conditions using the ElseIf keyword. The syntax is:

```
If condition-1 Then
     block-1
ElseIf condition-2 Then
     block-2
...

ElseIf condition-n Then
     block-n
Else
     block-else
End If
```

When this is encountered during execution, each condition is tested, starting at the top. The block associated with the first true condition is executed; then execution passes to the code after the End If statement. If no condition is true, the block associated with the Else keyword is executed. The Else keyword and its associated block are optional. If omitted, there is the possibility that no code within the If...End If structure will be executed.

The short program in Listing 6-1 demonstrates the use of If.

Listing 6-1 *Demonstration of the If statement*

```
Public Sub IfDemo()
    Dim num

    num = InputBox("Enter a number between 5 and 10:")
    If num < 5 Then
        MsgBox("That's too small.")
    ElseIf num > 10 Then
        MsgBox("That's too large.")
    Else
        MsgBox("Thank you!")
    End If
End Sub
```

When you have more than a few conditions to test, the Select Case statement is usually a better choice than using a lot of ElseIfs. Either will work, but a Select Case almost always requires less programming effort.

The IIf Function

VBA's IIf function is related to the If...Then statement and is used to return one of two values, depending on whether a condition is True. The syntax is:

```
IIf(condition, exp1, exp2)
```

If condition is True, the function returns exp1; if condition is False, it returns exp2. Here's an example that sets the variable Z equal to the larger of X or Y:

```
Z = IIf(X > Y, X, Y)
```

The Select Case Statement

**20 Min.
To Go**

The Select Case statement lets your program make multiple choices based on the value of a single expression. The syntax is as follows:

```
Select Case expression
        Case template-1
                block-1
        Case template-2
                block-2
        ...
        Case template-n
                block-n
        Case Else
                block-else
End Select
```

Here's how it works. The program starts by evaluating expression. It then goes down the list of Case statements, comparing the value of the expression against each template. If a match is found, the associated block of statements is executed. If there is no match, the block of statements associated with the Case Else is executed. You can have as many Case statements as desired. The Case Else is optional. Note than even if there are multiple templates that match that value of expression, only one (the first one found) is executed.

The template in a Case statement can contain a single comparison value, or multiple comparison values separated by commas. Each comparison value can be one of the following:

- Any expression (must be matched exactly).
- A range of values indicated by the To keyword. For example, 10 To 20.
- The Is keyword followed by a comparison operator and an expression. For example, Is < 100.

Here's an example that would match numerical values that are equal to 12, greater than or equal to 20, or between 1 and 4.

```
Case 12, Is >= 20, 1 To 4
```

You can also use To and Is with strings.

Please refer back to Session 5 for details on how VBA performs string comparisons.

The Do...Loop Statement

The Do...Loop statement, or Do for short, is used to execute a block of statements repeatedly — in other words, to loop through the statements. For instance, suppose your program needed to look through a column of numbers in a worksheet until it found a value of zero — a Do...Loop statement would be the ideal way to write the required code. This statement comes in several variations that can meet essentially any program need. They are described in Table 6-1.

Table 6-1   *Variations on the Do Statement*

Syntax	Action	Notes
Do While *condition*		
statements		
Loop	Repeatedly executes statements as long as condition remains true.	If condition is initially false, statements do not execute at all.
Do Until *condition*		
statements		
Loop	Repeatedly executes statements until condition becomes true.	If condition is initially true, statements will not be executed at all.
Do		
statements		
Loop While *condition*	Executes statements once; then repeats as long as condition remains true.	statements are always executed at least once.
Do		
statements		
Loop Until *condition*	Executes statements once; then repeats until condition becomes true.	statements are always executed at least once.

You can exit a Do loop early by including the Exit Do statement within the loop. When this statement is encountered, execution immediately passes to the code following the Loop statement regardless of the value of the condition that the loop is testing. The following example loops until the variable X is either zero or greater than 50:

```
Do Until X > 50
    ...
    If X = 0 Then Exit Do
    ...
Loop
```

Sometimes it is useful to set up a loop that would execute forever, and use Exit Do to terminate it. This loop repeatedly prompts the user to give an answer until he answers the question correctly:

```
Do While True
    str = InputBox("What's the capital of France?")
    If str = "Paris" Then Exit Do
Loop
```

Of course, the same result could be obtained as follows:

```
Do
    str = InputBox("What's the capital of France?")
Loop Until str = "Paris"
```

This demonstrates VBA's flexibility — there is almost always more than one way to do something.

When programming loops, you must be careful not to create an infinite loop — one that repeats forever. This can happen if the loop's condition is expressed incorrectly, or if code within the loop does not take any action to change the condition. Here's an example:

```
Do Until X < 5 And X > 10
...
Loop
```

Perhaps you already see the problem — it is impossible for X to be less than 5 and more than 10 at the same time, so the condition will never be met and the loop will repeat forever. If a VBA program stops responding and seems to be "frozen," an infinite loop might be the problem.

VBA supports the obsolete While...Wend statement, a holdover from earlier versions of Basic. Its syntax is:

```
While condition
...
Wend
```

Stopping an Infinite Loop

When an infinite loop is running, you usually have to resort to the Windows Task Manager to stop it. The steps are:

1. Press Ctrl+Alt+Del to open the Windows Security dialog box.
2. Click the Task Manager button to display the Task Manager dialog box.
3. On the Applications tab, select the Microsoft Visual Basic entry.
4. Click the End Task button.

This terminates the VBA Editor. Unsaved changes to your programs will be lost.

The loop repeats as long as condition is True. You can see that this is functionally equivalent to the following Do variant:

```
Do While condition
...
Loop
```

While...Wend is support only for backward compatibility. You should not use it in your programs.

The For...Next Statement

10 Min. To Go

The For...Next statement repeats a block of code a specified number of times. Its simplest form is:

```
For index = start To stop
...
Next index
```

- Index is a variable that is used to count loop repetitions. It is usually declared to be type Integer.
- Start is an expression specifying the starting value of index.
- Stop is an expression specifying the ending value of index.

When a For...Next statement is encountered, index is set equal to start, and the statements between the For and the Next are executed. Index is incremented by 1, and the process repeats. The statements are repeated until index is greater than stop. Note that for the last repetition, index is equal to stop.

Including the name of the counter variable in the Next statement is optional. If you simply use Next alone, VBA automatically matches it with the previous For.

Optionally, For...Next can use an increment value other than 1. The syntax for this is:

```
For index = start To stop Step step
...
Next index
```

In the preceding example, *step* specifies the increment value. Note the following:

- If step is negative, start must be greater than stop.
- If step is a floating-point value, index must be declared as a floating-point type.

This example counts down from 10 to 5 as follows: 10, 9.9, 9.8 ... 5.1, 5:

```
Dim index As Single
For index = 10 To 5 Step -0.1
...
Next index
```

Never: Change the value of the loop counter inside the loop. You can use the value, but you should let the For...Next statement make changes as the loop counts down.

Use the Exit For statement to exit from a For...Next loop early. The following example loops through all the elements in an array and exits if an element equal to zero is found:

```
Dim found As Boolean
Dim index As Integer
found = False
For index = LBound(MyArray) To UBound(MyArray)
    If MyArray(index) = 0 Then
            found = True
            Exit For
    End If
Next index
```

The For Each...Next Statement

You use the For Each...Next statement to iterate through all the members of a collection or array. The syntax for collections is:

```
For Each item in collection
...
Next
```

Item is a variable that has been declared as an appropriate type to reference the objects in the collection (type Object, type Variant, or the specific type of the collection). The loop starts by setting item to reference the first object in the collection and then executing the statements between the For and the Next. Item is then set to reference the next object in the collection, and the process repeats for all elements of the collection. If the collection is empty, the statements in the loop are not executed at all.

The following example uses For Each...Next to print all the worksheets in the active workbook:

```
Dim ws As Worksheet
For Each ws In ActiveWorkbook.Worksheets
     ws.PrintOut
Next
```

To loop through an array, the syntax is similar:

```
For Each var in array
...
Next
```

In this case, n is a variable of the same data type as array, or type Variant. The following code calculates the sum of all elements in the array (assuming MyArray is type Single):

```
Dim var As Single
Dim total As Single
total = 0
For Each var In MyArray
    total = total + var
Next
```

Note that you could perform the same task using a For...Next loop and the LBound and UBound functions, but For Each...Next permits somewhat easier and simpler programming.

As with For...Next, you can use the Exit For statement to exit a For Each...Next loop before all of the elements of the collection or array are processed.

The Goto Statement

The Goto statement instructs program execution to go to the specified location in the code. The syntax is:

```
Goto label
```

Label is a location identifier, consisting of a label followed by a colon on a line by itself in the code. Goto is limited to branching within a procedure — that is, both the Goto statement, and its target label must be within the same procedure. Here's an example:

```
Dim val As Integer
val = InputBox("Enter an even number:")
If val mod 2 <> 0 Then Goto NotEven
MsgBox("Thank You!")
Goto Finished
NotEven:
MsgBox("That's not an even number, pal!")
Finished:
' More code
```

A label itself has no effect on program operation — it serves only as the target of a Goto.

My advice is to avoid the Goto statement altogether (except, as you'll see later in the book, in error-handling code). Its use can result in confusing and buggy code, and I have yet to see a programming situation that could not be handled better by VBA's other control constructs.

Done!

REVIEW

The VBA language provides a number of control constructs that let you modify the execution of code in your program. You'll find that these statements are important in all but the simplest Excel programs. In this session, you learned:

- The If and Select Case statements are used to execute, or not execute, specified statements depending on conditions in the program.
- The For...Next statement lets you repeat execution a specified number of times.
- The Do...Loop statement repeats execution while, or until, a specified condition is met.
- The For Each...Next statement is used to iterate through all the members of a collection or all the elements of an array.
- You can jump to another program location with Goto, but this statement is best avoided.

QUIZ YOURSELF

1. When would you want to use a Select Case statement in preference to an If statement? (See the "The If...Then Statement" section.)

2. How would you use an If statement to execute code when a condition is False? (Hint: there's more than one way to do this.) (See the "The If...Then Statement" section.)

3. How would you ensure that the code in a Do...Loop construct is executed at least once? (See the "The Do...Loop Statement" section.)

4. Describe two ways to iterate through all the elements in an array. (See the "The For...Next Statement" and "The For Each...Next Statement" sections.)

5. When should you use the Goto statement? (See the "The Goto Statement" section.)

Procedures and Modules

Session Checklist

✔ Defining sub and function procedures

✔ Specifying procedure arguments

✔ Using optional and `ParamArray` arguments

✔ Calling procedures

✔ Declaring variables in procedures

✔ Procedure scope

✔ Storing and organizing procedures

**30 Min.
To Go**

You learned in a previous session that the procedure is VBA's fundamental unit of code organization. If you record a macro, it is saved as a VBA procedure. Furthermore, the simplest VBA programs consist of a single procedure. More complex programs, on the other hand, consist of many interacting procedures, and you must know how to create and work with procedures to create Excel programs.

Session 2 explains how procedures are used to organize VBA code.

There are five different types of procedures in VBA:

- A sub procedure is a named, independent section of code.
- A function procedure is similar to a sub procedure with the added feature of returning data to the program that called it.
- A method is a procedure (either sub or function) within a class module.

- A property procedure defines a property in a class.
- An event procedure is executed when an event, such as a keypress or mouse click, occurs.

Sub and function procedures, the most fundamental types, are covered in this session. Methods, property procedures, and event procedures are more specialized and are covered in later sessions.

Methods and property procedures are covered in Session 26. Event procedures are covered in Session 27.

Sub Procedures

A sub procedure is defined using the Sub and End Sub keywords. The syntax is:

```
Sub ProcName(arguments)
...
End Sub
```

The procedure name follows the usual VBA naming rules and must be unique within its scope. Arguments (data that is passed to the procedure) are covered in the next section. Use an empty set of parentheses when the procedure takes no arguments. Within the procedure you can include essentially any VBA code, with the following exceptions:

- Another procedure definition
- A class definition
- A user-defined type definition
- An enumeration definition

The length of code in a procedure is unlimited, but good programming practice dictates that procedures be kept to reasonable lengths. What is reasonable? There's no single correct answer to that question, but in my experience I have almost never found it necessary to create a procedure continuing more than 30 to 40 lines of code. When a procedure reaches that length, it almost always can, and should, be broken into two or more separate procedures. This results in code that is easier to read, understand, and debug.

When planning your procedures, you should try to create a separate procedure for each discrete task that needs to be performed. For example, suppose you are writing a program that calculates both the amount of a mortgage a person can afford based on his or her income and other debts, and the monthly payments on that mortgage for different interest rates. You could certainly place all the code in one procedure, but it would be preferable to separate the program into at least two procedures — one to determine the mortgage amount and the other to calculate the monthly payments. By keeping tasks that are logically separate in their own procedures, you reduce the chance of unintended code interactions and the resulting bugs and errors. Also, procedures are more likely to be reusable in other programs when designed this way.

Procedure Arguments

An *argument* is a piece of data that is passed to a procedure when the procedure is called. A procedure can be defined to take as many arguments as are needed. When defining the procedure, the argument list should contain one element for each argument. Each element has the following syntax:

```
argumentname As type
```

Argumentname is the name of the argument, following VBA's naming rules. Type is the data type of the argument. An argument can be any of VBA's data types, an object type from the Excel object model, a user-defined type, or an enumeration type. If the data type is not specified, the argument defaults to type Variant. Multiple arguments are separated by commas, as shown in the following example:

```
Sub MyProcedure(count As Integer, deadline As Date, overdue As Boolean)
...
End Sub
```

To pass an array as an argument, use an empty set of parentheses following the argument name. The following specifies one argument that is an array of type Single:

```
Sub AnotherSub(data() As Single)
```

Within the body of the procedure, each argument is available as a variable of the specified type and initially has the value that was assigned to the argument (see the following section, "Calling Procedures").

Assign argument names that are descriptive of the data the argument holds.

Optional Arguments

By default, procedure arguments are required — that is, when the procedure is called, a value must be passed for each of the procedure's defined arguments or an error occurs. You can, however, define one or more procedure arguments as optional. The syntax is:

```
Optional argname As type = default
```

Argname and type are the same as for nonoptional argument. You can assign a default value to the argument — this is the value the argument will have in the procedure if a value is not passed when the procedure is called. If you do not want to assign a default value, omit the = default part of the argument definition. In the procedure definition, all optional arguments must come at the end of the argument list, following any nonoptional arguments.

Execution exits a procedure when it reaches the End Sub **statement. You can also exit a procedure by executing the** Exit Sub **statement anywhere within the procedure.**

ParamArray Arguments

Additional flexibility in passing arguments to procedures is provided by the `ParamArray` keyword. Here's the syntax:

```
Sub SubName(ParamArray ArrayName())
```

This specifies that an array of arguments will be passed to the procedure. The array is always type `Variant`, but its length is flexible. Here's how it works. Suppose a procedure has been defined as follows:

```
Sub MySub(ParamArray Data())
...
End Sub
```

The procedure is then called as follows:

```
Call MySub("hello", 55, #12/25/2003#)
```

Within the procedure, the array `Data` contains three elements, with `Data(0)` containing the string "hello," `Data(1)` containing the value 55, and `Data(2)` containing the date 12/25/2003. The array size depends on the number of arguments passed. Use the `UBound` function to determine the size of the array.

You can combine `ParamArray` arguments with regular required arguments. There can be only one `ParamArray` in a procedure definition, and it must be the last item in the argument list. You cannot use the `Optional` keyword with `ParamArray`. Here's an example:

```
Sub MySub(A As Integer, B As String, ParamArray pa())
```

Now the procedure is called as follows:

```
Call MySub("first", "second", "third", "fourth")
```

The values "first" and "second" are passed as the arguments A and B. The values "third" and "fourth" are passed in the array `pa()`.

ByVal and ByRef Arguments

The terms `ByVal` and `ByRef` refer to the two ways in which a variable can be passed to a procedure as an argument. `ByRef`, which stands for "by reference," is the default. In this case, a reference to the argument is passed to the procedure — in other words, a pointer to where the argument is stored in memory. For example:

```
Dim str As String
str = "hello"
MySub str
```

Here, it is the memory address of the variable `str` that is passed to the procedure. Having this address, code in the procedure can access the value of `str`. Furthermore, code in the procedure can modify the value of `str`. This means that if code in the procedure changes the argument, the change is reflected in the original variable. Here's a demonstration:

```
Sub MySub(s As String)
    s = "changed"
End Sub

Dim str As String
str = "original
MySub str
```

After this code executes, the string `str` contains "changed."

You can also pass an argument by value using the `ByVal` keyword in the procedure definition:

```
Sub MySub(ByVal s As String)
```

When a procedure is called, `ByVal` arguments are passed by making a copy of the argument variable and then passing that copy to the procedure. Code in the procedure has access to the argument value, but it does not have access to the original variable and therefore cannot modify it. This is shown here:

```
Sub MySub(ByVal s As String)
    s = "changed"
End Sub

Dim str As String
str = "original
MySub str
```

After this code executes, the variable `str` still contains "original."

VBA's default is to pass variable arguments by reference because it is more efficient than passing by value. The ability to change the variable inside the procedure is a side effect of the way reference arguments work and should not regularly be employed as a programming technique. When a procedure needs to return data to the calling program, it is better to use a function procedure (covered later in this session). Modifying argument values within the procedure should be used only when really necessary, and then with great care.

Calling Procedures

You can call, or execute, a procedure from Excel's Macros dialog box (Alt+F8), but more often you will call procedures from code. In most cases, each Excel program you write will have one starting procedure that is the entry point to the program. From there, execution passes to the program's other procedures by means of procedure calls.

There are two equivalent forms for calling a procedure. The first uses the `Call` keyword:

```
Call procname(arglist)
```

If the procedure takes no arguments, omit the parentheses:

```
Call procname
```

The second method omits the `Call` keyword and uses the procedure name alone:

```
procname arglist
```

Note that when the `Call` keyword is omitted, the parentheses around the arguments are also omitted.

When a procedure takes arguments, each argument must be an expression that evaluates to the correct data type (the type defined for the argument). To pass an array, use the array name followed by empty parentheses.

Argument Type Checking

Each procedure argument has a defined data type. When the program passes a variable as an argument to a procedure, the type of the variable is checked against the argument's declared type. If the types differ, a "ByRef Argument Type Mismatch" error occurs. The following code snippet causes this error (at the `Call` statement):

```
Sub MySub(val As Single)
...
End Sub

Dim X As Long
X = 12345
Call MySub(X)
```

There are two ways to get around this problem. One is to use VBA's data conversion functions, which convert an expression to a specified data type. Thus, the `CSng` function converts an expression to type `Single` and could be used in the above example as follows:

```
Call MySub(CSng(X))
```

You can refer to the VBA documentation for details on the other data conversion functions.

The other way to avoid type-checking errors is to enclose the argument in an extra set of parentheses, as shown here:

```
Call MySub((X))
```

The parentheses convert the argument into a typeless expression, so the type mismatch error is not triggered.

The Insert ⇨ Procedure Command

The easiest way to add a new procedure to a VBA module is with the Insert ⇨ Procedure command. In the dialog box that's displayed, you enter the name of the procedure and select whether it is a sub or a function procedure. The editor enters the outline of the procedure in the module. You then edit the procedure to add arguments and code.

**10 Min.
To Go**

Function Procedures

A function procedure is identical to a sub procedure in almost every respect, including the way arguments are declared and the types of code it can contain. The difference is that a function procedure returns a value to the calling program, where a sub procedure does not. A function procedure is defined using the Function...End Function keywords:

```
Function FunctionName(arguments) As type
...
End Function
```

The type element specifies the data type of the value that the function returns and is one of VBA's data types, a user-defined type, or an enumerated type. If the As type portion of the function definition is omitted, the return type defaults to Variant.

The value returned by a function is specified by assigning a value to the function name within the body of the function:

```
Function MyFunction() As Integer
    ...
    MyFunction = expression
End Function
```

This assignment is often at the end of the function, but it can also be located elsewhere within the body of the function. Making this assignment does not in itself end the function. You can terminate the function early with the Exit Function statement.

If you do not assign a value to the function name, no error occurs. The value returned by the function will in this case be the value for an uninitialized variable of the specified return type (zero for numeric return types, a blank string for String and Variant return types, and Nothing for object return types).

The fact that a function returns a value affects the way it is called. Because it returns a value, a function call can be considered an expression and therefore can be used anywhere an expression can be used. Function arguments must be enclosed in parentheses. Here are some examples;

```
X = Func1() + Func2()
X = Func3(Func4())
Debug.Print Func5(a, b, c)
```

This code uses the Debug.Print **statement to display data in the VBA Editor's Immediate Window. The Immediate Window is covered in Session 2.**

You can also call a function in the same way that a sub procedure is called (as detailed earlier in this session). In this case the function's return value is ignored.

Variables in Procedures

Most of the variables that a program uses are declared within procedures. Such variables are called *local* variables because their scope is local to the procedure in which they are declared. In other words, a local variable does not exist outside the procedure.

 See Session 4 for information on declaring VBA variables.

 Do not try to define a user-defined type or an enumeration within a procedure — it is not permitted. You can, however, declare variables of a UDT or Enum type that is defined elsewhere.

Each time a procedure is called, its local variables are created and initialized. This means that a local variable does not retain its value between calls to the procedure. Usually this is fine, but there may be situations where you want a local variable to "remember" its value. This is done using the Static keyword. You can make a single variable static by using the keyword in the variable declaration:

```
Static X As Integer
```

Alternatively, you can make all variables static by using the keyword in the procedure definition:

```
Static Sub SubName()
...
End Sub
```

The code in Listing 7-1 demonstrates this.

Listing 7-1 *Demonstrating static variables*

```
Public Sub TestStatic1()
    Dim i As Integer

    For i = 1 To 5
            TestStatic2
    Next
End Sub

Public Sub TestStatic2()
    Static A As Integer
    Dim B As Integer
    Debug Print A, B
    A = A + 1
    B = B + 1
End Sub
```

When you run `TestStatic1`, the output in the Immediate Window is as follows:

```
0    0
1    0
2    0
3    0
4    0
```

The Debug.Print statement and the Immediate Window are covered in Session 2.

You can see that the static variable A maintained its value between calls to the procedure, while variable B did not.

Procedure Scope

You learned about the concept of variable scope in Session 4. Like variables, procedures also have scope, controlling the parts of the program from which the procedure can be called. There are three levels of procedure scope:

- **Public.** The procedure is visible to all modules in all projects. This is the default if the procedure is defined with no keyword. You can also use the `Public` keyword, which has the same effect.

- **Private.** The procedure is visible only within its own module. To create a private procedure, use the `Private` keyword:

  ```
  Private Sub MyuSub()
  ```

- **Restricted public.** If the `Option Private` statement is included at the start of the module, procedures defined with the `Public` keyword or with no keyword are visible to all modules in the current project, but not in other projects.

Storing Procedures

Procedures are stored in modules, but which modules? There is no single correct answer to this question. Aside from possible limitations imposed by procedure scope, there are really no limitations on where you place your procedures. You may want to give some thought to organizing them in a convenient manner.

When you first start programming, it may be practical to combine all your VBA procedures in a single module and then import that module into each project that you create. Later, as your collection of useful procedures grows larger, you may want to organize them into functional categories, each in its own module. Then, you can include a module in other VBA projects as needed.

Done!

REVIEW

Sub and function procedures provide the basic structure for organizing your VBA code. An Excel program consists of at least one procedure, and more complex programs contain many procedures. Among the items covered in this session are:

- A procedure is an independent section of code that has been assigned a name and can be called (executed) from other code.

- Function procedures return a value to the calling program; sub procedures do not.

- A procedure can accept arguments that are used to pass data to the procedure. Each argument has a specific, assigned data type.

- You can place essentially any VBA code in a procedure. The main exceptions are other procedure definitions, user-defined type definitions, and enumeration definitions.

- By default a procedure's scope is public, making the procedure available to all modules in all projects.

QUIZ YOURSELF

1. What is the main difference between a sub procedure and a function procedure? (See the "Function Procedures" section.)

2. How many arguments can a procedure take? (See the "Procedure Arguments" section.)

3. Do you need to enclose the arguments in parentheses when calling a sub procedure? (See the "Calling Procedures" section.)

4. What happens if you pass an argument to a procedure that has a different data type than the argument was declared to be? (See the "Argument Type Checking" section.)

5. How do you define an optional procedure argument with a default value? (See the "Optional Arguments" section.)

6. What is the default scope of a procedure? (See the "Procedure Scope" section.)

Working with Dates and Times

Session Checklist

✔ How the `Date` data type stores date and time information

✔ Creating date values from literal dates

✔ Reading the date and time from the system clock

✔ Obtaining details about a date

✔ Formatting dates and times for display

**30 Min.
To Go**

Excel programs frequently need to work with dates and, less often, times. Excel has excellent tools for working with these data types. These capabilities extend to the VBA language, which provides a special data type designed specifically to store date/time information.

The Date Data Type

VBA provides a special `Date` data type to store dates and times. Internally, the `Date` type stores a date and/or a time as a floating-point number, as follows:

- The integer part of the value specifies the date as the number of days since December 30, 1899.

- The fractional part of the value specifies the time as a fraction of the 24-hour day (.25 is 6a.m., .5 is noon, and so on).

- A fractional number with no integer part represents a dateless time.

For the user or the programmer, dates and times represented in this way are essentially meaningless. Fortunately you'll never (or at most, rarely) need to work with date and time values in this raw format. VBA provides all the tools you need for working with dates and times in more familiar formats. The underlying floating-point representation is completely hidden from your view.

Date/Time Values

VBA can recognize specific dates and times in almost all of the commonly used formats. To identify date/time literal constants as such, they must be enclosed in # characters. You can assign a specific date to a type Date variable with a simple assignment statement:

```
Dim dt As Date
dt = #01/05/2003# ' Or #5 Jan 03#, #January 5, 2003#, etc.
```

The DateValue function performs essentially the same task, converting a string representation of a date into a Date value:

```
Dim dt As Date
dt = DateValue("January 5, 2003")
```

If the argument contains time information, it is ignored, but improperly formatted time information will cause an error.

The DateSerial function creates a Date value from separate month, day, and year values:

```
DateSerial(year, month, day)
```

Each argument is an integer expression specifying the corresponding date component. To represent specific dates, month can range from 1 to 12, day from 1 to 31, and year from 100 to 9999. You can also create a value that represents a relative date. For example, a month value of -2 would create a relative date that is two months prior to another date. For example, you could determine the date that is two months before a project's due date, then use that date as a reminder to check on the project's status. You use such relative dates in the date calculations that are covered later in the session.

Dates and System Settings

The way that dates are handled depends to some extent on your Windows system settings, specifically those found under Regional Options. Among other things, these settings specify:

- How short dates are formatted (m/d/y, d/m/y, and so on).
- The separator character for short dates.
- How two-digit year values are interpreted. The default is for values 0 to 29 to be interpreted as the years 2000 to 2029, and values 30 to 99 to be interpreted as 1930 to 1999.

Dates are always interpreted and calculated according to the calendar in use on the system. The Regional Options also has settings that affect time values.

The System Date and Time

Each computer has a system clock that maintains the system date and time. You can read and set this value in your programs. To read the system clock, use these functions:

- Now: Returns the system date and time as a type Date.
- Date: Returns the system date (no time information).
- Time: Returns the current system time (no date information).

To set the system clock, use the Date and Time statements. It would be unusual, however, for an Excel program to need to set the system clock.

If the year is omitted from a date, VBA uses the current year as set on the system clock.

Use the TimeValue and TimeSerial functions to create time values for type Date variables. They work similarly to the parallel functions for dates. These three statements evaluate to a value for 5:21 p.m. (zero seconds).

```
TimeValue("5:21PM")
TimeValue("17:21")
TimeSerial(17, 21, 0)
```

For TimeSerial, the values are normally in the range 0 to 23 for hours, and 0 to 59 for minutes and seconds. Larger values wrap to the next larger unit; therefore, a seconds value of 90 corresponds to one minute and 30 seconds:

```
TimeSerial(12, 15, 30)  ' 12:15:30 PM
TimeSerial(12, 14, 90)  ' also 12:15:30 PM
```

Excel has a date bug that incorrectly reports that the year 1900 was a leap year. VBA's date functions do not have this bug.

Date Calculations

20 Min.
To Go

VBA has a function that lets you add and subtract dates. More specifically, it lets you add or subtract an interval (a relative date) from a date. For example, you could use this function to determine the date eight weeks from another date. The syntax is:

```
DateAdd(interval, number, date)
```

- Interval: A string expression specifying the interval being added. See Table 8-1 for the permitted values for this argument.
- Number: The number of intervals being added. Use a negative value to subtract.
- Date: The original date.

Table 8-1   *Values for the Interval Argument to the DateAdd Function*

Argument	Interval
yyyy	Year
q	Quarter (3 months)
m	Month
y, w, or d	Day of year
ww	Week
h	Hour
n	Minute
s	Second

Here are some examples of using the DateAdd function:

```
DateAdd("q", 2, Date)             ' The date 2 quarters from today.
DateAdd("d", -60, #12/25/2003#)   ' The date 60 days before Christmas 2003
DateAdd("n", 1000, Time)          ' The date (time) 1000 minutes from now.
```

The DateAdd function always returns a valid date and takes leap years into account.

If you need to work directly with date serial numbers, use the Single **data type. You can assign a date value directly to a type** Single **variable, and** *vice versa.* **For example:**

```
Dim d As Date
Dim s As Single
s = #1/1/2002#          ' s now equals 37257, the number of days between
                        ' December 30, 1899 and January 1, 2002.

d = s                   ' d now contains the date value for 1/1/2002.
```

If you are working only with date values that contain no time part, you can also use the Long **data type.**

Date and Time Details

Once you have a date, how can you obtain details about that date, such as the day of the week it falls on? You can use VBA's DatePart and DateDiff functions for this purpose.

DatePart offers a great deal of flexibility. The syntax is:

DatePart(*interval*, *date*, *firstdayofweek*, *firstweekofyear*)

- Interval: The date interval of interest. Possible values for this argument were shown earlier in this session, in Table 8-1, with these exceptions: "y" means day of the year (1–365 or 366), "d" means the day of the month (1–31 for August, for example), and "w" means weekday (1–7).
- Date: A type Date specifying the date of interest.
- Firstdayofweek: A constant specifying which day is considered to be the first day of the week. See Table 8-2 for permitted values. This argument is optional; the default is Sunday.
- Firstweekofyear: A constant specifying which week is considered the first week of the year. See Table 8-3 for possible values for this argument. The argument is optional; the default is the week in which January 1 occurs.

Table 8-2   *Constants for the DatePart Function's Firstdayofweek Argument*

Constant (value)	Meaning
vbUseSystem (0)	Use the system setting
vbSunday (1)	Sunday (the default)
vbMonday (2)	Monday
vbTuesday (3)	Tuesday
vbWednesday (4)	Wednesday
vbThursday (5)	Thursday
vbFriday (6)	Friday
vbSaturday (7)	Saturday

Table 8-3   *Constants for the DatePart Function's Firstweekofyear Argument*

Constant (value)	Meaning
vbUseSystem (0)	Use the system setting
vbFirstJan1 (1)	The week in which January 1 falls (the default)
vbFirstFourDays (2)	The first week containing at least four days of the new year
vbFirstFullWeek (3)	The first seven-day week of the year

**10 Min.
To Go**

The following are some examples of using the `DatePart` function:

```
DatePart("y", #July 4, 2003#)            ' Returns 185 because July 4
                                         ' is the 185th day of 2003.

DatePart("w", #July 4, 2003#)            ' Returns 6 because July 4, 2003
                                         ' is a Friday and by default
                                         ' Sunday is the first day
                                         ' of the week.

DatePart("w", #July 4, 2003#, vbMonday)  ' Returns 5 because July 4, 2003
                                         ' is a Friday and when Monday is
                                         ' specified as the first day of
                                         ' the week, Friday is day 5.

Dim d As Date                            ' Returns 36 indicating that the
d = DateAdd("m", 2, "7/4/2003")          ' date 2 months after July falls
DatePart("ww", d)                        ' in the 36th week of the year.
```

The `DateDiff` function is used to calculate the number of intervals between two dates. The syntax is:

```
DateDiff(interval, date1, date2, firstdayofweek, firstweekofyear)
```

- `interval`: Specifies the interval of interest as string value (see Table 8-1).
- `date1, date2`: The dates of interest. `Date1` should be the earlier date; if it is not, the function returns a negative value.
- `firstdayofweek`: A constant specifying which day is considered to be the first day of the week. See Table 8-2 for permitted values. This argument is optional; the default is Sunday.
- `firstweekofyear`: A constant specifying which week is considered the first week of the year. See Table 8-3 for possible values for this argument. The argument is optional; the default is the week in which January 1 occurs.

You can use `DateDiff` to create a function that determines whether a year is a leap year. If there are 364 days between January 1 and December 31 of a given year, it is not a leap year; if there are 365 days, it is. This function is shown in Listing 8-1.

Listing 8-1 *Function to determine if a year is a leap year*

```
Function IsLeapYear(year As String) As Boolean

' The year argument is a string specifying the year of interest
' For example, "2003".
' Returns True if the year is a leap year, False if not.

Dim d1 As String, d2 As String

d1 = "1/1/" & year
```

```
d2 = "12/31/" & year

If DateDiff("d", d1, d2) = 365 Then
    IsLeapYear = True
Else
    IsLeapYear = False
End If

End Function
```

Table 8-4 describes the other date information functions provided by VBA. In each case, date is a type Date or a numeric or string expression that can be interpreted as a date.

Table 8-4   *More Date and Time Functions in VBA*

Function	Description
Day(date)	Returns a value 1–31 representing the day of the month
Hour(date)	Returns a value 0–23 representing the hour of the day
Minute(date)	Returns a value 0–59 representing the minute of the hour
Month(date)	Returns a value 1–12 representing the month of the year
Second(date)	Returns a value 0–59 representing the second of the minute
Weekday(date, firstdayofweek)	Returns a value 1–7 representing the day of the week. The optional firstdayofweek argument specifies the first day of the week; the default is Sunday. See Table 8-2 for other values for this argument.
Year(date)	Returns the year

Formatting Date/Time Values

VBA is rather smart when it comes to displaying date and time values. Without any special effort on your part, a date/time value will be displayed using the "short date format" as specified in your system settings. With Windows 2000, in the United States, this is as follows:

```
12/01/2003 9:35:00 AM
```

 Date display settings are found in the Windows Control Panel under Regional Settings or Regional Options (depending on your Windows version).

If you need more control over how dates and times are displayed, use the FormatDateTime function. The syntax for this function is:

```
FormatDateTime(Date, NamedFormat)
```

Date is the date expression to be formatted. NamedFormat is an optional constant that specifies how the date is formatted. See Table 8-5 for possible settings. The function returns a string containing the formatted date.

Table 8-5 *Constants for the FormatDateTime Function's NamedFormat Argument*

Constant (value)	Format
vbGeneralDate (0)	Displays the date (if present) in short date format, and the time (if present) in long time format. This is the default setting.
vbLongDate (1)	Displays the date in long date format
vbShortDate (2)	Displays the date in short date format
vbLongTime (3)	Displays the time in long time format
vbShortTime (4)	Displays the time in short time format

If the FormatDateTime **function does not provide what you need, you can create your own custom date and time formats using the** Format **function. See the VBA documentation for details.**

Done!

REVIEW

VBA makes programming with date and time date relatively easy. The Date data type is specialized for holding date and time information, and there are numerous functions at your disposal for manipulating and formatting date and time information.

- The Date data type stores a date/time value as a floating-point number, with the integer part representing the date and the fractional part representing the time.
- VBA recognizes literal dates in many common formats. Date literals must be enclosed in # characters.
- DatePart is one of several VBA functions that provide detailed information about a date or time.
- Details of how dates and times are displayed are controlled to some degree by your system settings.
- VBA automatically formats date and time values for display, but you can have additional control of the formatting by using the FormatDateTime function.

QUIZ YOURSELF

1. How is the date stored in a date value? (See the "The Date Data Type" section.)

2. How would you convert the string representation of a date to a Date data type? (See the "Date/Time Values" section.)

3. What function reads the date on the system clock? (See the "Date/Time Values" section.)

4. What function would you use to determine the day of the week that a specific date falls on? (See the "Date and Time Details" section.)

5. What function gives you maximum control for defining custom date and time display formats? (See the "Formatting Date/Time Values" section.)

Working with Text

Session Checklist

✔ Displaying text data to the user

✔ Accepting input from the user

✔ Searching for text

✔ Comparing strings

✔ Working with ASCII values

✔ Modifying strings

**30 Min.
To Go**

An Excel program often needs to work with data that is in the form of text (or *strings*, as it is called in VBA). The VBA language has a special data type, String, to hold text data. It also provides a powerful collection of functions and statements to work with text data in various ways. These are the topics of this session.

Text Input and Output

An Excel program often needs to get some input from the user or to display a short message. VBA's tools for these tasks are covered in this section.

The MsgBox Function

To display a message to the user, use the MsgBox function. This function displays a message to the user in a small dialog box and returns a value indicating how the user responded to the message. Figure 9-1 shows an example.

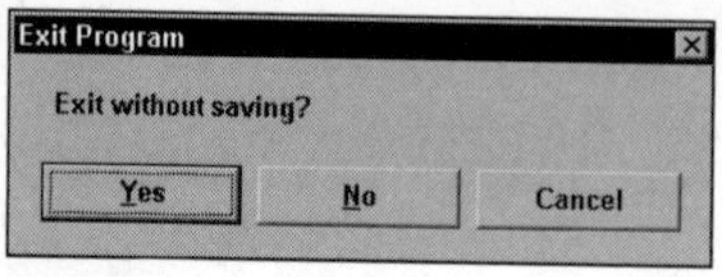

Figure 9-1   *A message displayed with the* MsgBox *function*

The syntax for the MsgBox function is as follows:

MsgBox(*prompt, buttons, title, helpfile, context*)

- Prompt. A string specifying the message to display.
- Buttons. A constant specifying the buttons and icons that display in the dialog box, and also which button is the default (you select this by pressing Enter). Permitted values are described in Table 9-1. If this argument is omitted, only an OK button is displayed.
- Title. A string specifying the dialog box title (displayed in the title bar). Optional. If omitted, the name of the application is used.
- HelpFile. The name of the help file that provides context-sensitive help for the dialog box (activated by pressing F1). Optional argument.
- Context. The context identifier for the dialog box's context-sensitive help. Optional. If the HelpFile argument is provided, context must be provided as well (and *vice versa*).

Table 9-1   *Constants for the MsgBox Function's buttons Argument*

Constant (value)	Description
vbOKCancel (1)	Displays OK and Cancel buttons
vbAbortRetryIgnore (2)	Displays Abort, Retry, and Ignore buttons
vbYesNoCancel (3)	Displays Yes, No, and Cancel buttons
vbYesNo (4)	Displays Yes and No buttons
vbRetryCancel (5)	Displays Retry and Cancel buttons
vbCritical (16)	Displays Critical Message icon
vbQuestion (32)	Displays Warning Query icon
vbExclamation (48)	Displays Warning Message icon
vbInformation (64)	Displays Information Message icon
vbDefaultButton2 (256)	Sets the second button as the default
vbDefaultButton3 (512)	Sets the third button as the default

Providing online help for your Excel applications is covered in Session 30.

The value passed to the buttons argument determines three things: which buttons are displayed, which icon is displayed, and which button (if more than one is displayed) is the default and will be selected when the user presses Enter. To specify two or three items in this argument, combine the corresponding constants from Table 9-1 using the Or operator. For example, to display the Yes, No, and Cancel buttons, a question mark icon, and have the second button (No in this case) be default, you would use the following syntax:

```
vbYesNoCancel Or vbQuestion Or vbdefaultButton2
```

Here's a real example that displays the message "Exit without saving" along with Yes, No, and Cancel buttons, a question mark icon, with the No button as the default:

```
reply = MsgBox("Exit without saving?", vbYesNoCancel Or vbQuestion Or _
        vbdefaultButton2)
```

Instead of the Or operator you can simply add button constants together when needed.

The MsgBox function returns an integer value that identifies the button the user selected to close the dialog box. These return values are represented by the following constants, whose meanings should be clear; the value of each constant is given in parentheses:

```
vbOK (1)
vbCancel (2)
vbAbort (3)
vbRetry (4)
vbIgnore (5)
vbYes (6)
vbNo (7)
```

Here's an example of using the return value:

```
Dim reply As Integer

reply = MsgBox("Exit without saving?", vbYesNoCancel Or vbQuestion Or _
        vbdefaultButton2)
If reply = vbYes Then
    ' Code to exit without saving here.
Elseif reply = vbNo Then
    ' Code to save then exit here.
Else
    ' Code to return to program here.
End If
```

If you do not care about the value returned by the MsgBox **function, you can simply ignore it — in other words, call** MsgBox **like a sub procedure.**

InputBox Function

The InputBox function displays a dialog box with a prompt and an entry field where the user can enter text. The text entered by the user is returned to the calling program. Figure 9-2 shows an example.

Get Name	✕
Please enter your first name:	OK
	Cancel

Figure 9-2   *The dialog box displayed by the* InputBox *function*

The syntax of the InputBox function is:

```
InputBox(prompt, title, default, xpos, ypos, helpfile, context)
```

- Prompt. The prompt displayed in the dialog box.
- Title. A string specifying the dialog box title (displayed in the title bar). Optional. If omitted, the name of the application is used.
- Default. The text displayed in the entry field when the dialog box is first displayed. Optional; the default is an empty string.
- Xpos, ypos. Numerical values specifying the position of the dialog box relative to the upper left corner of the screen. The units are twips, with 1,440 twips per inch. Both arguments are optional. If xpos is omitted, the dialog box is centered horizontally. If ypos is omitted, the dialog box is positioned about one-third of the way from the top of the screen.
- HelpFile. The name of the help file that provides context-sensitive help for the dialog box (activated by pressing F1). Optional argument.
- Context. The context identifier for the dialog box's context-sensitive help. Optional. If the HelpFile argument is provided, context must be provided as well (and vice versa).

This example uses the InputBox function to get the user's favorite flavor of ice cream, with "Chocolate" as the default response:

```
flavor = InputBox("Your favorite flavor?", "Ice cream", "Chocolate")
```

Sessions 19–22 show you how to use User Forms for more sophisticated data entry tasks than are possible with InputBox.

Searching for Text

To locate an occurrence of one string within another string, use the `InStr` and `InStrRev` functions. `InStr` starts looking at the beginning of the target string, while `InStrRev` starts at the end. The syntax for these functions is:

```
InStr(start, string1, string2, compare)
InStrRev(string1, string2, start, compare)
```

- `Start`. The character position at which to start the search. Optional; if omitted, the search starts at the first (`InStr`) or last (`InStrRev`) position. Even though `InStrRev` searches from the end of the string, it interprets the `start` argument as a position relative to the start of the string.
- `String1`. The string being searched.
- `String2`. The target string (the string being searched for).
- `Compare`. A constant specifying how string comparisons are performed. See Table 9-2 for permitted settings for this argument. Optional. If omitted, a binary (case-sensitive) comparison is performed.

Table 9-2   *Constants for the InStr and InStrRev Functions' Compare Argument*

Constant (value)	Meaning
`vbUseCompareOption (-1)`	The setting of the Option Compare statement is used.
`vbBinaryCompare (0)`	A binary (case-sensitive) comparison is performed.
`vbTextCompare (2)`	A textual (noncase-sensitive) comparison is performed.

Use the `Len` **function, covered later in this session, to determine the length of a string.**

The functions return the character position at which `string2` is found within `string1`, or 0 if it is not found. Character positions are always counted from the start of the string, with 1 being the first character. They also return 0 if either string is zero length or if `start` is greater than the length of `string1`.

The `Option Compare` **statement specifies how text comparisons are performed within a VBA module. Place the statement at the start of a module, outside of any procedures. Use** `Optional Compare Text` **for case-insensitive comparisons, or** `Option Compare Binary` **for case-sensitive comparisons.**

Table 9-3 shows some examples of using the `InStr` and `InStrRev` functions.

Table 9-3   *InStr and InStrRev Examples*

Function call	Return value
InStr(, "Microsoft", "o")	5
InStrRev("Microsoft", "o")	7
InStrRev("Microsoft", "o", 6)	5
InStr(,"Microsoft", "MICRO", vbBinaryCompare)	0

To find the second and subsequent occurrences of one string within another, call InStr **repeatedly. For the second and subsequent calls, set the** start **argument equal to one more than the value returned by the previous call.**

Comparing Strings

The StrComp function compares two strings. The syntax is as follows:

```
StrComp(str1, str2, compare)
```

Str1 and str2 are the strings to compare. Compare is a constant that specifies how the comparison is to be performed. This is the same as the values for the InStr and InStrRev function, explain in Table 9-1 earlier in this session. The function returns:

- -1 if str1 is less than str2.
- 0 of str1 and str2 are equal.
- 1 if str1 is greater than str2.
- Null if either str1 or str2 is Null.

The concepts of "less than" and "greater than" are interpreted using the ASCII values of the characters in the strings. For the letters, this corresponds to alphabetical order with the caveat that all uppercase letters are less than the corresponding lowercase letters when a binary comparison is used.

String Conversions

VBA provides various functions for converting string data between one form and another. These functions are covered in this section.

The StrConv Function

The StrConv function performs a variety of conversions. Its syntax is:

```
StrConv(string, conversion)
```

String is the string to be converted, and conversion is a constant specifying the conversion to be performed (see Table 9-4). The function returns the converted string.

Table 9-4 *Constants for the Conversion Argument to the StrConv Function*

Constant (value)	Conversion
vbUpperCase (1)	Converts all letters in the string to uppercase (see also the Ucase function)
vbLowerCase (2)	Converts all letters in the string to lowercase (see also the LCase function)
vbProperCase (3)	Converts the string to proper case (first letter of each word uppercase, all others lowercase)
vbUnicode (64)	Converts the string to Unicode characters
vbFromUnicode (128)	Converts a Unicode string to the default system code page

The StrConv function has some addition conversions, omitted from the table, that are relevant only in far East locales and Japan. See the online documentation for details.

The LCase and UCase Functions

These functions convert all the letters in a string to either uppercase (UCase) or lowercase (LCase). The syntax is:

```
LCase(string)
UCase(string)
```

String is any string expression. Nonletter characters are not affected.

The Val Function

The Val function converts a string into its numerical equivalent. The syntax is:

```
Val(string)
```

The function returns a numeric value corresponding to the part of string that is recognized as a number. The function starts at the first character of string and continues until it encounters a nonnumeric character. Numeric characters are digits, leading plus and minus signs, a decimal point, and the octal and hexadecimal prefixes (&O and &H respectively). Dollar signs and commas are not included. White space is ignored. If the function does not recognize a number, it returns 0. Here are some examples:

```
Val("55 23rd Street")     ' returns the value 5523
Val("-1.12")              ' returns the value -1.12
```

```
Val("1,000")                    ' returns the value 1
Val("A123")                     ' Returns the value 0.
```

Some areas of the world use a comma instead of a period as a decimal point. Val will not recognize this even if the operating system is set to the proper locale. In this case you can use the CDbl function to convert a string such as "1,234" to a numerical value. Unlike Val, however, CDbl will generate an error if there are any nonnumeric characters in the string.

The Str Function

The Str function converts a numerical value into a string. Specifically, it returns a type Variant containing a string representation of the number. The syntax is:

```
Str(value)
```

Value is any numeric expression. The returned string includes a leading space for positive numbers.

Working with ASCII Values

Computers use numerical values internally for all data. Text is represented by assigning a numerical value to each letter, digit, and symbol. Obviously, for computers to be able to share text data, they have to all use the same codes. The first widely adopted standard was the ASCII character set which used the values 0 to 127 to represent the letters, numerals, and commonly used punctuation marks and characters. For example, lowercase letters a through z are represented by the values 97 to 122. The ANSI (American National Standards Institute Code) expanded on the ASCII code by adding values 128 to 255 to represent less frequently used symbols as well as letters with diacritical marks (such as _ and é) that are used in many languages. ANSI is sometimes called extended ASCII.

The ASCII codes 0 to 31 represent nonprinting characters such as line feed, carriage return, and tab. (ASCII stands for American Standard Code for Information Interchange and is pronounced "ass-key.")

It soon became apparent that the 255 possible ANSI values were not sufficient for the number of characters that computers needed to work with. As a result, the Unicode standard was developed, using values from 0 to 65,535 to represent a much wider range of characters, including mathematical symbols and dingbats. Only about 39,000 of these codes are currently assigned, leaving plenty of room for future expansion.

VBA provides functions for working with both ASCII and Unicode character codes.

Displaying Unicode Characters

While Windows supports Unicode, this does not mean that you can automatically display any Unicode character on-screen (or, for that matter, print it). The operating system's regional settings, and specifically which languages are installed, determine which characters are available.

The Asc, AscB, and AscW Functions

You learned earlier that VBA uses numbers internally to represent letters, numbers, and other characters. Theses three functions return the numerical code corresponding to a character. The syntax is:

```
Asc(str)
AscB(str)
AscW(str)
```

The str argument is a string containing the character of interest. If str contains more than one character, the first one is used. If str is an empty string, an error occurs. The three functions differ as follows:

- Asc. Returns the ASCII code for the character.
- AscB. Returns the first byte of the character's Unicode code.
- AscW. Returns the character's Unicode code.

The Asc function is useful when you need to determine what characters are in a string. For example, you might want to verify that text entered by the user contains only letters — no numbers or punctuation marks. Sure, you could go through the text a character at a time and compare each one with "a," "b", and on through "z," but that's rather clunky. Using Asc, you can take advantage of the fact that the codes for the letters are 97 to 122 (for lowercase) and 65 to 90 (uppercase), greatly simplifying the comparisons you need to make.

The function shown in Listing 9-1 provides an example. This function verifies that a string is a number — that is, contains only the characters 0, 1, and so on, through 9. It returns True if the passed string is all numbers; otherwise, it returns False. The function makes use that the ASCII codes for the digits 0 through 9 are 48 through 57 respectively. The function works by going through the string a character at a time and seeing if the ASCII value is within that range. If only a single character fails the test, the string is not a number, and the function returns False. The code makes use of VBA's Len and Mid functions. You may be able to figure out what they do on your own; however, they are covered later in this session.

Listing 9-1 *Determining if a string represents a number*

```
Public Function IsNumber(s As String) As Boolean

' Returns True if the argument is a number
' containing only the digits 0-9.
' Returns False otherwise.

Dim i As Integer
Dim buf As String * 1

IsNumber = True

' Return False if an empty string was passed.
If Len(s) = 0 Then
    IsNumber = False
    Exit Function
End If

' Loop thru all characters in s.
For i = 1 To Len(s)
    ' Extract the ith character.
    buf = Mid(s, i, 1)
    If Asc(buf) < 48 Or Asc(buf) > 57 Then
        IsNumber = False
        Exit For
    End If
Next i

End Function

Public Sub TestIsNumber()

Dim str As String
Dim InputOK As Boolean

' The default for Boolean values is False,
' but it never hurts to explicitly initialize
' the value in code.
InputOK = False

Do
    str = InputBox("Please enter an integer number:")
    InputOK = IsNumber(str)
Loop Until InputOK

MsgBox "Thank you!"

End Sub
```

Listing 9-1 also includes a procedure named `TestIsNumber` that lets you test the `IsNumber` function. The code in this procedure uses the `InputBox` function to prompt the user to enter an integer number. The `IsNumber` function then tests whether the text entered by the user is, in fact, a number. The loop repeats until a valid number is entered.

It would be a good programming exercise for you to modify the `IsNumber` function so it also accepts numbers with a decimal point or a leading minus sign.

To run this demonstration, follow these steps:

1. Open the VBA Editor.
2. Open the code-editing window for one of the modules in the Project Explorer window. Because this program does not interact with a worksheet, it does not matter which module you use.
3. Insert the code from Listing 9-1 into the module.
4. Place the editing cursor anywhere inside the `TestIsNumber` procedure.
5. Press F5 to run the program.

In addition to pressing F5, you can run a VBA procedure by clicking the Run Sub button on the toolbar, or by selecting Run Sub from the Run menu.

The Chr Function

This function returns the character that corresponds to a specific numeric code. The syntax is:

```
Chr(code)
```

The code argument is the numeric code of interest. The function returns a string containing the corresponding character. If code is out of range, an error occurs.

Extracting or Modifying Parts of Strings

10 Min. To Go

The VBA functions that are covered in this section are used when you need to extract or modify part of a string.

The Left and Right Functions

These functions extract a specified number of characters from either the left or the right end of a string. The syntax is:

```
Left(string, length)
Right(string, length)
```

String is the original string, and length is the number of characters to extract. If length is more than the length of string, the entire string is returned.

As with most of VBA's string manipulation functions, the original string is never modified by Left or Right functions. The return value of the function is a new string with the specified modifications.

The Mid Function

The Mid function extracts characters from the middle of a string. The syntax is:

```
Mid(string, start, length)
```

String is the string to extract from, and start is the character position at which to start extracting. Length specifies the number of characters to extract. The length argument is optional; if it is omitted, all characters from start to the end of string are returned. If start is greater than the length of string, an empty string is returned. The following are some examples of using the Mid function:

```
Mid("Bill Gates", 4, 5)     ' Returns "l Gat"
Mid("Bill Gates", 4)        ' Returns "l Gates"
Mid("Bill Gates", 12)       ' Returns "" (an empty string)
```

The Mid Statement

The Mid statement replaces part of one string with another string. The syntax is:

```
Mid(string1, start, length) = string2
```

- String1. The string to modify.
- Start. The character position in string1 at which to start.
- Length. The number of characters in string1 to be replaced. This argument is optional; if omitted, the number of characters replaced is equal to the length of string2.
- String2. The string to insert into string1.

All or part of string2 will be inserted into string1. The length of string1 always remains unchanged.

Be aware that the Mid statement is distinct from the Mid function, which does something totally different. The Mid function returns part of a string without changing the original string, while the Mid statement modifies a string. Note also that the Mid statement is the only one of VBA's string manipulation tools that modifies the original string.

Table 9-5 shows some examples of using the Mid statement. The original value of s is "123456789" in all examples.

Table 9-5 *Mid Statement Examples*

Statement	Result
Mid(s, 4) = "abcd"	s contains "1234abcd9"
Mid(s, 4, 2) = "abcd"	s contains "1234ab789"
Mid(s, 8) = "abcd"	s contains "1234567ab"

Other String Functions

Table 9-6 describes VBA's remaining string manipulation functions.

Table 9-6 *Additional String Manipulation Functions*

Syntax	Description	Example
Len(*str*)	Returns the length (number of characters) of a string	Len("hello") returns 5
LTrim(*str*)	Returns a string with any leading spaces removed	LTrim(" ABC ") returns "ABC "
RTrim(*str*)	Returns a string with any trailing spaces removed	RTrim(" ABC ") returns " ABC"
Space(*n*)	Returns a string consisting of n spaces	Space(5) returns " "
String(*n, char*)	Returns a string consisting of n copies of the single character char	String(6, "!") returns "!!!!!!"
Trim(*str*)	Returns a string with both leading and trailing removed	Trim(" ABC ") returns "ABC"

Done!

REVIEW

One of VBA's strengths is its powerful collection of string functions. It's hard to imagine a text-handling task that VBA could not handle. Among the things you learned in this session are:

- The MsgBox function displays a text message to the user.
- The InputBox function accepts text input from the user.
- You can search for text starting at either the start (InStr function) or the end (InStrRev function) of the text.
- String comparisons can be case-sensitive or case-insensitive.
- Characters are represented by numbers, and the Asc and Chr functions let you convert from one to the other.
- The Left, Right, and Mid functions are used to extract parts of strings.

QUIZ YOURSELF

1. What does the MsgBox function's return value tell you? (See the "The MsgBox Function" section.)
2. How do the Mid function and the Mid statement differ? (See the "The Mid Function" and "The Mid Statement" sections.)
3. In VBA, is the string "apple" always considered equal to the string "APPLE"? Please explain. (See the "Comparing Strings" section.)
4. How do the Asc and AscW functions differ? (See the "The Asc, AscB, and AscW Functions" section.")
5. What functions are used to trim leading and trailing spaces from strings? (See the "Extracting or Modifying Parts of Strings" section.)

Using Ranges and Selections

Session Checklist

✔ Using the Range object

✔ Understanding relative ranges

✔ Worksheet comments

✔ Using columns and rows to determine range location and size

✔ Naming ranges

**30 Min.
To Go**

Many of the actions carried out by a VBA program target a specific part of a worksheet. Clearly, you need a way to identify parts of a worksheet, from a single cell to the entire worksheet. VBA uses the Range object as well as its cousin the Selection object for this purpose.

The Range Object

The Range object is designed to refer to a group of cells in a worksheet. This can be a single cell, or it can be a rectangular block of cells of any size up to the limits of the worksheet itself. When you want to perform some action in a worksheet, such as applying formatting or entering data, you almost always start by obtaining a Range object that refers to the cells upon which to be acted.

The most common way to obtain a Range reference is from the Worksheet object's Range property:

```
wsRef.Range(ref)
```

In this syntax, `wsRef` is a reference to the worksheet, and *ref* identifies the cells that the range will include, as follows (note that range references are given as strings in quotes):

- For a single cell range, use the column letter and row number. For example, "A8" or "Z29."
- For a multicell range, use the upper left cell and the lower right cell separated by a colon. For example, "A8:B12."

An alternative way to reference a multicell range is to identify the top left and bottom right cells separately, separated by a comma. Thus, `Range("A8", "B12")` is equivalent to `Range("A8:B12")`. Also remember that your program can define as many different `Range` objects as needed.

The following code references the single cell A8 in the currently active worksheet:

```
ActiveSheet.Range("A8")
```

You could use this reference to perform various actions, such as placing the numeric value 123 or the text "Hello" in the cell:

```
ActiveSheet.Range("A8") = 123
ActiveSheet.Range("A8") = "Hello"
```

You can also create a variable that refers to a range:

```
Dim MyRange As Range
Set MyRange = ActiveSheet.Range("A8")
```

Now, `MyRange` refers to cell A8 and can be used to manipulate it.

If you set a range equal to a value (numeric or text), and the range refers to more than one cell, the value is placed in all cells of the range. Existing data in the cells is overwritten without warning.

Setting a range to a value is the same as using the `Range` object's `Value` property. Thus, this line of code:

```
ActiveSheet.Range("A8") = 123
```

has exactly the same effect as this one:

```
ActiveSheet.Range("A8").Value = 123
```

Manipulating Ranges

After you have a reference to a range, what can you do with it? You saw above how to insert data into a range — simply assign the data to the range. You can place numeric data, text data, or a formula in a cell this way. When inserting a formula, use a string containing the formula, being sure to include the leading equal sign that tells Excel that the entry is a formula and not just text. This code places a formula in cell B12 that adds the values in cells B10 and B11:

```
ActiveSheet.Range("B12") = "=B10+B11"
```

Please refer to Sessions 12 and 13 for more information on using Excel formulas in your code.

Many of the actions you can take with Range objects are covered in upcoming sessions.

Relative Ranges

The ranges you have seen so far are defined with respect to a worksheet and are always identified in terms of the row numbers and column letters in that worksheet. Excel and VBA also allow you to define relative ranges — a range that is not defined in terms of its location in the worksheet, but in terms of its position relative to another range. This can be very useful for writing code that acts on different worksheet locations depending on the circumstances. Look at this code:

```
Dim range1 As Range
Set range1 = ActiveSheet.Range("B3")
```

Now, the range r1 refers to cell B3 in the worksheet. Another way to look at it is that it refers to the cell that is one column to the right, and two rows down, from the upper left cell of the worksheet. This is illustrated in Figure 10-1.

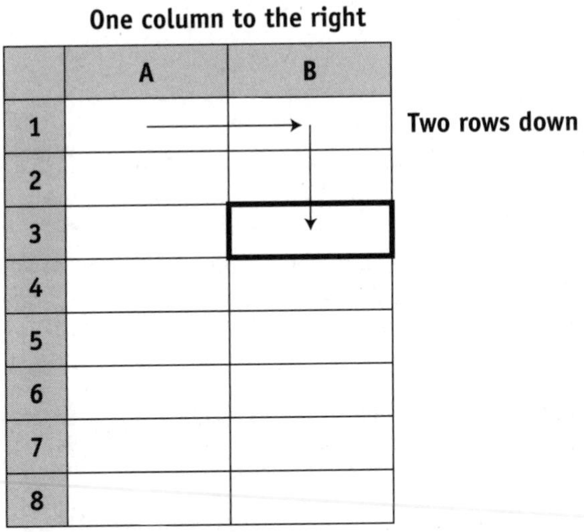

One column to the right

	A	B
1		
2		
3		
4		
5		
6		
7		
8		

Two rows down

Figure 10-1 *A range location can be thought of in terms of its position relative to the top left cell in the worksheet.*

Instead of using the Range property of a Worksheet object, suppose you use the Range property of an existing Range object. For example:

```
Set range2 = range1.Range("B3")
```

In this code, the "B3" still means "one column to the right and two rows down," but this time it is in relation to range1 and not in relation to the worksheet. If range1 refers to worksheet cell B3 (as from the previous code snippet), the result is that range2 refers to "one column to the right and two rows down from cell B3" or, in worksheet terms, cell C5. This is illustrated in Figure 10-2.

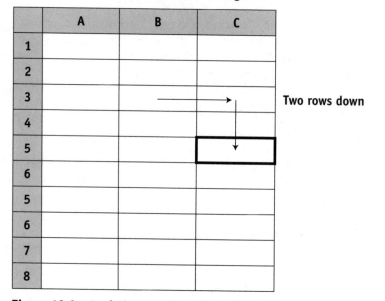

Figure 10-2 *A relative range location is defined in terms of its position relative to another range.*

When defining a relative range using the Range **property, the size of the original range has no effect on the size or location of the relative range that you create. Only the location of the upper left cell of the original range matters.**

If you want to create a relative range containing more than one cell, use a cell range as the argument to the Range property. Here's an example:

```
Dim range1 As Range, range2 As Range
Set range1 = ActiveSheet.Range("B3")
Set range2 = range1.Range("C4:E5")
```

In the last line of code, the "C4" part of the argument specifies the position of the new range with respect to range1, and the "E5" part of the argument specifies the size of the new range. The result is that range2 refers to cells D6:F7. Here's how this works:

1. The original range, range1, refers to cell B3.

2. The "C4" part of the argument says "two columns to the right and three rows down." Starting from the original cell B3, this takes you to cell D6 as the upper left corner of the new range.

3. The argument "C4:E5" specifies a range that is 3 columns wide and 2 rows high. Because the new range starts at cell D6, this means it extends to column F and row 7; therefore, the final range2 is D6:F7.

Another way to create a relative range is using the Range object's Offset property. This differs from the Range object's Range property because you specify the new range as a numerical offset from the original range (as opposed to a row/column designation). It also differs in that the new range automatically has the same size as the original range. The syntax is:

```
OriginalRange.Offset(RowOffset, ColumnOffset)
```

The RowOffset and ColumnOffset arguments are numerical values that specify rows below, and columns to the right, of OriginalRange. Use negative argument values to specify columns to the left or rows above the original range. Here's an example:

```
Dim range1 As Range, range2 As Range
Set range1 = ActiveSheet.Range("D4:E5")
Set range2 = range1.Offset(-2, 3)
```

After this code executes, range2 refers to the range G2:H3. Here's why:

1. The original range had its top left cell at D4.

2. The ColumnOffset argument to the Offset property specified "3 columns to the right," or column G.

3. The RowOffset argument specified "2 rows up," or row 2; therefore, the new range has its top left corner at cell G2.

4. The original range was 2 × 2 cells in size, so the new range will be the same size.

When would you want to use relative ranges? They can be useful when you want to write code to perform some action on the worksheet, but do not know ahead of time exactly where that will be. For example, suppose that you want to format a column of numbers with alternate rows in boldface. You could write a program that starts at the active cell, which the user would be instructed to place at the top of the column. This could be anywhere in the worksheet. Then the program would do the following:

1. Get a range that references the active cell.

2. Make that cell boldface.

3. Use the Offset property to get a new range that is two cells below the original range.

4. Return to step 2, and repeat until an empty cell is encountered.

The program shown in Listing 10-1 demonstrates this use of a relative range. To use this program, do the following:

1. Place a column of data (numbers and /or text) in a worksheet.

2. Move the cell pointer to the first cell in the column.

3. Open the VBA Editor.

4. Use the Project Explorer to open a module. You can use the module associated with the worksheet that you put the data in, or you can add a new module.

5. Add the code from the listing to the module.

6. Run the program using one of the techniques you have learned so far.

20 Min. To Go

Listing 10-1   *Demonstration of using a relative range to format worksheet cells*

```
Public Sub AlternateRowsBoldface()

' Starting at the active cell, formats
' cells in the column below with alternate
' rows in boldface. Stops when it encounters
' an empty cell.

Dim r1 As Range

' Set r1 to the active cell
Set r1 = ActiveCell

' Loop until an empty cell is found.
Do While r1.Value <> ""
    ' Set the font to boldface.
    r1.Font.Bold = True
    ' Get a new range two rows below the current one.
    Set r1 = r1.Offset(2, 0)
Loop

End Sub
```

Empty Cells

A blank cell's `Value` property seems to return an empty string, as was used in Listing 10-1; however, it actually returns the special value `Empty`. You can test for this situation using the `IsEmpty` function:

```
If IsEmpty(Range("B2").Value) Then
    ' cell B2 is blank.
Else
    ' cell B2 is not blank.
End If
```

Other Range References

Excel and VBA provide several other useful ways to obtain references to Range objects. They are described in Table 10-1.

Table 10-1 *Additional Ways to Obtain Range References*

Reference	Returns a Range **object that references**
The ActiveCell keyword	The active cell in the currently active worksheet.
A Range object's CurrentRegion property	A range bounded by (but not including) empty rows and columns and the worksheet borders.
A Worksheet object's UsedRange property	The smallest range that contains all of the used cells in the worksheet.

The CurrentRegion property can be useful. Its utility is based on the fact that the data in most Excel worksheets is arranged in sections, or tables, that have blank rows and columns between them. For example, look at the worksheet in Figure 10-3. You can see that there are two tables of data, separated by a blank row. With the CurrentRegion property, you can easily define a region that includes an entire table without knowing its exact size beforehand.

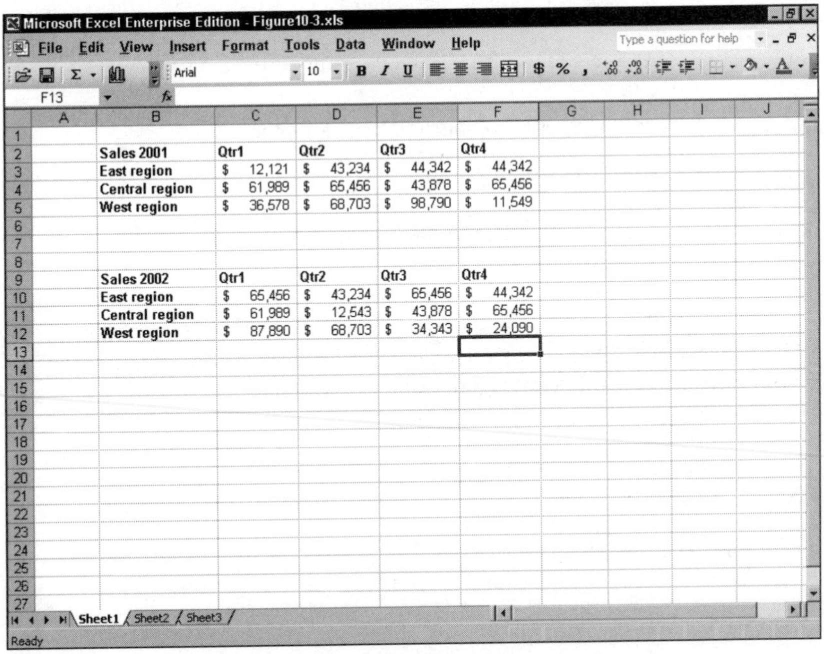

Figure 10-3 *Excel data is often organized in tables separated by blank rows or columns.*

Suppose that you know a table has its upper left corner in cell B2 (as in Figure 10-3), but you do not know how many rows and columns the table contains. You can create a Range object that references the entire table as follows (this code assumes that the worksheet containing the table is active):

1. Create a Range object that references cell B2.
2. Get the CurrentRegion property from the Range object created in step 1.

The following code illustrates these steps:

```
Dim TableRange As Range
Dim CellRange As Range
Set CellRange = ActiveSheet.Range("B2")
Set TableRange = CellRange.CurrentRegion
```

Note that the above code could be shortened to the following, which accomplishes the same thing:

```
Dim TableRange As Range
Set TableRange = ActiveSheet.Range("B2").CurrentRegion
```

After this code executes, the variable TableRange references the entire table (cells B2:F5) and can be used to perform various actions such as changing the format.

Working with Comments

An Excel worksheet cell can have a comment attached to it. When a cell that contains a comment is active, the comment displays in a balloon next to the cell, as shown in Figure 10-4. You can use comments for many purposes, such as documenting what data a cell holds or providing reminders to the user.

To add a comment to a cell AddComment method of the Range object:

```
SomeRange.AddComment "Comment text"
```

Because of the way that Excel and VBA handle comments, you cannot simply modify a comment by editing it or by adding a new comment to the cell. If you call the AddComment method for a cell that already contains a comment, an error is generated; therefore, you must see if the cell already contains a comment and, if so, remove it. Only then can you safely add a comment to the cell.

To determine if a cell has a comment, compare its Comment property with the special value Nothing. This is illustrated in the following code snippet:

```
If SomeRange.Comment Is Nothing Then
    ' Cell does not have a comment.
Else
    ' Cell has a comment.
End If
```

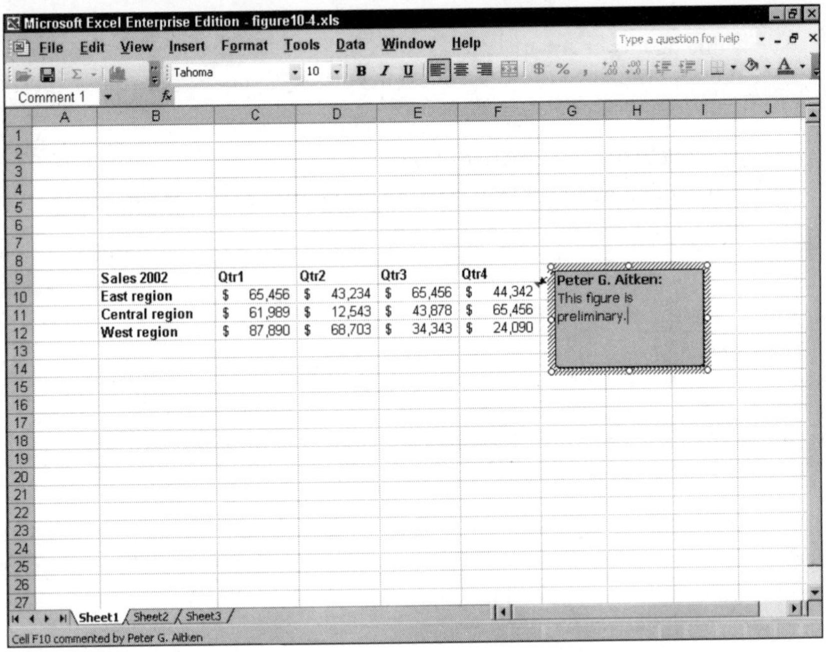

Figure 10-4 *A worksheet cell can have a comment associated with it.*

To delete a comment, call the `ClearComments` method. Combining this with the code above, you can create a procedure that safely adds a comment to a range, as shown in Listing 10-2. Note the use of the `Not` logical operator in this code. By reversing the logical value returned by the expression `r.Comment Is Nothing`, the code in the `If` block executes only if the range has a comment associated with it.

Listing 10-2 *A procedure to add a comment to a cell*

```
Public Sub AddComment(Comment As String, r As Range)

' Adds the specified comment to the cell
' specified by Range r. Deletes any existing
' comment from the cell.

If Not r.Comment Is Nothing Then
    r.ClearComments
End If
r.AddComment Comment

End Sub
```

Never try to add a comment to a cell without first verifying that it does not already have a comment.

To read a cell's comment, use the `Comment.Text` property. If you try to read this property on a cell that does not have a comment, an error occurs; therefore you should verify that a cell has a comment first, as shown here. This code uses the `Debug.Print` statement to display the comment text in the Immediate Window.

```
If Not SomeRange.Comment Is Nothing Then
    Debug.Print SomeRange.Comment.Text
End If
```

Range Columns, Rows, and Size

You can determine the location of a range using its `Column` and `Row` properties. They work as follows:

- `Column`. Returns a number identifying the first column (the left-most column) in the range (1 = A, 2 = B, and so on).
- `Row`. Returns the number of the first (top-most) row in the range.

To determine the size of a range, use the `Columns.Count` and the `Rows.Count` properties. These properties return the number of columns and rows, respectively, in the specified range.

Reading Data from Ranges

If a range points to a single cell, its `Value` property returns whatever is in the cell. What happens when a range points to a block of two or more cells? The `Value` property then returns an array (as a type `Variant`) that contains the data in all the cells.

When you are not sure that a range refers to a single cell, your code needs to check to see whether the data returned by the `Value` property is an array. This is done using the `IsArray` function:

```
Dim x
x = SomeRange.Value
If IsArray(x) Then
  ' SomeRange pointed to multiple cells, and x contains an array.
Else
  ' SomeRange pointed to one cell, and x contains a single value.
End If
```

The array that is returned has two dimensions and is the same size as the range. The first dimension of the array indexes the rows in the range, and the second dimension indexes the columns. To illustrate, look at the selected range in Figure 10-5, comprising cells B4:C7. If you created a range that included these cells and obtained its `Value` property, you would get an array as follows:

- The first dimension of the array has four elements, for the four rows in the range.
- The second dimension of the array has two elements, for the two columns in the range.

- Element (1,1) contains the value 1.
- Element (2,1) contains the value 2.
- Element (4,2) contains the value 8.

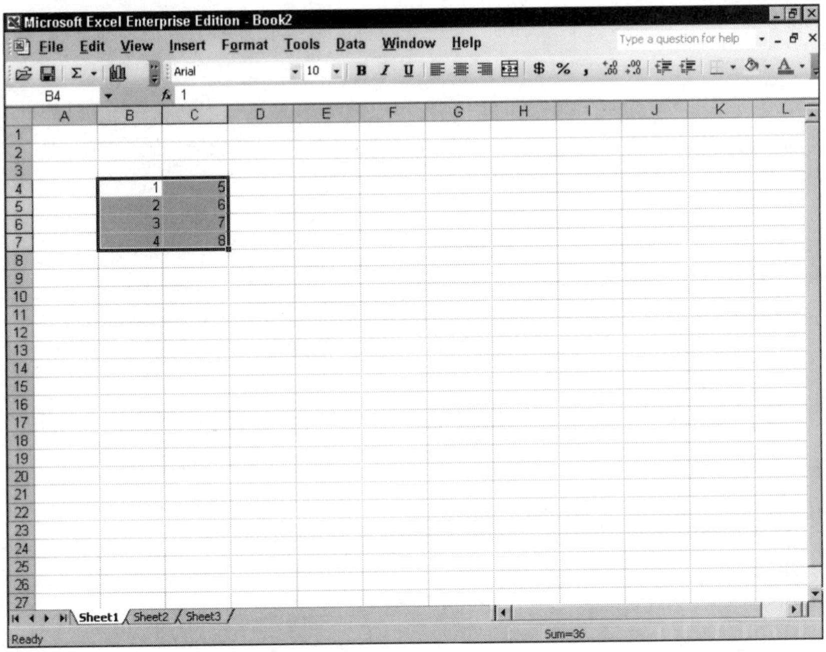

Figure 10-5 *A multiple cell range used in the example in the text*

The program that is presented in Listing 10-3 demonstrates how to read data from single- and multiple-cell ranges. The program reads data from the current selection and displays it in the immediate window using the `Debug.Print` statement. To try this program:

1. Place the code from the listing into a module in the VBA Editor.
2. Switch to Excel, and select a range that contains data. It can be a single cell range or a multiple cell range.
3. Run the program.

Listing 10-3 *Reading values from single and multiple cell ranges*

```
Public Sub DisplayRangeData()

Dim r1 As Range
Dim i As Integer, j As Integer
Dim x As Variant

Set r1 = Selection
```

Continued

Listing 10-3 *Continued*

```
If r1 Is Nothing Then
    Debug.Print "Please select some cells first."
    Exit Sub
End If

x = r1.Value
If IsArray(x) Then
    Debug.Print "You selected a multiple cell range."
    For i = 1 To UBound(x, 1)
        For j = 1 To UBound(x, 2)
            Debug.Print "Cell " & j & "," & i; " contains " & x(i, j)
        Next j
    Next i
Else
    Debug.Print "You selected a single cell."
    Debug.Print "Its value is " & x
End If

End Sub
```

Sample program output is shown in Figure 10-6. This was generated using the range from Figure 10-5.

```
Immediate                                    [X]
 You selected a multiple cell range.          [▲]
 Cell 1,1 contains 1
 Cell 2,1 contains 5
 Cell 1,2 contains 2
 Cell 2,2 contains 6
 Cell 1,3 contains 3
 Cell 2,3 contains 7
 Cell 1,4 contains 4
 Cell 2,4 contains 8                           
 [◄] [                                    ] [►]
```

Figure 10-6 *Sample output from the program in Listing 10-3*

Naming Ranges

10 Min.
To Go

Any defined range can be assigned a name. One way to do this is by using the Range object's Name property:

```
SomeRange.Name = "Sales Total"
```

The name that you assign must be unique within the workbook (not assigned to another range). After a range has been named in this way, you can access the range from the workbook's Range collection using the following syntax:

```
Range(RangeName)
```

Suppose you want cell B6 to display the sum of cells B1:B5. The following code uses a named range to put the required formula in cell B6:

```
Dim r As Range
Set r = Range("B6")
r.Name = "Total"
Range("Total").Value = "=Sum(B1:B5)"
```

Now, the cell B6 contains the formula =Sum(B1:B5).

 The syntax for the `Names.Add` method is given using named arguments to remind you of this option. Remember, you can use named arguments with any Excel method, or you can identify arguments by position as has been done in many other examples in this book.

Range names that are assigned in this manner exist only as long as the code is running. In other words, they are not saved with the workbook. When you want to define named ranges that are persistent and should remain in effect the next time the workbook is opened, you must explicitly add them to the workbook's `Names` collection using its `Add` method:

```
Names.Add Name:=name, RefersTo:=reference
```

name is the name for the range and must be unique within the workbook, and *reference* identifies the cells that name refers to. This argument is a string containing the following parts:

1. An equal sign.
2. The name of the worksheet containing the cells.
3. An exclamation point.
4. The column and row of the top left cell in the range.
5. Optional, for multicell ranges: a colon followed by the column and row of the lower right cell.

When creating the cell references, you need to be aware of the difference between relative and absolute references. (These are covered in more detail in Session 11.)

*   An absolute reference refers to a specific location in the worksheet, as identified by the row number and column letter. To create an absolute reference, include dollar signs in the reference. For example, "$B$6" always refers to cell B6.
*   A relative reference refers to a location relative to the current active cell, in the same way that a relative range is defined. To create a relative reference, omit the dollar signs. For example, "B6" refers to the cell five rows down and one column to the right of the active cell.

The following are examples of creating persistent named ranges in a workbook. This code creates a named range "Sales Data" that refers to the cells B4:F10 in sheet1:

```
ActiveWorkbook.Names.Add Name:="Sales Data",
RefersTo:="=sheet1!$B$4:$F$10")
```

This code creates a named range that refers to the single cell that is one row below the active cell in the active workbook:

```
ActiveWorkbook.Names.Add Name:="Total" RefersTo:=ActiveSheet.Name & "!A2"
```

Ranges that are created in this way are referred to in the same way as the temporary named ranges discussed earlier. For example:

```
Range("Total").Value = 123
```

The following code has the same effect as the previous example:

```
Dim r As Range
Set r1 = Range("Total")
r1.Value = 123
```

The Selection Property

The Selection property is similar to a Range object in that it refers to a range of one or more cells. Specifically, it refers to the cell(s) that have been selected by the user by clicking or dragging with the mouse, or using the keyboard. A given worksheet can have only one selection at a time. This is different from ranges, where there is no limit.

Another difference is that while a Range object always refers to a range of one or more cells, the Selection property may refer to something else, such as a chart in the worksheet. You can verify that the Selection property is pointing to a range of cells using the TypeName function. When passed the Selection property as its argument, this function returns the string "Range" if one or more cells is selected. If something else is selected, it returns a different string. (If nothing is selected, the Selection property returns Nothing.) Therefore, rather than assuming that Selection indicates a range, you would use code such as the following:

```
If TypeName(Selection) = "Range" Then
    ' Selection is a range.
Else
    ' Selection is not a range.
End If
```

The Selection property returns a Range object that references the selected cells. After you have this Range object, you use it to perform whatever actions are needed. The previous code snippet would be modified to the following:

```
Dim r1 As Range
If TypeName(Selection) = "Range" Then
    Set r1 = Selection
    ' Now use r1 to work with the selected cells.
End If
```

Why would you use the Selection object in place of a Range object? There is only one situation where I have found this useful: when you want to let the user select the cells that the program will act on. There are two approaches to letting the user specify a range. One is to instruct the user to select a range of cells and then run your program. An example of this technique can be found in Session 11. The other approach is to use a RefEdit control, which is covered in Session 29.

Display a Range to the User

To display a range to the user, use the Range object's Select method. The range will be selected in the worksheet, just as if the user had selected it. This lets the user verify that the range is correct. Here's the code required:

```
Do
  Range1.Select
  reply = MsgBox("Is this the correct range?", vbYesNo)
  If replay = vbYes Then
    ' Code to process Range1 goes here.
  Else
    ' Code to change Range1 goes here.
  End If

Loop While reply <> vbYes
```

Remember that to let the user verify a range, the worksheet must be visible.

The Range.Activate method selects the one cell at the top left corner of the range, regardless of how large the range is. The Range.Select method selects the entire range. For a range that points to a single cell, the Select and Activate methods are equivalent.

REVIEW

Done!

- The Range object is essential for many aspects of Excel programming.
- A Range can identify anything from a single cell up to an entire worksheet.
- Your program can have as many Range objects defined at the same time as are needed.
- You can assign a name to a Range object and then use the name to refer to it.
- A Range can be defined in terms of absolute row and column locations, or relative to the location of another range.
- The Range.Value property is used to write data to, and read data from, cells in a range.
- The Selection property returns a Range object that represents the current selection.

QUIZ YOURSELF

1. How many ranges can you define in a given worksheet? (See the section "The Range Object.")
2. If you assign a name to a range, is the name remembered the next time the workbook is opened? (See the section "Naming Ranges.")

3. How do you obtain a reference to the active cell? (See the section "Other Range References.")

4. How many comments can be associated with a single worksheet cell? (See the section "Working with Comments.")

5. How do you tell if the Value property has returned data from more than one cell? (See the section "Reading Data from Ranges.")

PART

II

Saturday Morning
Part Review

1. What does the expression 11 mod 3 evaluate to?
2. If A is True and B is False, what does the expression A Or B evaluate to?
3. Does the comparison expression "Smith"="smith" evaluate to True or False?
4. Suppose that Obj1 and Obj2 are both object references. How can you determine if they reference the same object?
5. Do the expressions 4 + 2 * 8 and (4 + 2) * 8 evaluate the same? Please explain.
6. Will some VBA statements within an If...End If block always be executed?
7. When can you omit the Else part of a Select Case statement?
8. What does the Iif function do?
9. How can you ensure that the statements in a Do...Loop statement will be executed at least once?
10. When should you use the While...Wend statement?
11. How many Exit For statements can you put in a For...Next loop?
12. How does a function procedure differ from a sub procedure?
13. What's the limit on the number of lines of code in a procedure?
14. How do you pass an array as an argument to a procedure?
15. How do you specify the value to be returned by a function?
16. Can a local variable in a procedure "remember" its value between calls to the procedure? If so, how?
17. VBA can recognize dates in common formats such as 12/25/2003. In VBA code, how do you indicate that such a value is a date?
18. Which VBA function is used to add an interval to a date?
19. Which two functions are used to search for text (to find one string within another)?

20. How do you convert a string so that the first letter of each word is uppercase and all other letters are lowercase?

21. Do the characters "A" and "a" have the same ASCII values?

22. How would you extract a certain number of characters from the start of a string?

23. Which Excel object do you use to refer to a block of worksheet cells in a VBA program?

24. Suppose a range references a single worksheet cell. How can you tell if that cell is empty?

25. What does the Worksheet object's UsedRange property reference?

26. How do you add a comment to a cell?

27. How many Selection objects can a worksheet have?

28. How do the Range.Activate and Range.Select methods differ?

PART

III

Saturday
Afternoon

Working with Columns, Rows, and Cells

Session Checklist

✔ Use the `Cells` property to reference single cells in a range

✔ Use the `SpecialCells` property to access selected cells based on their content

✔ Access and manipulate entire rows and columns in a worksheet

✔ Add and delete worksheet rows and columns

**30 Min.
To Go**

The previous session showed you how to use the `Range` object to identify and manipulate specific parts of a worksheet. Sometimes your program needs to work with columns, rows, and individual cells. This session shows you how to perform these tasks.

Referencing Cells with the Cells Property

When you need to work with worksheet cells, the `Cells` property of the `Range` and `Worksheet` objects is one of the most useful tools available to you. The `Cells` property enables you to access single cells within a range in a manner that is convenient in programming. The `Cells` property works in a similar manner for the `Worksheet` and `Range` objects, but with this difference:

- The `Range.Cells` property references just the cells in that range.
- The `Worksheet.Cells` property references all the cells in the worksheet (not just the used cells).

There are three ways to use the `Cells` property, explained in the following sections.

The `Application` **object also has a** `Cells` **property. It works similar to the** `Worksheet.Cells` **property but always references the cells on the active worksheet.**

Referencing All Cells

If the `Cells` property is used without any arguments, it references all the cells in the range (the `Range.Cells` property) or worksheet (the `Worksheet.Cells` property); therefore, you could use the following line of code to change the font style and size of all cells in the specified worksheet:

```
Worksheets("Sales Data").Cells.Font.Name = "Arial"
Worksheets("Sales Data").Cells.Font.Size = 10
```

Likewise, the following code changes the background color of Range1 to a light purple color:

```
Range1.Cells.Interior.Color = RGB(220, 220, 255)
```

Setting cell background color and other aspects of worksheet formatting, including fonts, are covered in detail in Session 14.

**20 Min.
To Go**

Referencing by Row and Column

You can use the `Cells` property to reference individual cells using the following syntax:

```
Cells(RowIndex, ColumnIndex)
```

The RowIndex and ColumnIndex arguments are numerical values that identify the cell by its row and column. A value of 1 specifies the first row or column within the range and then increases to the right and downward. Cells(1,1) references the top left cell in the range.

The utility of this version of the `Cells` property is that it enables you to iterate through all the cells in a range. In effect, you can treat the range as a two-dimensional array. The procedure is as follows:

1. Use the `Range.Rows.Count` property to determine the number of rows in the range.
2. Use the `Range.Columns.Count` property to determine the number of columns in the range.
3. Create a `For...Next` loop that iterates through all the rows.
4. Inside the first `For...Next` loop, create another loop that iterates through all the columns.
5. Inside the inner loop, perform whatever action is required on the current cell.

For the range r1, for example, the code would look similar to this:

```
For r = 1 to r1.Rows.Count
  For c = 1 To r1.Columns.Count
    ' Code to manipulate r1.Cells(r, c) goes here.
  Next c
Next r
```

The Range **object has** Width **and** Height **properties. You might think that these properties give the size of the range in terms of rows and columns, but they do not. Rather, they give its size in terms of screen pixels. You must use the** Rows.Count **and** Columns.Count **properties to determine the number of rows and columns in a range.**

The program in Listing 11-1 illustrates the use of the Cells property. The program goes through all the cells in the current selection and determines the largest and smallest values in the cells; then displays a dialog box with the results (as shown in Figure 11-1).

Listing 11-1 *Using the Cells property to loop through all cells in a range*

```
Public Sub LargestSmallestValues()
' Displays a dialog box with the largest
' and smallest values in the current selection.

Dim row As Integer, col As Integer
Dim largest_value, smallest_value
Dim r As Range
Dim s As String

' Make sure selection is a range.
If TypeName(Selection) <> "Range" Then
    MsgBox ("There is no range selected")
    Exit Sub
End If

Set r = Selection

' Start with the first cell value.
largest_value = r.Cells(1, 1).Value
smallest_value = r.Cells(1, 1).Value

' Loop thru all rows.
For row = 1 To r.Rows.Count
    ' Loop thru all columns.
    For col = 1 To r.Columns.Count
        If r.Cells(row, col).Value > largest_value Then
```

Continued

Listing 11-1

Continued

```
            largest_value = r.Cells(row, col).Value
        End If
        If r.Cells(row, col).Value < smallest_value Then
smallest_value = r.Cells(row, col).Value
        End If
    Next col
Next row

s = "The largest and smallest values are "
s = s & largest_value & " and " & smallest_value
MsgBox s

End Sub
```

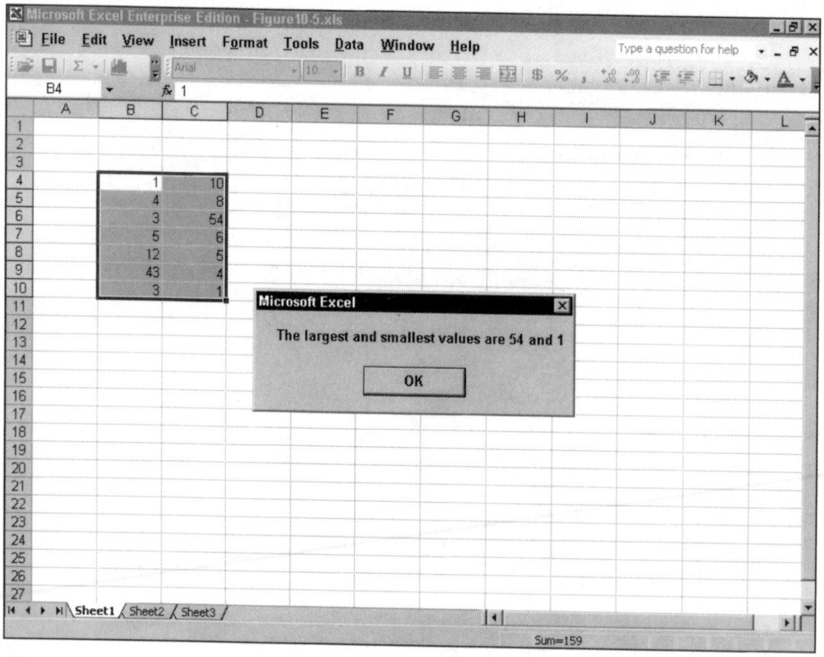

Figure 11-1   *The output of the program in Listing 11-1*

To see this program in action, complete the following steps:

1. Enter the code from the listing into the VBA Editor.
2. Switch to Excel, and enter numerical values in all cells of a range in the worksheet.
3. Select the range by dragging over it with the mouse.
4. Run the program from the macros dialog box (Alt+F8).

Screen Updating

By default, any changes that a program makes to a worksheet are immediately reflected on the screen (only if the worksheet is visible, of course). When there's no need for the user to see the changes as they are made, you can turn screen updating off. This has the added advantage of making your programs run faster. To do so, set the `Application.ScreenUpdating` property to False at the start of a program. Be sure to set it back to True when the program is done.

When you run the program, be sure that all cells in the selected range contain numerical values. Blank cells or text entries will fool the program.

Referencing by Cell Position

The third way to reference cells with the `Cells` property is by the position of the cell in the range. The syntax is:

```
Cells(CellPosition)
```

`CellPosition` is a numerical value specifying the position of the cell in the range. Cells are numbered starting at 1 for the top left cell, and move across and down. For example, in a range that is four columns wide and three rows high, the cells in the first row is, from left to right, positions 1, 2, 3, and 4. The next row is 5, 6, 7, and 8, and the last row is 9, 10, 11, and 12.

This syntax for the `Cells` property does not offer any advantages over the row and column addressing described in the previous section. To use this syntax to iterate through all cells in a range, use the following code (assume that r is the range of interest):

```
For pos = 1 To r.Columns.Count * r.Rows.Count
  ' Code to work with r.Cells(pos) goes here.
Next pos
```

The SpecialCells Method

You can use the `SpecialCells` method to select certain cells within a range, based on their contents and other characteristics. You can then perform an operation on only the selected cells. The syntax is:

```
SomeRange.SpecialCells(Type, Value)
```

The Type argument is required and identifies the type of cells to be selected. Permitted values for this argument are listed in Table 11-1. The `Value` argument is optional and used only when Type is either `xlCellTypeConstants` or `xlCellTypeFormulas`. Permitted values for this argument are given in Table 11-2. The `SpecialCells` method returns a Range object that references the selected cells. You can use this Range object to manipulate the cells as required by your program, for example, to format formula cells differently from other cells.

Table 11-1 *Constants for the SpecialCells Method's Type Argument*

Constant	Cells selected
xlCellTypeAllFormatConditions	Cells of any format
xlCellTypeBlanks	Blank cells
xlCellTypeComments	Cells that contain comments
xlCellTypeConstants	Cells containing number or text values
xlCellTypeFormulas	Cells containing formulas
xlCellTypeLastCell	The last cell in the range
xlCellTypeSameFormatConditions	Cells having the same format
xlCellTypeVisible	Cells that are visible

Table 11-2 *Constants for the SpecialCells Method's Value Argument*

Constant	Description
xlErrors	Formula cells with an error
xlLogical	Cells containing a logical formula
xlTextValues	Cells containing text data
xlNumbers	Cells containing number data

The following are examples of using the SpecialCells method. If the worksheet cursor is positioned in a table of data, this code activates the last (lower right) cell in the table.

```
ActiveCell.CurrentRegion.SpecialCells(xlCellTypeLastCell). _
    Activate
```

The CurrentRegion property was explained in Session 10.

This code sets all cells in the range r1 that contain numerical data to 0:

```
r1.SpecialCells(xlCellTypeConstants, xlNumbers).Value = 0
```

The program in Listing 11-2 presents a more sophisticated example of using the SpecialCells method. Within the worksheet region that is selected, it formats all cells containing text as boldface and all cells containing numbers in blue text, making it easy for the user to tell them apart.

Listing 11-2   *Using the SpecialCells method to apply selective formatting*

```
Public Sub FormatRegion()

Dim r As Range

If TypeName(Selection) <> "Range" Then
    MsgBox "You must select a range of cells."
    Exit Sub
End If

Set r = Selection
r.SpecialCells(xlCellTypeConstants, xlNumbers).Font.Color = RGB(0, 0, 255)
r.SpecialCells(xlCellTypeConstants, xlTextValues).Font.Bold = True

End Sub
```

Using the RGB function to specify colors is covered in Session 14.

Manipulating Columns and Rows

**10 Min.
To Go**

When you need to work with entire columns or rows, you use the Columns and Rows properties. These properties return a Range object that references one or more entire columns or rows. There are three ways to access this property:

- The Application.Columns (or Rows) property refers to columns (or rows) in the active worksheet.

- The Worksheet.Columns (or Rows) property refers to columns (or rows) in the specified worksheet.

- The Range.Columns (or Rows) property refers to columns (or rows) in the specified range.

Because the Application **object is always available as an implicit reference in VBA programs written in Excel, referring to the** Columns **or** Rows **property alone is the same as referring to the** Application.Columns **or** Application.Rows **property.**

Be aware that the Range.Columns property does not return a reference to full columns, but only that part of the columns that fall within the range. The same is true for rows and the Range.Rows property.

Referencing Entire Rows and Columns

You can use the `EntireRow` and `EntireColumn` properties to access full rows and columns within a range. For example, `Range("B1").EntireColumn` references the entire column B, and `Range("B9").EntireRow` references all of row 9. I present an example of using these properties in the section "Adding and Deleting Rows and Columns" later in this session.

You can use the Rows property with or without an argument (`Columns` works the same way):

- Rows without an argument returns a range containing all rows in the range or worksheet.

- Rows(*n*) returns the *n*th row in the range or worksheet.

The following are some examples. To reference the first column in the active worksheet:

```
Columns(1)
```

To reference the second row in the range r1:

```
r1.Rows(2)
```

To reference all columns that are spanned by range r1:

```
r1.Columns
```

To reference the third column (column C) in the specified worksheet:

```
Worksheets("Summary").Columns(3)
```

Remember that the Rows and Columns properties return a Range object, and you can use any of the Range object's properties and methods to work with the columns.

The Range **object was covered in detail in Session 10.**

For a more complete example of using the Columns property, look at the program in Listing 11-3. This program assigns the Currency format to the specified columns in the active worksheet.

Listing 11-3   *Using the Columns property*

```
Public Sub FormatColumnsAsCurrency(first As Integer, number As Integer)

' Assigns the currency format to columns in
' the active worksheet. The "first" argument
' identifies the leftmost column (A=1, etc.)
```

```
' and the "number" argument specifies how many columns.

Dim i As Integer

For i = first To first + number - 1
    Columns(i).NumberFormat = "$#,##0.00"
Next i

End Sub
```

After inserting this procedure into the VBA Editor, you cannot simply run it directly because it requires arguments. To try it out, you must create another procedure that calls the FormatColumnsAsCurrency procedure. This other procedure might look similar to this:

```
Sub Test()

FormatColumnsAsCurrency 2, 3

End Sub
```

The arguments passed in this example apply the format to columns B through D. To test the program, enter your test procedure code in the same module as the FormatColumnsAsCurrency procedure; then run it.

Adding and Deleting Rows and Columns

The Range object has the properties EntireColumn and EntireRow that allow you to work with entire rows and columns, rather than just the portion that is contained within the range. You can use these properties to add and delete rows and columns.

To add one or more columns or rows:

1. Define a Range object that spans the desired number of columns or rows in the location where you want the new columns or rows located.
2. Call the Range object's EntireColumn.Insert or EntireRow.Insert method.

When you insert columns, existing data is shifted to the right. For example, look at this code:

```
Range("B2:C2").EntireColumn.Insert
```

The results are:

- Two columns (B and C) are inserted.
- The old column B has moved over to column D, and C has moved over to E.

When new rows are added, existing rows are shifted down in the same manner.

To delete entire rows or columns, use the EntireColumn.Delete or EntireRow.Delete method. For example, this code deletes rows 5 through 10:

```
Range("A10").EntireRow.Delete
```

Done!

REVIEW

A worksheet is composed of cells arranged in rows and columns. In this session, you learned about some of the tools available to the Excel programmer for working with cells, rows, and columns.

- The `Cells` property enables you to access single cells within a range or worksheet.
- The `SpecialCells` methods allows you to select cells from a range based on their content, such as number cells or formula cells.
- Use the `Columns` and `Rows` properties to refer to the columns or rows in a worksheet or range.
- The `EntireRow` and `EntireColumn` properties enables you to refer to the full rows or columns that are spanned by a range.
- Use the `EntireRow` and `EntireColumn` properties to add or delete rows and columns from the worksheet.

QUIZ YOURSELF

1. When used without an argument, what does the `Cells` property reference? (See the "Referencing All Cells" section.)

2. Which method would you use to access only those cells in a range that contain comments? (See the "The SpecialCells Method" section.)

3. Range r1 refers to cells B1:C1. Does `r1.Columns` refer to all of columns B and C? (See the "Manipulating Columns and Rows" section.)

4. Range r1 refers to cells A2:A4. To what does `r1.EntireRow` refer? (See the "Referencing Entire Rows and Columns" sidebar.)

5. You insert a new worksheet column at position B. What happens to data in the original column B? (See the "Adding and Deleting Rows and Columns" section.)

Programming with Custom Formulas

Session Checklist

✔ Creating cell references in formulas

✔ Using absolute versus relative cell references

✔ Referring to named ranges in formulas

✔ Linking formulas to other worksheets and workbooks

✔ Using operators in Excel formulas

✔ Avoiding circular references

✔ Controlling formula calculation

**30 Min.
To Go**

An Excel program often needs to perform calculations, and the programmer has two options in this regard. You can perform the calculations in VBA code using the operators that were covered in Session 5, or you can perform the calculations in the Excel worksheet by inserting formulas into worksheet cells. The latter approach is the topic of this session.

Cell References in Formulas

An Excel formula almost always uses data that is located in other worksheet cells. To write custom formulas, you need to understand how to reference these cells. There are three ways to reference cells:

- As a relative cell reference
- As an absolute cell reference
- As a named range

Relative Cell References

A relative cell reference consists of the cell's column letter and row number. For example, A3 is a relative reference. In this case, *relative* means the reference does not always refer to the specific cell A3. Here's how this works.

Suppose you enter the formula =A3+A4 into cell A5. This means add the values in cells A3 and A4. So far, there doesn't seem to be anything relative about these references, but to Excel, what it really means is add the values in the two cells immediately above this cell. This becomes evident only when you copy the formula to another cell. Suppose you copy it to cell B5. Excel changes the formula to =B3+B4. Note that it keeps the same relative meaning: add the values in the two cells immediately above this cell. No matter where you copy this formula, it changes so it always adds the two cells above the cell containing the formula.

Relative cell references are the default in Excel and with good reason. Relative references make it possible to create a formula and then copy it to different worksheet locations. For example, if you have 20 columns of numbers to add, you can create the formula for the first column and place it in the cell below the column; then, copy the formula to the cells below the other columns, and the references automatically adjust so that each copied formula sums the numbers in the column above it.

 All Excel formulas begin with an equal sign. This tells Excel that it is a formula and not text data.

Absolute Cell References

Just the opposite of the relative cell reference, an absolute cell reference does not change when it is copied. The reference always refers to the same worksheet cell. You create an absolute cell reference by including dollar signs in the reference: $A$2. Here's a formula that uses absolute references:

```
=$A$3+$A$4
```

If you copy this formula to another worksheet location, the reference does not change. The formula always adds the values in cells A3 and A4.

A cell reference can also be part absolute and part relative with the absolute part being either the column letter or the row number. For example:

- $A3 — Column absolute, row relative
- A$3 — Row absolute, column relative

When a formula containing such a reference is copied, the relative part is adjusted to maintain its original relative meaning, while the absolute part remains unchanged. Table 12-1 gives some examples.

Table 12-1 *Relative versus Absolute Cell References*

Formula in cell A2	When copied to cell D6
=A1	=D5
=$A$1	=$A$1
=$A1	=$A5
=A$1	=D$1

Here's an example of using absolute cell references. The goal is to create a table that calculated the volume of differently sized cylinders. Different values for the cylinder radius are listed down the left side of the table, and different values for its height are listed across the top. In each cell, the volume for the corresponding radius and height is displayed. The formula for cylinder volume is:

$$\pi r^2 h$$

- π is the geometric constant "pi," approximately 3.1416.
- r is the radius of the cylinder.
- h is the height of the cylinder.

Now, look at the worksheet in Figure 12-1. What would the required formula be for the top left cell of results (cell C5)? In pseudocode it would be:

```
(pi) times (cell B5 squared) times (cell C4)
```

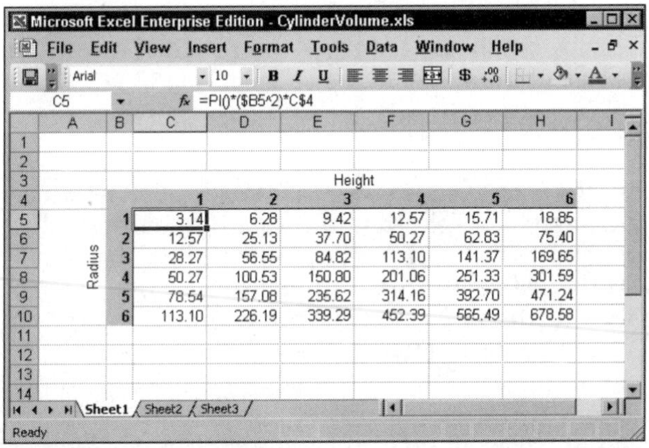

Figure 12-1 *A table that uses part absolute cell references for its calculations*

Many programmers find it useful to outline a program or procedure in "pseudocode" before writing the actual VBA code. Pseudocode is nothing more than plain English (or French, Spanish, and so on) descriptions of what the program will do at each point.

Note that you can obtain the value of pi from the Excel function PI(). The initial formula placed in cell C5 might be as follows:

```
=PI()*(B5^2)*C4
```

If, however, you were to copy this formula to the other cells in the table, the relative ranges would be changed, and the formulas would not refer to the proper cells. For example, when copied to cell D2, the result would be:

```
=PI()*(C6^2)*D5
```

Clearly this is not correct. The formula needs to use part absolute references, as follows:

```
=PI()*($B5^2)*C$4
```

When copied, the formula is correct, and the values in the table display properly.

Named Range References

As you learned in Session 10, you can assign names to ranges in a workbook. In your formulas, you can use an assigned name rather than a cell reference to refer to a cell. This applies only to ranges that refer to a single cell.

Please refer to Session 10 for more information on naming ranges.

To refer to a named cell in a formula, simply use the range name in the formula. For example, this formula displays the sum of the values in the cells SubTotal1 and SubTotal2:

```
=SubTotal1+SubTotal2
```

Using named cells instead of cell references offers several advantages. Cell references are not adjusted if rows or columns are inserted or deleted in the worksheet; therefore, if a formula refers to C5 and a row is inserted into the worksheet above row 5, the data that was in C5 will now be in D5. Any formulas that reference C5 will still reference C5. In contrast, a range name that had referred to C5 will refer to D5 after the row insertion, and the formula will still work. Also, if data is moved from one location in the worksheet to another, the assigned range names go along with it.

You can use multiple cell ranges in some of Excel's built-in functions, which are covered in Session 13.

**20 Min.
To Go**

Referencing Cells in Other Worksheets and Workbooks

A formula can reference a cell in another worksheet (within the same workbook) using the following notation:

    sheetname!CellReference

For example, the following formula displays 10 times the value in cell A2 of the worksheet sheet1:

    =10*sheet1!A2

You can reference a cell in another workbook that is currently open in Excel by using this syntax:

    [WorkbookFileName]Worksheetname!CellReference

For example, this formula displays one half the value in cell D5 on sheet1 in Sales.xls:

    =0.5*[Sales.xls]sheet1!D5

If the name of the linked workbook contains one or more spaces, you must enclose it in single quotes:

    =0.5*'[Sales Data.xls]sheet1'!D5

If the linked workbook is not currently open, the reference must include the complete path to the file and must also use single quotes:

    =0.5*'c:\data\[Sales.xls]sheet1'!D5

In Excel, use the Edit ⇨ Links command to view all links to sources outside the current workbook.

Use Caution When Using Links Between Workbooks

There are some situations that can play havoc with links between workbooks, and you must be aware of them. If the source workbook (the one being linked to) and the target workbook (the one containing the link reference) are both open and you use the File ⇨ Save As command to make a backup copy, Excel automatically updates the target links to reflect this new name. This may not be what you want. If you rename the source workbook when the target workbook is not open, the new name is not reflected in the link references.

Operators

Excel provides a number of operators that can be used in formulas: mathematical, conditional, and logical, and as you will see, these operators are almost identical to VBA's own operators.

Mathematical Operators

Excel's mathematical operators are identical to those used in VBA, and they include the standard operations of addition (+), subtraction (-), multiplication (*), and division (/), as well as the following less common operations:

- **Integer division (\\).** Performs a division and returns the integer part of the answer.; therefore, 11\3 evaluates to 3.
- **Exponentiation (^).** Raises a number to a power. In VBA, 4^2 means four to the second power or 4^2, and evaluates to 16.
- **Modulus (mod).** Performs a division and returns the remainder. For example, 18 mod 5 evaluates to 3. Floating-point numbers are rounded to integers when used with mod.

Excel does not have an assignment operator. The equal sign is used to indicate the start of a formula and also as a comparison operator.

Comparison Operators

Excel's comparison operators are identical to VBA's. These operators perform a comparison between two values and return either True or False. For example, you can use these operators to determine if numbers in worksheet cells are less than, equal to, or greater than some comparison value. They are reviewed here:

- = Equal to
- > Greater than
- < Less than
- >= Greater than or equal to
- <= Less than or equal to
- <> Not equal to

Logical Operators

As you learned in Session 5, logical operations are used to work with True/False values. Excel does not have logical operators *per se*, but rather provides the programmer with three functions that perform the same tasks as the AND, OR, and NOT operators in VBA:

- AND(cond1, cond2). Returns True only if cond1 and cond2 are both True; returns False otherwise.

- OR(cond1, cond2). Returns False only if cond1 and cond2 are both False; returns True otherwise.
- Not(cond). Returns True if cond is False; returns False if cond is True.

For more details and examples of using the logical operators, please refer to Session 5.

Avoiding Circular References

**10 Min.
To Go**

A *circular reference* exists when the formulas in two or more cells are mutually dependent. Here's a simple example:

- In Cell A2: =B2/2
- In cell B2: =A2*10

You can see that the value of cell A2 depends on cell B2, and the value of cell B2 depends on cell A2. Excel cannot calculate when there is a circular reference. If you create a circular reference manually, Excel displays a warning dialog box. You can then display the Circular Reference toolbar (View ⇨ Toolbars ⇨ Circular Reference) which also displays a link between the cells that are involved. Also, the circular reference dialog box is displayed, letting you examine and resolve the problem. This is shown in Figure 12-2.

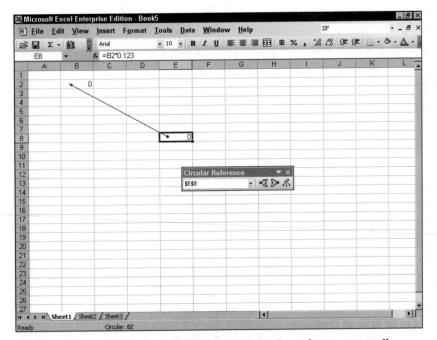

Figure 12-2   Excel does not let you enter a circular reference manually.

If you enter a circular reference from a VBA program, however, Excel does not object. The involved cell, however, is not calculated but instead displays 0. To detect circular references in code, use the Worksheet object's CircularReference property. This property returns a Range object that references the first circular reference on the worksheet, or Nothing if there are no circular references. You can use this property to indicate the source of the circular reference in the worksheet. The program in Listing 12-1 shows how.

Listing 12-1 *A program to detect circular references*

```
Sub ShowCircularReferences()

If ActiveSheet.CircularReference = Nothing Then
  MsgBox "No circular references on " & ActiveSheet.Name
Else
  ActiveSheet.CircularReference.Select
End If

End Sub
```

When run, this program checks for circular references on the active worksheet. If none is found, a message to that effect is displayed. If one is found, it is selected in the worksheet.

Use of the CircularReference property is usually restricted to program development. As a programmer, you can use the program in Listing 12-1 or something similar to it to verify that your programs do not result in circular references in the project's worksheets.

Controlling Formula Calculation

Excel's default is to automatically recalculate all formulas in a workbook as needed. With most workbooks this is fine, because calculation is performed so quickly that it does not cause noticeable delays or other problems. There can be situations, however, in which automatic calculation is not desirable. In particular, some large, complex workbooks with lots of formulas and links can take a while to calculate, even on a fast computer. For this reason, Excel offers you the option of manual recalculation.

When you are working in Excel, you set the calculation mode by selection Tools ➪ Options to display the Options dialog box; then, on the Calculation tab (see Figure 12-3), select either Automatic or Manual.

When manual calculation mode has been selected, it affects all open workbooks. The calculation mode is a property of the Excel application and not of individual workbooks or worksheets. Then while still in Excel, do the following:

- Press F9 to calculate all open workbooks.
- Press Shift+F9 to calculate only the active worksheet.

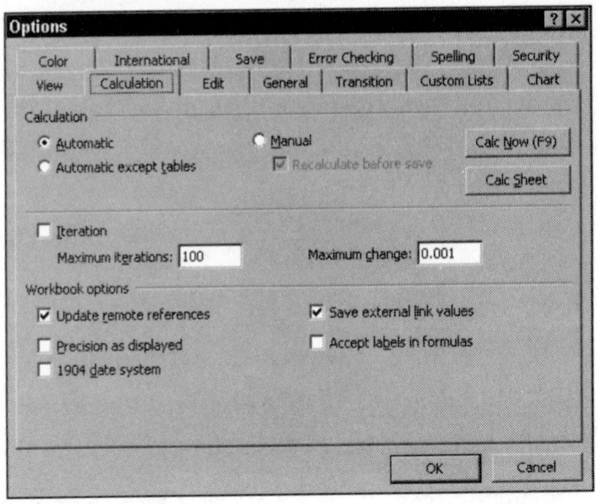

Figure 12-3　Selecting automatic or manual calculation in Excel

In your VBA programs, you can control workbook calculation as required by your program. To set calculation to manual, set the `Application` object's `Calculation` property to `xlCalculationManual`:

```
Application.Calculation = xlCalculationManual
```

To return to automatic calculation, set this property to `xlCalculationAutomatic`.

If your program sets the calculation mode to manual, it should always set it back to automatic before exiting.

When calculation is set to manual, a VBA program can force calculation to occur by calling the `Calculate` method. This method can be called on three objects, as follows:

- The `Application` object calculates all open workbooks.
- The `Worksheet` object calculates a single worksheet.
- The `Range` object calculates the specified range.

Here are some examples. This line of code calculates all open workbooks. Note that because the `Application` reference is implicit, the `Calculate` keyword can be used alone:

```
Calculate
```

This code calculates all formulas in the Sales worksheet in the active workbook:

```
ActiveWorkbook.Worksheets("Sales").Calculate
```

This code calculates all formulas in columns A through D of the active worksheet:

```
ActiveSheet.Columns("A:D").Calculate
```

Done!

REVIEW

One of Excel's most powerful features is the capability to perform customized calculations by creating formulas in worksheet cells. This session showed you how to create these formulas in your VBA programs.

- Most formulas perform calculations on data in other cells and must include a reference to the source cell(s).
- A cell reference can be either absolute or relative.
- A formula can reference a cell in another worksheet or workbook.
- The operators available for use in Excel formulas are similar to the VBA operators.
- Circular references, in which two cells refer to each other, must be avoided.
- Worksheet formulas can be calculated automatically or under the control of your program.

QUIZ YOURSELF

1. What is the difference between an absolute and a relative cell reference? (See the "Cell References in Formulas" section.)
2. How does a formula reference a cell in another worksheet in the same workbook? (See the "Referencing Cells in Other Worksheets and Workbooks" section.)
3. Does Excel have the same logical operators as VBA? (See the "Logical Operators" section.)
4. How would you determine if a worksheet contains any circular references? (See the "Avoiding Circular References" section.)
5. When would you want to use manual formula calculation? (See the "Controlling Formula Calculation" section.)

SESSION

Programming with Excel's Built-In Functions

Session Checklist

✔ Using Excel functions in VBA code

✔ Excel function overview

✔ The `WorksheetFunction` object

**30 Min.
To Go**

Excel's calculation abilities go well beyond the custom formulas you learned about in the previous session. You also have access to a library of predefined functions to use in your worksheet calculations.

Excel's Built-in Functions

Excel provides a complete library of functions that you can use in a worksheet. Each function performs a commonly needed (or, in some cases, not-so-commonly-needed) calculation. Rather than figuring out the details yourself — for example, to calculate payment on a loan or depreciation for tax purposes — you can just plug in the appropriate function. You must know which function to use, of course, and later in this session you'll learn the details of some of the more commonly used ones.

When you work directly in Excel, you access functions using the function bar. When you click the fx button, the Insert Function dialog box is displayed as shown in Figure 13-1. In this dialog box you can select functions alphabetically or by category, and view a brief description of the selected function below the function list. Using this dialog box is a good way for you to gain some familiarity with the functions in Excel.

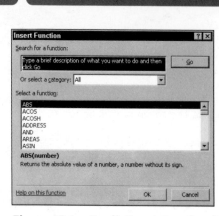

Figure 13-1   *Excel's Insert Function dialog box*

Excel offers a large number of functions, too many to cover in this session. The latter part of this session provides information and examples for some of the more commonly needed functions, but this is merely scratching the surface. You can refer to Excel's online help or use the Insert Function dialog box to get information on functions that are not covered here.

Using Excel Functions in Formulas

An Excel function consists of the function name followed by parentheses. Almost all functions take one or more arguments that specify the data the function is to use. An argument may be a literal value, a cell reference, a range reference, or even another function. It is important that the argument be of the appropriate type, no matter what form it takes. A function that performs a numerical calculation, for example, should not be passed text data as an argument.

To use a function, include it in the formula and then insert it in the desired cell. A formula may contain nothing but a function, as in the following example that uses the Sum function to add the values in cells B1:B9 in the worksheet named "Sales" and display the result in cell B10:

```
Worksheets("Sales").Range("B10") = "=Sum(B1:B9)"
```

A function can also be part of a more complicated formula, as in the following example that sums the values in cells B1:B9 and multiplies that value by the number in the cell named InterestRate:

```
Worksheets("Sales").Range("B10") = "=Sum(B1:B9)*InterestRate"
```

Cell and range references in function arguments work the same as they do in formulas. See Session 11 for details.

**20 Min.
To Go**

Excel Function Overview

The remainder of this session provides information on some of the more frequently used functions, along with some examples. Excel divides its functions into categories, and this session follows the same arrangement. Not all categories are included. Some of the more specialized, such as statistical functions, are beyond the scope of this book.

Logical functions are covered in Session 12, and database functions are covered in Session 27.

Financial Functions

Excel's financial functions can perform a variety of sophisticated calculations, including annuities, depreciation, and so on. The function that is perhaps used most often is PMT, which calculates the payments on a loan. For example, if you were thinking about taking out a car loan of $20,000 at 5% for four years, this function could tell you what your monthly payments would be.

The syntax for the PMT function is:

```
PMT(rate, nper, pv, fv, type)
```

- **Rate.** The interest rate being charged, per period.
- **Nper.** The number of periods, or term, of the loan.
- **Pv.** The amount of the loan (present value).
- **Fv.** Optional. The amount owed at the end of the payments (future value). For most loans this is 0, which is the default value if this argument is omitted.
- **Type.** Optional. Set to 0 (the default) if payments are due at the end of each period. Set to 1 if the payments are due at the beginning of each period.

The return value of the function is the payment due per period. It is essential that the period used for the `rate` argument and the `nper` argument are the same. Most loans quote an annual interest rate but require payments monthly. Continuing with the example given previously, you would use months and would have:

- 5% interest per year is the same as 0.05/12 per month.
- Four-year loan period is the same as 4*12 months.

Real-world monthly payments may be different from the results returned by the PMT function because of extra fees tacked onto the loan payment.

The formula to calculate the monthly payment on this loan would be:

```
=PMT(0.05/12, 4*12, 20000)
```

The PMT function returns a negative number for the loan payment because it is money going out rather than money flowing in. Simply place a minus sign in front of the function to get a positive result.

The program shown in Listing 13-1 shows how to use this function in a loan calculator worksheet. It also shows one approach to creating custom applications using VBA programming. This approach is to write a program that creates a worksheet, complete with the required labels, data entry cells, and formulas. After this has been done, the program is not used again; the finished worksheet is itself the custom application.

Listing 13-1   *A VBA program to create a loan calculator worksheet*

```
Public Sub CreateLoanWorksheet()

Dim wb As Workbook
Dim ws As Worksheet

'Create a new, blank workbook.
Set wb = Workbooks.Add
'Rename the first worksheet.
wb.Worksheets(1).Name = "Loan Calculator"
Set ws = wb.Worksheets("Loan Calculator")

'Add a title to the worksheet.
ws.Range("A1") = "Loan Calculator"

'Put identifying labels in column B.
ws.Range("B4") = "Loan amount"
ws.Range("B5") = "Annual interest rate"
ws.Range("B6") = "Loan term in years"
ws.Range("B7") = "Monthly payment"

' Increase the width of column B to
' accomodate the labels.
ws.Range("B1").EntireColumn.AutoFit

'Put the loan payment formula in C7
ws.Range("C7").Value = "=-PMT(C5/12, C6*12, C4)"

'Save the workbook.
wb.SaveAs Filename:="LoanCalculator"

End Sub
```

The design of the finished worksheet is fairly simple. It contains a label to identify the application, three more labels to identify the cells where the user enters the loan information (amount, interest rate, and term), and a final label to identify the result. The result cell will contain the PMT formula to calculate the loan payment. In sum, the steps that the VBA program has to perform are:

1. Create a new workbook.
2. Rename the first worksheet to "Loan Payment" so the worksheet tab displays that name.
3. Insert the required labels in the target cells.
4. Insert the required PMT formula into the result cell.
5. Save the workbook.

One more task is required. The labels that are placed in the worksheet are wider than the default column width, which means that the width of the column must be increased to accommodate them. This is done using the column's AutoFit method, which automatically increases the column width as needed to fit the data in the column. You'll see this in the following code.

Figure 13-2 shows the worksheet created by this program. The result cell, C7, displays #DIV/0! because the input cells for the PMT formula are empty and the function cannot calculate properly. When values are entered in the three input cells, this display is replaced by the result.

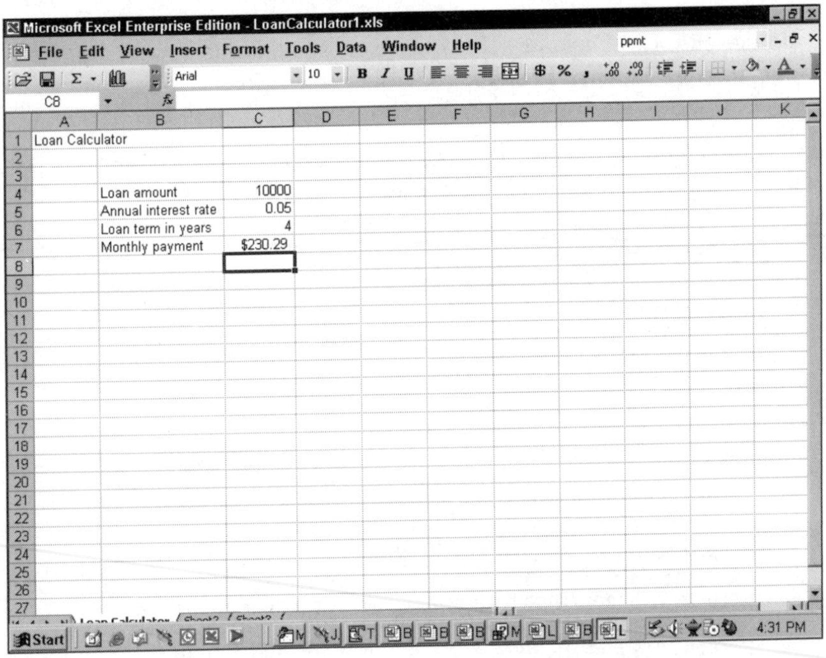

Figure 13-2   *The worksheet created by the program in Listing 13-1*

> **Percentages must be entered as decimals. For example, you would enter 0.05 for 5%.**

Looking at Figure 13-2, there are several potential improvements that are immediately obvious, plus one other that may not be so obvious:

- The worksheet is rather plain in appearance. Some formatting would result in a more appealing product.
- The loan amount should display as a currency amount, and the interest rate as a percentage.
- A careless user could erase or change labels or the worksheet's formula.

I will revise this project in later sessions. After I have covered the relevant programming topics, these shortcomings will be addressed.

Date and Time Functions

10 Min. To Go

Excel maintains dates and times using the same approach that VBA does for a type `Date` variable — a floating-point number in which the integer part represents the date, as the number of days since December 31, 1899, and the fractional part represents the time as a fraction of the 24-hour day. The earliest date that Excel can understand is January 1, 1900, which has the serial number 1. When you work in a worksheet, you can enter dates in any commonly used format, and Excel recognizes it as a date. It is converted to the corresponding serial number for storage, but displayed in a readable date format. The same is true of times.

Unlike VBA, Excel cannot use negative date serial numbers to represent dates before January 1, 1899.

Excel's date and time functions parallel those found in VBA to some extent. They are listed with brief descriptions in Table 13-1. Refer to the online help for more details.

Table 13-1 *Excel's Date and Time Functions*

Function	Description
Date	Converts year, month, and day data into a date serial number.
DateValue	Converts a string containing a formatted date into a date serial number.
Day	Returns the day of the month (1–31) for a specified date.
Hour	Returns the hour of the day (0–23) for a specified time.
Minute	Returns the minute of the hour (0–59) for a specified time.
Month	Returns the month of the year (1–12) for a specified date.
Now	Returns the current date and time formatted as a date/time.
Second	Returns the second of the minute (0–59) for a specified time.
Time	Converts an hour, minute, and second data into a time value.
TimeValue	Converts a string containing a formatted time into a time value.
Today	Returns the current date formatted as a date.

Function	Description
Weekday	Returns the day of the week (1–7) for a specified date.
Year	Returns the year of a specified date.

Math and Trig Functions

Excel's math and trig (trigonometry) functions perform a variety of related calculations. For example, all the trig functions, such as sine and cosine, are available. Logarithms, matrix operations, and exponentials, just to name a few, are also available. One math function that can be useful in various situations is RAND, which returns pseudo-random numbers. The syntax is:

```
RAND()
```

The return value is a pseudo-random number equal to or greater than 0 and less than 1. Note that the return value of this function changes each time the worksheet is recalculated. If your programs need a table of data for testing purposes, you can fill the cells with the RAND function to get what you need. If you need numbers in a range other than 0–1, add a multiplier to the formula. For example, the formula

```
=RAND()*100
```

returns random values in the range 0–100.

Nonchanging Random Numbers

Excel's RAND function has the limitation that its return value changes each time the worksheet is recalculated. To fill cells with nonchanging random numbers, you can use VBA's RND function. RND works the same way, returning a pseudo-random number equal to or greater than 0 and less than 1; however, by using a short program to fill the cells with these values, you'll get a table of data that does not change with each worksheet recalculation. The program in the following listing does just this.

```
Public Sub FillRangeWithRandomValues(r As Range, max As Single)

' Fills the specified worksheet range with random
' numbers in the range 0-max.

Dim i As Integer, j As Integer
For i = 1 To r.Columns.Count
    For j = 1 To r.Rows.Count
    r.Cells(j, i) = max * Rnd()
```

Continued

Nonchanging Random Numbers   *Continued*

```
      Next j
   Next i


   End Sub
```

Pass this procedure a range and a maximum value, and the code fills the range with random values ranging from 0 to the specified maximum.

Text Functions

The text functions offered by Excel provide text-handling capabilities that are similar to those provided by the VBA language. Some of the functions even have the same names. Table 13-2 describes some of Excel's text functions.

Table 13-2   *Description of Some of Excel's Text Functions*

Function	Description
Clean(*text*)	Removes all nonprintable characters from text.
Dollar(*number, decimals*)	Converts a number to currency format text with the specified number of decimal places.
Exact(*text1, text2*)	Returns True only if text1 and text2 match exactly (case-sensitive).
Rept(*text, num*)	Repeats text the specified number of times.
T(*value*)	If value is text, returns that text. If value is not text, returns an empty string.
Trim(*text*)	Removes all spaces from text except for single spaces between words.
Value(*text*)	Converts a text representation of a number to a numeric value.

Suppose you want to sum the values in cells A1:A10 and then display the result formatted as currency (for example, "$1234.00"). The following formula does the trick:

```
=Dollar(Sum(A1:A10), 2)
```

VBA Functions or Excel Functions?

There's a lot of overlap between the functions provided by VBA and those provided by Excel. When a task could be performed either way, how do you decide which to use? It is usually fairly easy to decide, based on the nature of your project.

- When the purpose of your code is to create all or part of a worksheet, which the user will then use, you usually choose Excel functions. Because Excel functions exist in worksheet cells and are evaluated whenever the worksheet is recalculated, they can perform their job without the need to run VBA programs. You'll also tend toward using Excel functions when the results need to be displayed in the worksheet.

- VBA functions are often more appropriate when your code plays a more active role in an application, beyond that of simply creating a worksheet with in-place labels and formulas. If the result of a function will be used internally, and not displayed, a VBA function is also more appropriate

Another way to display a number in currency format is by applying the "Currency" format to the cell, as you learn in Session 14. This is one of many situations where Excel and VBA provide you with more than one way to obtain a given result.

The WorksheetFunction Object

Excel provides many worksheet functions that do not have VBA parallels. If you want to use one of these functions in code, you can use the WorksheetFunction object. This object lets you evaluate an Excel worksheet function in VBA code without having to place the function in a worksheet cell, which is useful when your program needs to use a function result but does not need to display it to the user. The syntax is:

```
WorksheetFunction.FunctionName(arguments)
```

FunctionName can be any of the Excel worksheet functions. The argument list must be appropriate as defined for that function. For example, the following code sets the variable x to the smallest value in the range A1:A10:

```
x = WorksheetFunction.Min(ActiveSheet.Range("A1:A10"))
```

This technique is useful considering Excel provides many functions that are not part of the VBA language.

Done!

REVIEW

Excel provides a rich library of worksheet functions for financial, mathematical, and other calculations.

- Your VBA program can use Excel's worksheet functions by including them in formulas that are inserted into cells.
- The date and time worksheet functions are similar to VBA's date and time functions, representing dates and times as serial numbers.
- The WorksheetFunction object enables you to use Excel worksheet functions in your VBA code.

QUIZ YOURSELF

1. How is a worksheet function different from a VBA function? (See the "VBA Functions or Excel Functions?" sidebar.)

2. How do you use a worksheet function in a worksheet formula? (See the "Using Excel Functions in Formulas" section.)

3. Can you use the date and time worksheet functions with dates prior to January 1, 1900? (See the "Date and Time Functions" section.)

Formatting a Worksheet

Session Checklist

✔ Formatting numbers

✔ Font formatting

✔ Changing text alignment and orientation

✔ Adding borders and backgrounds to ranges

✔ Changing column widths and row heights

**30 Min.
To Go**

The term *formatting* refers to the appearance of a worksheet. Because a worksheet's formatting does not affect the way it works, formatting is sometimes considered to be a nonessential extra that does not require much attention. This is a big mistake! An important aspect of any worksheet is how easy it makes the user's job. Appropriate application for formatting not only makes a worksheet easier to use, but it can reduce the chance for errors as well. This session covers the most important aspects of worksheet formatting.

Cell Formatting

Much of the formatting that can be applied to a worksheet is called *cell formatting* because in general, the formatting is applied to individual cells. In Excel, you access cell formatting options by selecting Format ➪ Cells from the menu to display the dialog box that is shown in Figure 14-1. Each tab in this dialog box is related to a specific type of formatting, as follows:

- **Number.** This controls how numbers are formatted.
- **Alignment.** This is for text alignment with respect to the sides, top, and bottom of the cell, as well as text rotation.
- **Font.** Here is where you can set the style, color, and size of the font used to display cell data.

- **Border.** This is where you can specify the style and placement of borders around the cell edges.
- **Patterns.** This determines the color and pattern of the cell background.
- **Protection.** This locks and hides cells.

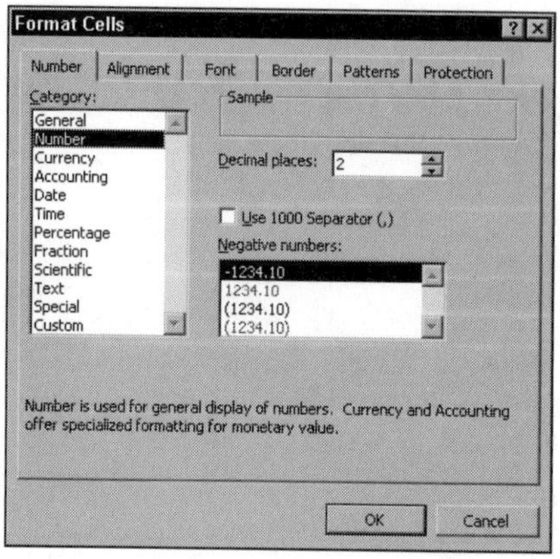

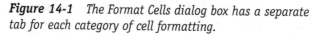

Figure 14-1 *The Format Cells dialog box has a separate tab for each category of cell formatting.*

Changing cell formatting in a VBA program requires that you obtain a range reference to the cell(s) of interest and then use the Range object's properties to set the desired formatting. These properties are covered in detail in the following sections. Be aware, however, that Excel's formatting capabilities are very sophisticated and complete, and it is beyond the scope of this book to go into detail on more than a small fraction of the possibilities. For this reason, I have the following two suggestions:

- Work in Excel to become familiar with the formatting options that are available to you. Explore the various settings in the Format Cells dialog box, as well as the other commands on the Format menu. Use the online help as needed for clarification and assistance.
- Use the macro-recording feature to learn about the code required to apply specific formatting.

See Session 10 for more information on defining ranges. The steps required to record a macro were presented in Session 2.

When using the macro-recording feature, be aware of the way that Excel records macros. If you record the actions of using the Format Cells dialog box to change one aspect of formatting, the macro includes not only the aspect(s) of formatting that you changed, but also those aspects that were not changed. Here's an example. I recorded the action of changing the alignment of the selected cells from the default to "centered." The recorded macro is shown as follows:

```
Sub Macro1()
'
' Macro1 Macro
' Macro recorded 1/30/2003 by Peter G. Aitken
'
    With Selection
        .HorizontalAlignment = xlCenter
        .VerticalAlignment = xlBottom
        .WrapText = False
        .Orientation = 0
        .AddIndent = False
        .IndentLevel = 0
        .ShrinkToFit = False
        .ReadingOrder = xlContext
        .MergeCells = False
    End With

End Sub
```

The one line of code that reflects the formatting that I changed is:

```
.HorizontalAlignment = xlCenter
```

The other lines of code are related to additional aspects of formatting that are located on the same tab in the Format Cells dialog box as the Alignment option. Even though I did not change these, Excel included them in the recorded macro code. This means that when you are using recorded macros to learn what the code is for making formatting changes, you need to pay attention to locate the specific code that is relevant.

Number Formatting

Number formatting controls how numbers are displayed; it has no effect on cells that contain text. When you apply number formatting using the Format Cells dialog box, you have a variety of named categories and options from which to choose (see Figure 14-1). In code, however, things are not this simple. Number formats are set using formatting codes that use a special syntax to describe how a number is to be displayed. These format codes are assigned to the NumberFormat property of the Range object. For example, to display numbers with no commas or special characters, and two decimal places, the code would be as follows:

```
SomeRange.NumberFormat = "0.00"
```

Excel's number formats are flexible and permit you to display numeric data in almost any imaginable way. Each number formatting code is made up of certain characters, as described in Table 14-1.

Table 14-1 *Elements of Number Formatting Codes*

Character	Meaning	Code example	Format example
#	Significant digit	##.#	12.67 displays as 12.7
0	Nonsignificant 0	#.000	1.2 displays as 1.200
.	Decimal point	##.##	12.34 displays as 12.34
$	Currency symbol	$#.##	21.98 displays as $21.98
%	Percent symbol	#.#%	0.05 displays as 5.0%
,	Thousands separator	#,###	98000 displays as 98,000

You can also display positive and negative numbers differently. In accounting, for example, negative numbers may be displayed in red and/or enclosed in parentheses. To do this, include two format specifiers in the format code separated by a semicolon. The first format applies to positive numbers, the second to negative numbers. For example:

`$#.##;($#.##)`

This format will display positive numbers with a dollar sign and two decimal places. Negative numbers will be formatted the same but will also be enclosed in parentheses.

To specify a display color, include the color name enclosed in square brackets at the start of the format code. The available color names are:

- Black
- Cyan
- Magenta
- White
- Blue
- Green
- Red
- Yellow

The following code, for example, displays positive numbers in the default font color of the cell and negative numbers in red.

`$#.##;[Red]$#.##`

A display color specified in this way overrides the font color that is set for the cell (see the next section on font formatting).

For more details on Excel's formatting codes, refer to the online help.

**20 Min.
To Go**

Font Formatting

Excel provides complete control over the font used to display data in worksheet cells. The aspects of formatting that you can control are as follows:

- The style, or face, of the font
- The size of the font
- Use of italics, boldface, and underlining
- Special effects such as strikethrough, superscript, and subscript

When working in Excel, you use the Font tab in the Format Cells dialog box (shown in Figure 14-2) to make changes. In VBA, you control the display font by means of the Font object. This object has a set of properties that correspond to various aspects of the font's appearance. They are described in Table 14-2.

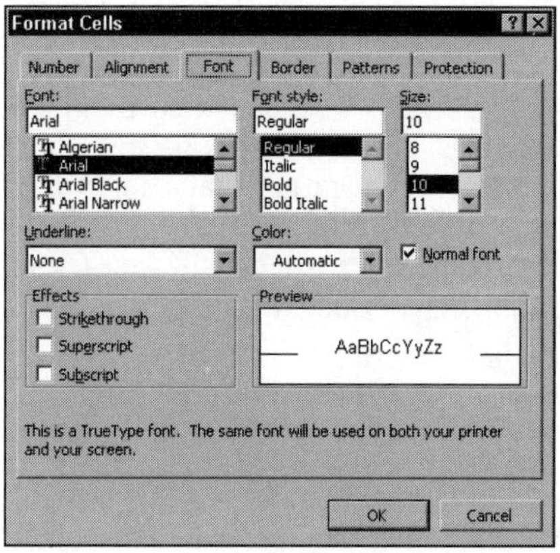

Figure 14-2 *The Font tab of the Format Cells dialog box*

Table 14-2 *Properties of the* Font *Object*

Property	Description
Name	The name of the font (its typeface)
Color	The color of the font, as an RGB value
Size	The vertical size of the font, in points (1 point = 1/72 inch; Excel's default font is 10 points)
Bold	True/False value specifying whether the font is boldface
Italic	True/False value specifying whether the font is italic

Continued

Table 14-2   *Continued*

Property	Description
Underline	A constant specifying the underlining of the font, which can be set to xlUnderlineStyleNone, xlUnderlineStyleSingle, or xlUnderlineStyleDouble
Strikethrough	True/False value specifying whether the font is displayed with strikethrough (horizontal lines through the characters)
Subscript	True/False value specifying whether the font is displayed as a subscript
Superscript	True/False value specifying whether the font is displayed as a superscript

Specifying the name of a font requires that you know the name of the desired font. Windows and Excel support a wide range of fonts, some of the more popular being Arial, Courier New, Georgia, MS Sans Serif, and Times New Roman. It's a safe bet that these and many other fonts will be available on all Windows systems, but you cannot be sure about some other fonts that may be installed as part of specific applications rather than as part of the operating system. Fortunately, the Font property is very forgiving. If you assign a nonexistent font name to this property, no error occurs — the cell displays Excel's default font (Arial).

The Color property uses an RGB value, which identifies a color in terms of its red, green, and blue components. To set this property, use the RGB function:

```
RGB(r, g, b)
```

Each argument is a number in the range 0 to 255 that specifies the relative level of the red, green, or blue component. RGB(0, 0, 0) is black, RGB(255, 255, 255) is white, RGB(122, 122, 122) is gray, RGB(0, 0, 255) is blue, and so on (you can experiment to get some experience with the colors produced by various RGB settings). For example, this code sets the font of the current selection to lime green:

```
Selection.Font.Color = RGB(122, 255, 0)
```

 VBA provides a set of predefined constants for a few colors. They are vbBlack, vbRed, vbGreen, vbYellow, vbBlue, vbMagenta, vbCyan, **and** vbWhite. **You can use these constants in place of the** RGB **function when setting the** Color **property.**

Alignment and Orientation of Data

You can control the alignment of data in a cell, both horizontally and vertically. Figure 14-3 shows the appearance of the various settings for vertical and horizontal alignment.

RGB Color Definitions

The RGB color model defines a color in terms of the three primary colors: red, green, and blue. You may remember from art class that the primaries are red, blue, and yellow, so what gives? Red, blue, and yellow are the *subtractive* primaries that are important when you are mixing paints. In contrast, red, green, and blue are the *additive* primaries that apply when you are mixing light, as in the light emitted by a computer monitor. With 255 possible levels for each of the three primaries, this model allows for over 16 million distinct colors.

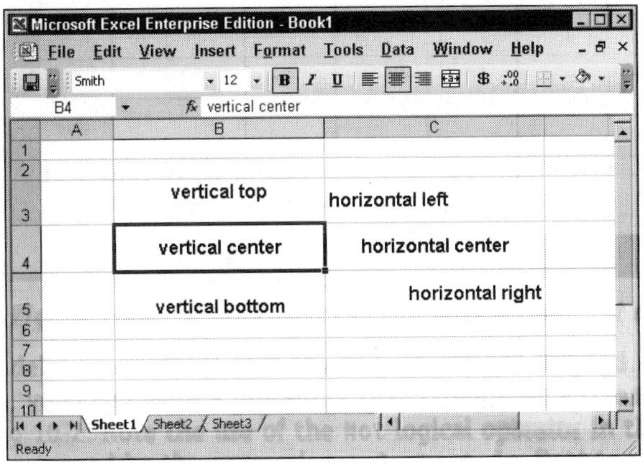

Figure 14-3 *Illustration of different horizontal and vertical alignment settings*

To change alignment, use the following properties of the Range object:

- `HorizontalAlignment.` Set to `xlLeft`, `xlCenter`, or `xlRight`.
- `VerticalAlignment.` Set to `xlTop`, `xlCenter`, or `xlBottom`.

Excel's default is to use bottom alignment for vertical position. Horizontally, numbers are right-aligned, and text is left-aligned.

You can also change the orientation of text from the default horizontal to vertical or anything in between using the `Range.Orientation` property. Orientation is specified as degrees rotated counter-clockwise from the default horizontal orientation. For example, orientation of 90 degrees results in vertical text that reads from bottom to top. Permitted values for orientation range from -90 to 90 degrees. Figure 14-4 shows examples of some orientation settings.

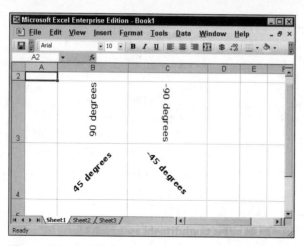

Figure 14-4 Cell data can be oriented at various angles.

 If you change the orientation of cell data, Excel will not automatically increase the row height to fit the new orientation. You'll have to do that manually.

Cell Borders

Excel can display borders around individual cells or groups of cells. For ranges of two or more cells, the borders can be around the outer edges only or can include the boundaries between cells within the range as well. Any Range object has a Borders collection that contains the borders for that range. Each individual border is represented by a Border object. Each border has an associated constant, as described in Table 14-3.

Table 14-3 *Range Borders and the Associated Constants*

Border	Constant
Bottom edge of range	xlEdgeBottom
Top edge of range	xlEdgeTop
Left edge of range	xlEdgeLeft
Right edge of range	xlEdgeRight
Vertical borders inside the range	xlInsideVertical
Horizontal borders inside the range	xlInsideHorizontal

You can manipulate the borders of a range in two ways:

- If you use the Borders collection without an argument, you affect all borders.
- If you use the Borders collection with one of the constants from Table 14-3 as an argument, you affect only the specified border.

For example, this code places double borders on all four edges and the interior borders of the current selection:

```
Selection.Borders.LineStyle = xlDouble
```

In contrast, this code places a double border only at the top edge of the selection:

```
Selection.Borders(xlEdgeTop).LineStyle = xlDouble
```

The aspects of a border that you can control are described in Table 14-4.

Table 14-4 *Properties of the* Border *Object*

Property	Description	Settings
Color	The color of the border	An RGB value (as described earlier in this session); the default is black
LineStyle	The style of the border, such as a continuous line, a dashed line, a dotted line, and so on	xlContinuous, xlDash, xlDashDot, xlDashDotDash, xlDot, xlDouble, xlSlantDashDot, xlLineStyleNone
Weight	The thickness of the border, from hairline to a thick rule	xlHairline, xlThin, xlMedium, xlThick

To remove a border, set its LineStyle **property to** xlLineStyleNone.

The program in Listing 14-1 demonstrates using VBA code to add borders to a worksheet. It also uses some of the font formatting techniques that were covered earlier in this session. The objective is to format a data table that has a row of column headings and a column of row headings. The format that is applied is described in comments in the listing. The program formats the table (using the CurrentRegion property) that the active cell is in. Figure 14-5 shows the results of running this program.

Listing 14-1 *A program to format a worksheet table*

```
Public Sub FormatTable1()

' Formats the table that the active cell is
' in as follows:
```

Continued

Listing 14-1 *Continued*

```
'  - Thick border below the top row.
'  - Thick border to the right of the left column.
'  - Thin horizontal borders between other cells.
'  - Top row text in boldface and centered horizontally.
'  - Left column text in boldface and right-aligned.

Dim r As Range, r1 As Range

' Make sure the selection is a region.
If TypeName(Selection) <> "Range" Then
    MsgBox "A worksheet cell must be active to run this program."
    Exit Sub
End If

' Get a region for the entire table.
Set r = Selection.CurrentRegion

' Put thin horizontal borders inside the region.
r.Borders(xlInsideHorizontal).LineStyle = xlContinuous
r.Borders(xlInsideHorizontal).Weight = xlThin

' Get the top row of the region
Set r1 = r.Rows(1)

'Put a thick border at the bottom of the row.
r1.Borders(xlEdgeBottom).LineStyle = xlContinuous
r1.Borders(xlEdgeBottom).Weight = xlThick

' Make text in the row bold and centered.
r1.Font.Bold = True
r1.HorizontalAlignment = xlCenter

' Get the left column of the region.
Set r1 = r.Columns(1)

' Put a thick border at the right edge of the column.
r1.Borders(xlEdgeRight).LineStyle = xlContinuous
r1.Borders(xlEdgeRight).Weight = xlThick

' Make text in the column bold and right-aligned.
r1.Font.Bold = True
r1.HorizontalAlignment = xlRight

End Sub
```

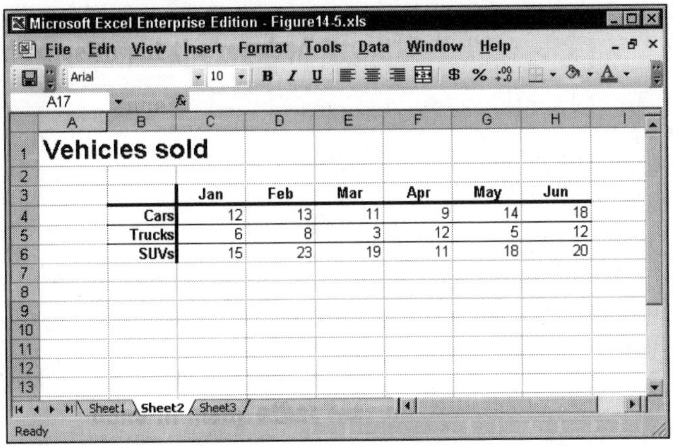

Figure 14-5 A table that has been formatted with the program in Listing 14-5

Cell Backgrounds

By default, all cells in an Excel worksheet have a white background. You can change a cell's background to a different color, and also display a background pattern. The background of a cell or range is represented by the Interior object. This object has properties that determine its color and pattern, as described in Table 14-5.

10 Min. To Go

Table 14-5 *Properties of the* Interior *Object Control a Cell's Background*

Property	Description	Settings
Color	The color of the background	An RGB value (as described earlier in this session)
Pattern	The pattern displayed	A constant specifying the pattern. Permitted values include xlPatternChecker, xlPatternDown, xlPatternHorizontal, xlPatternVertical, and xlPatternNone
PatternColor	The color of the pattern (if any)	An RGB value; the default is black

While Cell Protection is found in Excel's Format Cells dialog box, it is really an aspect of worksheet security rather than formatting. For this reason it is covered in Session 24.

Different color backgrounds can make a worksheet easier to read. You can use backgrounds to differentiate table headings from table data, for example.

At this point you have learned about the tools required to further improve the Loan Calculator application that was started in Session 13. Specifically, the goal is to apply font and background formatting to make the worksheet more attractive and clearly delineate which cells the user should enter data into. Here's what needs to happen:

- The worksheet title in cell A1 should be a larger font.
- The labels in cells B4:B7 should be boldface.
- Cells C4:C7 should have appropriate number formats.
- The entire area of the worksheet should have a gray background color with the three data input cells white.

The resulting program is presented in Listing 14-2. New code that has been added to the original program from Session 13 is bracketed in "***" comments.

Listing 14-2   *The improved program for creating a loan calculator worksheet*

```
Public Sub CreateLoanWorksheet()

Dim wb As Workbook
Dim ws As Worksheet

' Create a new, blank workbook.
Set wb = Workbooks.Add
' Rename the first worksheet.
wb.Worksheets(1).Name = "Loan Calculator"
Set ws = wb.Worksheets("Loan Calculator")

With ws
' Add a title to the worksheet.
  .Range("A1") = "Loan Calculator"

  '***
  ' Change the font of cell A1
  .Range("A1").Font.Size = 24
  .Range("A1").Font.Bold = True
  '***

  ' Put identifying labels in column B.
  .Range("B4") = "Loan amount"
  .Range("B5") = "Annual interest rate"
  .Range("B6") = "Loan term in years"
  .Range("B7") = "Monthly payment"

  '***

  'Change the font in B4:B7 to bold.
  .Range("B4:B7").Font.Bold = True
  '***

  ' Increase the width of column B to
```

```
' accommodate the labels.
.Range("B1").EntireColumn.AutoFit

' Put the loan payment formula in C7
.Range("C7").Value = "=-PMT(C5/12, C6*12, C4)"

'***
' Format cells C4 and C7 as currency.
.Range("C4").NumberFormat = "$#,###.00"
.Range("C7").NumberFormat = "$#.##"
' Format cell C5 as percent.
.Range("C5").NumberFormat = "0.00%"
' Set background to gray for all cells.
.Range("A1:D9").Interior.Color = RGB(200, 200, 200)
' Set background to white for input cells.
.Range("C4:C6").Interior.Color = vbWhite
'***
End With

' Save the workbook.
wb.SaveAs Filename:="LoanCalculator"

End Sub
```

The worksheet created by this new version of the program is shown in Figure 14-6. I think you'll agree that the worksheet is much more attractive than the original version. In addition, having the data entry cells differentiated from the other worksheet cells makes the user's job much easier. There are still more improvements that can be made, and those are covered in Session 24.

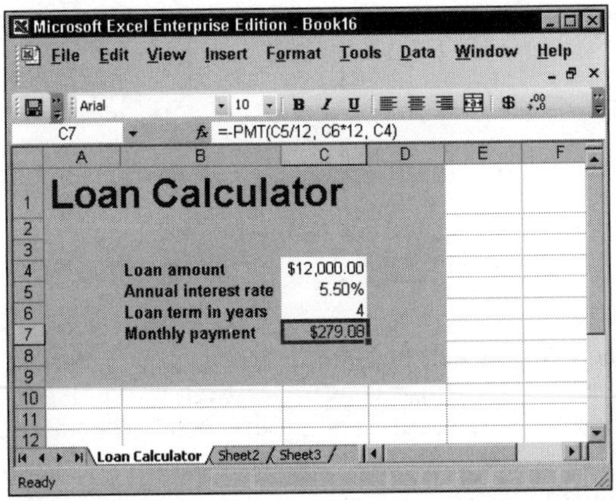

Figure 14-6 *The Loan Calculator worksheet created by the program in Listing 14-2*

Changing Row and Column Size

The width of columns and the height of rows in a worksheet can be changed to accommodate the data they contain. A column's width is measured in terms of characters — specifically, it is a multiple of the width of the 0 (zero) character in the default font. The default column width is approximately 8.5. Column width is controlled by the `ColumnWidth` property.

One way to set column width is used when you know the column(s) that needs to be changed. Use the `Worksheet` object's `Columns` collection to reference the columns. For example, this code sets the width of column B in the active worksheet to 16:

```
ActiveSheet.Columns("B") = 16
```

The following code doubles the width of columns C through E on Sheet1:

```
With Worksheets("Sheet1").Columns("C:E")
    .ColumnWidth = .ColumnWidth * 2
End With
```

The other way to set column width is to set the width of the columns in a range using the `EntireColumn` property. This lets you set column width without knowing the identity (letters) of the columns in advance. This code, for example, sets the width of columns in the current selection to 15:

```
Selection.EntireColumn.ColumnWidth = 15
```

One very useful technique is to set the width of columns as required by the data in the columns. The `AutoFit` method does this, setting the column to the width required to display the widest cell data in the column.

> `AutoFit` **works with data currently in the row. If you later add data that is wider, the column does not automatically resize to fit the new data — you must call** `AutoFit` **again.**

This code uses `AutoFit` to set the size of columns A:E in the active worksheet:

```
ActiveSheet.Columns("A:E").AutoFit
```

This code sets the width of the columns spanned by the specified range:

```
SomeRange.EntireColumn.AutoFit
```

Row height is measured in points; there are 72 points in an inch. Use of this measurement unit makes sense when you recall that font height is also measured in points, and that row height is usually adjusted to fit the fonts used. Excel automatically increases row height as needed to fit the largest font in the row, but you still may want to change the row height in your program for special formatting needs.

There are two Range properties that apply to row height. `Height` is read-only and is used to obtain information about row height. `RowHeight` is read/write and is used to set row height as well as to obtain information about row height. The information that is returned from these properties differs as described in Table 14-6.

Table 14-6 *Information Returned by Properties Related to Row Height*

Property	For single-row ranges	For multirow ranges
RowHeight	The height of the row	If all rows are the same height, the height of one row; if all rows are not the same height, Null
Height	The height of the row	The total height of all rows in the range

The following code changes the row height of a range. If the rows in the range are all the same height, the height is doubled. If they are not all the same height, they are all set to 22 points.

```
If SomeRange.RowHeight > 0 Then
    SomeRange.RowHeight = SomeRange.RowHeight * 2
Else
    SomeRange.RowHeight = 22
End If
```

Done!

REVIEW

This session explained the most important aspects of formatting an Excel worksheet.

- Numbers can be displayed in a wide variety of formats, appropriate for the data being displayed.
- Data can be displayed in different fonts. The size, color, and style of the font can be changed, too.
- Cell data can be displayed at any orientation from horizontal to vertical.
- You have full flexibility for displaying single or double borders around individual cells or multiple cell ranges.
- Row height and column width can be changed to fit the data contained in the worksheet.

QUIZ YOURSELF

1. When defining a numeric format, what's the different between the # and 0 characters? (See the "Number Formatting" section.)
2. If you increase the size of the font in a range, do you also need to increase the row height to fit the font? Explain. (See the "Changing Row and Column Size" section.)
3. How do you set the width of a column to fit the widest data that the column contains? (See the "Changing Row and Column Size" section.)
4. When dealing with fonts, what is a point? (See the "Font Formatting" section.)
5. How do you define a color in VBA? (See the "Font Formatting" section.)

Find and Replace Operations

✔ Using the Find method to search for data in a worksheet range

✔ Controlling search details with Find method arguments

✔ Using the FindNext and FindPrevious methods to continue a search

✔ Calling the Replace method to locate and replace data in a range

**30 Min.
To Go**

E xcel and VBA provide tools that enable you to search for data in a worksheet and optionally replace it with other data. These tools are the topic of this session.

Finding Data

There are three methods that you can use when finding data in a worksheet:

- Find. This starts a find operation and locates the first occurrence of the target.
- FindNext. This method locates the next occurrence of the target after a find operation is in progress.
- FindPrevious. This method locates the previous occurrence of the target after a find operation is in progress.

These methods are covered in the following sections.

The Find Method

The Find method locates data within a range, and although it is a rather complicated method, it offers a great deal of flexibility. The syntax is:

```
SomeRange.Find(What, After, LookIn, LookAt, SearchOrder, _
    SearchDirection, MatchCase, MatchByte)
```

- What is the data to find and can be any Excel data type. This is the only required argument of the Find method.

- After specifies the single cell in the range after which the search is to start. Optional; if omitted, the search starts in the top left cell of the range.

- LookIn specifies what type of data is to be searched. Possible values are xlFormula (search cells that contain formulas), xlValues (search cells that contain text or numeric values), and xlComments (search cell comments) Optional; the default is xlValues.

- LookAt can be either xlPart or xlWhole specifying whether the entire data item or only part of it is to be matched. The default is xlPart (searching for "Jack" will match "Jackson.")

- SearchOrder can be either xlByColumns or xlByRows specifying the order in which the cells in the range are searched. The default is xlByColumns (the search goes across then down).

- SearchDirection is either xlNext or xlPrevious specifying the direction of the search. The default is xlNext.

- MatchCase is True or False specifying whether the search is case-sensitive for text matches. The default is False.

- MatchByte is relevant only when double-byte language support is installed. True means that double-byte characters match only double-byte characters, while False means that double-byte characters match the single-byte equivalents. The default is False.

When you call the Find **method, values that are passed for the** LookIn, LookAt, SearchOrder, **and** MatchByte **arguments are saved and will be in effect the next time you call** Find **unless you explicitly change them.**

The Find method returns a Range object that references the first cell in the range in which there is a match. If there is no match, the method returns the special value Nothing. The following program finds the first occurrence of a target in a range. If it is found, the cell is selected. If it is not found, a dialog box to that effect displays. This program is shown in Listing 15-1, which also includes a program named TestFind that you run to call the procedure FindDataInRange. You should change the arguments that are passed to FindDataInRange as needed.

Listing 15-1 *Program to find and select data in a range*

```
Public Sub FindDataInRange(r As Range, target As Variant)

' Searches for target in a range r. If found, selects
' the cell. If not, displays a message.

Dim r1 As Range

Set r1 = r.Find(target)
If r1 Is Nothing Then
    MsgBox target & " was not found."
Else
    r1.Select
End If

End Sub

Public Sub TestFind()

' Tests the FindDataInRange procedure.

FindDataInRange ActiveSheet.Range("A1:G10"), "hello"

End Sub
```

The `Find` **method does not locate formula results. Thus, if a cell contains a formula that evaluates to the value 6, searching for "6" does not match that cell.**

The FindNext and FindPrevious Methods

After you call the `Find` method, you may want to look for other occurrences of the target within the range, and that's just what the `FindNext` and `FindPrevious` methods do. They are identical except that `FindNext` searches forward and `FindPrevious` searches backward. The syntax is:

```
FindNext(After)
FindPrevious(After)
```

The `after` argument is optional. It is a Range object specifying the single cell where the search is to commence. Typically you pass the range that was returned by the `Find` method or the previous call to `FindNext` or `FindPrevious`. This way the search continues from where it left off. If `After` is omitted, the search starts back at the first cell in the range being searched. Both methods return a Range object referencing the cell where a match was found or `Nothing` if no match is found.

Be aware that the various Find methods do not remember which cells they have already searched. By default, they — if called repeatedly — just loop back and search the range again and again. The trick to making sure the range is searched only once is to keep track of the cell where the first match is found, using the Range.Address property. The address of subsequent matches is then compared to this, and it is clear when the methods have completed searching the range and have looped back to the beginning.

The function CountStringsInRange in Listing 15-2 illustrates this technique. This function is passed a range and a target string as its arguments. It counts the number of times the target is found within the range and returns the result to the caller. This listing also contains a procedure, TestCountStrings, that you can run to try out the function.

Listing 15-2   *A function to count the number of times a string appears in a range*

```
Public Function CountStringsInRange(r As Range, target As String) As Long

' Counts the number of times the string target is
' found in a range, and returns the result.

Dim count As Long
Dim r1 As Range
Dim AddressOfFirstFind

count = 0

'Find the first instance.
Set r1 = r.Find(target)

' If the string is not found, return 0.
If r1 Is Nothing Then
    CountStringsInRange = 0
    Exit Function
' If found, loop to find any other instances.
End If

' Save the address of the first location.
AddressOfFirstFind = r1.Address
Do
    ' Increment the total.
    count = count + 1
    ' Find the next instance starting at the
    ' previous find location.
    Set r1 = r.FindNext(r1)
    ' Loop until the process returns to the first location.
Loop While r1.Address <> AddressOfFirstFind

' Return the result.
```

```
CountStringsInRange = count

End Function


Public Sub TestCountStrings()

Dim count As Long
Dim target As String
target = "Sales"
count = CountStringsInRange(Selection, target)
MsgBox "The string '" & target & "' was found " & count & " times"

End Sub
```

To try out this program, follow these steps.

1. Add the code from the listing to a module in your VBA editor.

2. Edit the `TestCountStrings` procedure so the variable named `target` contains the text for which you want to search.

3. Switch to Excel and then enter some text data in a section of the worksheet (or open a worksheet that already contains data).

4. Use the mouse or keyboard to select the range you want to search.

5. Press Alt+F8 to open the Macro dialog box.

6. Select the `TestCountStrings` macro and then click Run.

The program performs its task and displays the results in a dialog box, as shown in Figure 15-1.

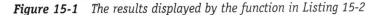

Figure 15-1　*The results displayed by the function in Listing 15-2*

It would be a good programming exercise for you to modify the `CountStringsInRange` **function so it performs a case-sensitive search.**

Replacing Data

You use the `Replace` method to replace data in a range. The syntax is:

```
SomeRange.Replace(What, Replacement, LookAt, SearchOrder, _
    MatchCase, MatchByte)
```

`What` is the data to be replaced, and `Replacement` is the replacement data. The other arguments are all optional and have the same meanings as they do for the `Find` method (described earlier in this session). The `Replace` method always returns True, so you cannot use its return value to determine whether any replacements were actually made.

> **If you need to know how many replacements are made, use the** `Find` **and** `FindNext` **methods to count the number of times the target string appears in the range (as demonstrated in Listing 15-1). You then know how many replacements will be made when you use the** `Replace` **method.**

`Replace` can work with any kind of Excel data. You can replace number values, even though the arguments to the method are strings. Here's an example:

```
Selection.Replace What:="1", Replacement:="9"
```

This code replaces all 1 digits with 9. For example:

- The value 1 changes to 9.
- The value 1.251 changes to 9.259.
- The string 15 Oak Street changes to 95 Oak Street.
- The formula =A1+1 changes to =A9+9.

The program in Listing 15-3 presents a useful example of using the `Replace` method. This procedure `ReplaceAllInActiveWorkbook` searches all data in all worksheets in the active workbook and makes the specified replacement. It replaces data in value cells only — formulas are not affected (this is the default for the `Replace` method). The program logic is as follows:

1. Use the `ActiveWorkbook` keyword to get a reference to the active workbook.
2. Loop through the `Worksheets` collection to get a reference to each worksheet in the workbook.
3. For each worksheet, use the `UsedRange` property to obtain a range that references the used part of the worksheet.
4. Call the `Replace` method on this range.

Listing 15-3　*A program to perform text replacement throughout a workbook*

```
Public Sub ReplaceAllInActiveWorkbook(target As String, _
        replacement As String)

Dim ws As Worksheet
Dim r As Range

' Make sure there is a valid target.
If target = "" Then Exit Sub

For Each ws In ActiveWorkbook.Worksheets
    Set r = ws.UsedRange
    r.Replace target, replacement
Next

End Sub

Public Sub TestReplaceAll()

Dim target As String, replacement As String

target = InputBox("Enter text to be replaced (blank to exit):")
If target = "" Then Exit Sub
replacement = InputBox("Enter replacement text:")
ReplaceAllInActiveWorkbook target, replacement

End Sub
```

Listing 15-3 also includes a procedure named `TestReplaceAll` that you can execute to test the program. This procedure uses the `InputBox` function to prompt the user for the text to replace and the replacement text. Note that entering a blank for the target exits the program without performing any replacements.

The `InputBox` function is covered in Session 9.

Cross-Ref

To test this program:

1. Enter the code from Listing 15-3 into a module in your VBA editor.
2. Open the workbook in which you want to make the replacements, or you can enter data in a blank workbook for testing purposes.
3. Make sure the desired workbook (from step 2) is active.
4. In Excel, open the Macro dialog box (Alt+F8) and then run the `TestReplaceAll` macro.

Done!

REVIEW

The Excel object model provides you with methods that let you search for and replace data in a worksheet range.

- The Range.Find method enables you to locate the first instance of a target within a specified range.
- A search can be restricted to value cells, formula cells, or cell comments.
- After calling Find, use the FindNext and FindPrevious methods to continue the search.
- The Replace method enables you to find and replace data in a range.

QUIZ YOURSELF

1. What type of worksheet cells does the Find method search by default? (See the "The Find Method" section.)

2. What data does the Find method return to the calling program? (See the "The Find Method" section.)

3. Does the Replace method match case when performing replacements? (See the "Replacing Data" section.)

4. True or false: The Replace method's return value gives the number of replacements that were made. (See the "Replacing Data" section.)

Creating Custom Toolbars

Session Checklist

✔ Creating a custom toolbar

✔ Adding and removing toolbar buttons

✔ Running a VBA program from a toolbar button

✔ Distributing toolbars with a workbook

✔ Controlling the visibility and position of toolbars

**30 Min.
To Go**

Excel offers over a dozen toolbars, each containing a set of buttons for related work-sheet commands. The Standard and Formatting toolbars are normally displayed all the time because they provide commonly needed commands. Other toolbars are more specialized, with commands related to specific tasks, such as working with pivot tables, drawing, and using XML. You can customize existing toolbars and also create your own new toolbars, specifically designed for the needs of your application.

Customizing Toolbars in Excel

You can customize the toolbars when working in Excel. This technique is useful when you create a workbook that will be distributed to end-users. You can ensure that the toolbars in the workbook are organized and displayed in the most effective way. Commands that your users will need frequently can be grouped together on a toolbar, and commands that are rarely if ever used can be hidden away until needed.

Displaying and Hiding Toolbars

Excel's default is to display the Standard and Formatting toolbars near the top of the Excel window. They may be displayed on two rows, or they may be combined into a single row. In the latter case, all buttons from the two toolbars usually do not fit on one row, so the buttons that you use least often are hidden and can be displayed by clicking the arrow at the right end of the toolbar.

To control which toolbars are displayed, select View ⇨ Toolbars from the Excel menu. A list of available toolbars is displayed, with a check mark next to the ones that are currently displayed (see Figure 16-1). To display a hidden toolbar (or hide a displayed one), click its name.

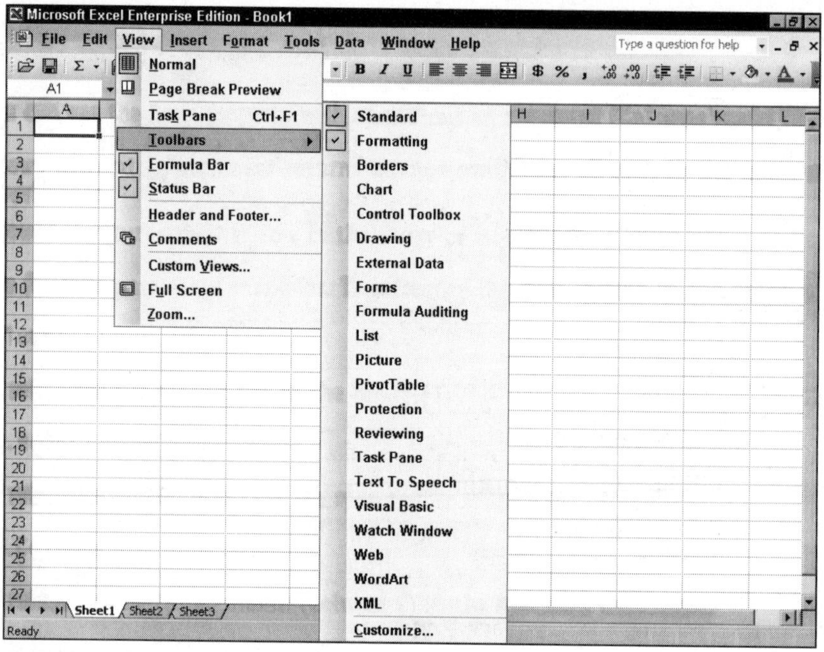

Figure 16-1 *Selecting toolbars to display*

When displayed onscreen, a toolbar can be docked along one edge of the screen, or it can float over the main Excel window. Table 16-1 summarizes the actions you can take when positioning toolbars.

Table 16-1 *Manipulating Toolbars*

To	Do this
Change the toolbar from docked to floating	Point at the vertical dotted line at the left or top edge of the toolbar and then drag it to the desired location.
Change toolbar from floating to docked	Point at the toolbar's title bar and then drag it to one edge of the screen.
Close a floating toolbar	Click the X button in its title bar.

To	Do this
Move a floating toolbar	Point at its title bar and then drag to the new location.
Close a docked toolbar	Select View ⇨ Toolbars from the menu and then deselect the toolbar.
Resize a floating toolbar	Point at an edge of the toolbar and then drag to the desired size.

Creating a New Toolbar

You can create a new toolbar and add whatever buttons you want to it. These can be Excel's existing toolbar buttons, which are already linked to specific commands, as well as custom buttons that are linked to VBA programs. Creating custom toolbars to be part of your application can be a great help to users.

To create a new toolbar:

1. Select View ⇨ Toolbars ⇨ Customize to display the Customize dialog box.
2. Click the Toolbars tab (see Figure 16-2).
3. Click the New button. Excel prompts you for a name for the new toolbar.
4. Enter a descriptive name; then click OK.

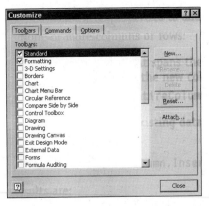

Figure 16-2   *The Toolbars tab in the Customize dialog box*

A newly created toolbar is empty, so you need to add buttons to it, as described in the next two sections.

> **Custom toolbars are listed along with Excel's built-in toolbars on the Toolbars tab of the Customize dialog box.**

Adding and Removing Toolbar Buttons

You can add buttons to and remove buttons from any Excel toolbar. You can also rearrange existing buttons on a toolbar. There are two ways to do this. The first method involves copying or moving buttons between toolbars:

**20 Min.
To Go**

1. Make sure all the required toolbars are visible.
2. Select View ➪ Toolbars ➪ Customize to display the Customize dialog box. This puts Excel into toolbar customization mode.
3. Drag a button from one toolbar to another. If you want to move the button, drag the button and drop it in its new location. To copy, hold down the Ctrl key while dragging.
4. To move a button to a different position on the same toolbar, drag it to the new position.
5. To remove a button from a toolbar, drag it off the toolbar and drop it anywhere but on another toolbar (the worksheet, for example).
6. When finished, click the Close button to close the Customize dialog box.

The second method of adding buttons involves dragging them from the Customize dialog box.

1. Make sure the toolbar(s) you want to customize are visible.
2. Select View ➪ Toolbars ➪ Customize to display the Customize dialog box.
3. Click the Commands tab (see Figure 16-3).

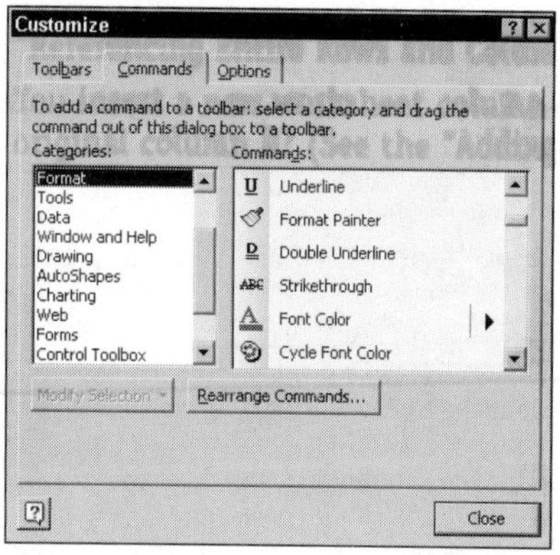

Figure 16-3   *The Commands tab in the Customize dialog box*

4. In the Categories list, select the category to which the desired command belongs. The Commands list displays the commands in that category.
5. Drag a command from the Commands list and drop it on the toolbar. Note that some commands do not have a button graphic associated with them. In this case, the toolbar displays a button with the command name on it.

6. Repeat as needed until the toolbar has all the desired commands on it.

7. Click the Close button to close the Customize dialog box.

Running Programs from Toolbar Buttons

So far I have described customizing toolbars with commands that are built into Excel. You can also create custom buttons that are linked to a macro or program. The first step is to place a custom button on a toolbar, as follows:

1. Make sure the toolbar you want to customize is visible.

2. Select View ⇨ Toolbars ⇨ Customize to display the Customize dialog box.

3. Click the Commands tab (see Figure 16-3).

4. In the Categories list, select the Macros category (see Figure 16-4).

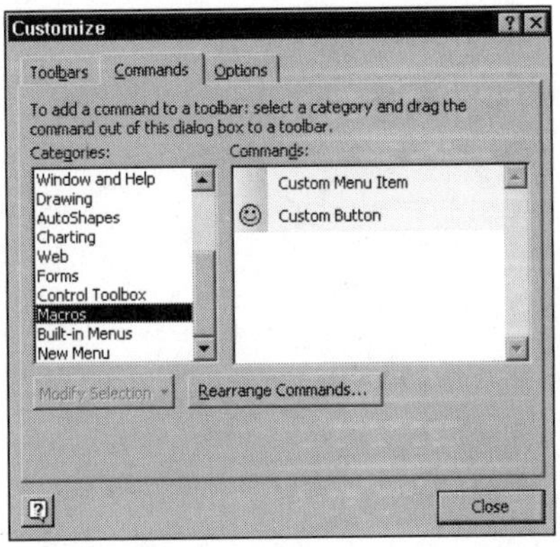

Figure 16-4   *Adding a custom button to a toolbar*

5. From the Commands list, drag the custom button item to the target toolbar; then drop the Custom Button item.

6. Repeat as needed if you need more than one custom button.

7. Click the Close button to close the Customize dialog box.

At this point you have a custom button on a toolbar, but it is not yet linked to a program. In addition, the button has a default smiley face graphic and the default title Custom Button. The following sets of steps deals with in order.

To link a program to a button:

1. Right-click the button on the toolbar.

2. From the pop-up menu, select Assign Macro. Excel displays the Assign Macro dialog box.

3. In the Macro Name list, select the macro that you want to assign to the button.

4. Click OK.

You can assign a macro to any toolbar button, not just custom buttons. This is best avoided, however, because users tend to associate the graphic on toolbar buttons with the default command that is assigned.

After you have assigned a program, or macro, to a toolbar button, clicking the button runs the program just as if you selected it from the macros dialog box.

To change the name of a custom button:

1. Right-click the button on the toolbar to display the pop-up menu (see Figure 16-5). You must do this while the Customize dialog box is displayed.

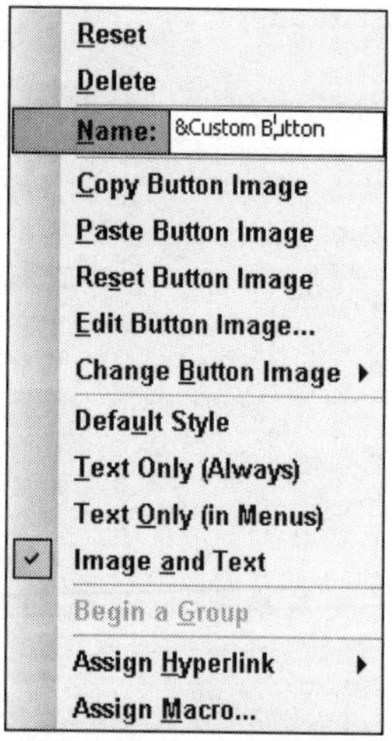

> Reset
> Delete
> **N**ame: [&Custom Button]
> **C**opy Button Image
> **P**aste Button Image
> Re**s**et Button Image
> **E**dit Button Image...
> Change **B**utton Image ▶
> Defa**u**lt Style
> **T**ext Only (Always)
> Text **O**nly (in Menus)
> ✓ Image **a**nd Text
> Begin a **G**roup
> Assign **H**yperlink ▶
> Assign **M**acro...

Figure 16-5   Changing a custom button's name

2. The third item on the menu is Name:. Click in the box next to this menu item and then edit/enter the new button name. Optionally, place an ampersand (&) character in front of the character that will serve as the button's access key.

3. Click outside the pop-up menu to close it.

 The access key for a toolbar button is a character — usually a letter — that can be pressed along with the Alt key to select the button (as an alternative to clicking the button). A button's access key is displayed underlined on the toolbar. A button's access key works only if the button's title is displayed; if only the button's image is displayed, the access key is inactive.

 Never assign an access key that is used by an Excel menu command, such as Alt+F for the File menu. Doing so is likely to result in confusion for the user.

To change the image on a toolbar button:

1. Right-click the button on the toolbar to display the pop-up menu (see Figure 16-5). You must do this while the Customize dialog box is displayed.

2. To use one of the supplied images, select Change Button Image from the menu, and select one of the images that are displayed (see Figure 16-6).

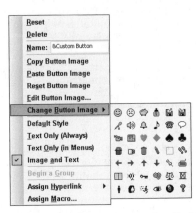

Figure 16-6   *Selecting a supplied image for a toolbar button*

3. To edit the existing image, select Edit Image from the menu to open the Button Editor (see Figure 16-7).

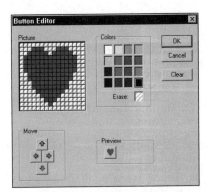

Figure 16-7   *Using the Button Editor to modify a button's image*

4. Edit the image as desired; then click Close.

Using the Button Editor

The Button Editor is a simple icon-editing tool. Icons are fixed at 16 × 16 pixel size and limited to 16 colors. Editing actions include the following:

- To change pixels, click the desired color in the Colors box and then click or drag over the image.
- To erase pixels, click the Erase item in the Colors box and then click or drag over the image. An erased pixel lets the toolbar's background show through.
- To clear the entire image, click the Clear button.
- To move the entire image within the frame, click the arrow buttons.
- Click OK to save your changes, or click Cancel to discard them.

A toolbar button can display only its icon, only its name, or both icon and name. To control what is displayed, right-click the button on the toolbar to display the pop-up menu. You must do this while the Customize dialog box is displayed, then:

- Select Default Style to display only the icon.
- Select Text Only (Always) to display only the button's name.
- Select Image and Text to display both.

Distributing Toolbars

**10 Min.
To Go**

By default, custom toolbars are stored as part of Excel and not associated with a particular workbook. To distribute a custom toolbar as part of an application, you must attach the toolbar to the workbook. Here are the required steps:

1. Open the workbook that will be distributed.
2. Select View ⇨ Toolbars ⇨ Customize to display the Customize dialog box.
3. Click the Toolbars tab, if necessary.
4. Click the Attach button. Excel displays the Attach Toolbars dialog box (see Figure 16-8).
5. The list on the left displays the names of the available custom toolbars. Select a name and then click the Copy button to attach the toolbar to the workbook.
6. Repeat as needed to attach additional toolbars.
7. When finished, click OK.

Restoring Toolbar Defaults

To return a built-in Excel toolbar to its default state by removing any added buttons and restoring any deleted buttons, follow these steps:

1. Select View ⇨ Toolbars ⇨ Customize to display the Customize dialog box.

2. Click the Toolbars tab.

3. In the Toolbars list, select the toolbar you want to reset.

4. Click the Reset button

You cannot reset custom toolbars because they do not have a default state associated with them.

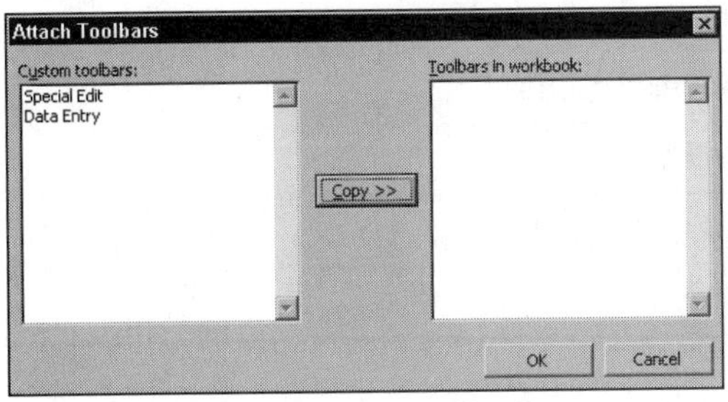

Figure 16-8 *Attaching a custom toolbar to a workbook*

Hiding and Displaying Toolbars in VBA Code

It is possible to manipulate toolbars in many ways using VBA code. In particular, you can display and hide toolbars as needed in code. This technique enables you to add a nice level of customization to your applications, having the needed custom toolbars displayed at the right times.

In VBA, a toolbar is referred to as a command bar. There are three types of command bars: toolbars, menu bars, and shortcut menus. Only the toolbar type is relevant to the present discussion.

All command bars are maintained in the Application object's CommandBars collection. This includes Excel's built-in toolbars plus any custom toolbars. This collection works similar to the other collections you have encountered in this book. You can refer to an individual item by its position in the collection:

```
CommandBars(4)
```

This is not particularly useful in most situations. It is much better to refer to the item by its name:

```
CommandBars(name)
```

To make a toolbar visible, set its `Visible` property to True. To hide it, set this property to False. For example, this code makes the toolbar named Data Entry visible:

```
CommandBars("Data Entry").Visible = True
```

You can also control the position of a toolbar by setting its `Position` property. The settings for this property are described in Table 16-2.

Table 16-2   *Settings for the CommandBar Object's Position Property*

Constant	Meaning
msoBarLeft	Docked on the left
msoBarRight	Docked on the right
msoBarTop	Docked at the top
msoBarBottom	Docked on the bottom
msoBarFloating	Floating

The program in Listing 16-1 shows an example that uses these properties. This program would be used in an Excel application that includes custom toolbars named Data Entry and Stats. When the program runs, it makes both toolbars visible and positions them docked at the top of the worksheet window.

Listing 16-1   *A program to display and position custom toolbars*

```
Sub DisplayCustomToolbars()

CommandBars("Data Entry").Visible = True
CommandBars("Data Entry").Position = msoBarTop
CommandBars("Stats").Visible = True
CommandBars("Stats").Position = msoBarTop

End Sub
```

Please see Session 24 for information about protecting custom toolbars from modification by the user.

Done!

REVIEW

This session showed you how to create custom toolbars and distribute them with your Excel application.

- You can add as many custom toolbars as needed to Excel.
- A custom toolbar can contain Excel's predefined buttons as well as custom buttons.
- To distribute a custom toolbar with a worksheet, you must first attach it to the worksheet.
- You use the CommandBars collection to access individual toolbars in VBA code.
- You can display or hide and change the position of toolbars in your VBA code.

QUIZ YOURSELF

1. When working in Excel, how do you display and hide toolbars? (See the "Displaying and Hiding Toolbars" section.)

2. How many different toolbars can a particular button be on? (See the "Adding and Removing Toolbar Buttons" section.)

3. What steps are required to distribute a custom toolbar with a workbook? (See the "Distributing Toolbars" section.)

4. In VBA code, how do you change the position of a toolbar? (See the "Hiding and Displaying Toolbars in VBA Code" section.)

Saturday Afternoon
Part Review

1. How can you determine the number of rows and columns in a range?
2. What does `Application.Columns` refer to?
3. Your program inserts one new column at position B. What happens to the old column B?
4. Assume that range R refers to cells A1:D6. To which cell does `R.Cells(6)` refer?
5. What does `Worksheets("Sales Data").Cells` refer to?
6. How could you refer to all blank cells in a range?
7. Cell A10 contains the formula `=SUM($A$1:$A$9)`. If you copy this formula to cell F20, what does it change to?
8. A formula contains the cell reference A$10. What happens when this formula is copied to another cell?
9. How can a formula in one worksheet reference a cell in another worksheet?
10. How does Excel tell a cell formula from text data?
11. What is a circular reference?
12. Which Excel function is used to calculate the payment on an installment loan?
13. Which Excel function formats a numeric value to currency format?
14. Is it possible to use an Excel function in VBA code? If so, how?
15. How do you change the numeric display format of a range?
16. What are the three primary colors that are used in defining colors in Excel?
17. Which property would you set to change the background color of cells?
18. Which unit is used to measure the width of columns in a worksheet?
19. Which method would you call to adjust the width of columns to fit the data they hold?

20. Which method would you call to find all instances of a search string in a range?
21. What value does the Find method return if it does not find the search string?
22. In Excel, how do you control which toolbars are displayed?
23. When you create a new toolbar, which buttons does it have by default?
24. How do you assign a macro to a custom toolbar button?
25. Are custom toolbars automatically distributed with the workbook?
26. What are the two main options for positioning a toolbar in Excel?

PART

IV

Saturday Evening

Introduction to Charts

Session Checklist

✔ Chart sheets versus embedded charts

✔ Specifying data to be plotted

✔ Selecting chart type

✔ Adding chart and axis titles

✔ Working with fonts in a chart

✔ Using the `ChartWizard` method

**30 Min.
To Go**

Excel provides truly sophisticated charting capabilities. You can create a wide variety of charts, including pie, line, and bar charts, as well as more specialized chart types such as radar, scatter, and doughnut charts. An Excel chart is linked to data in a worksheet and automatically updates to reflect changes in the data. This session and the next show you how to work with Excel charts in your VBA programs.

Embedded Charts and Chart Sheets

A chart can exist in a worksheet in two ways:

- As an *embedded chart* in a regular worksheet, along with data and/or other embedded charts.
- On a *chart sheet*, which is a special kind of worksheet that holds a single chart and nothing else.

Figures 17-1 and 17-2 show examples of these two options.

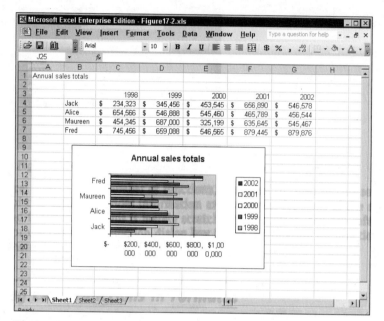

Figure 17-1   *An embedded chart in a worksheet along with the chart's data*

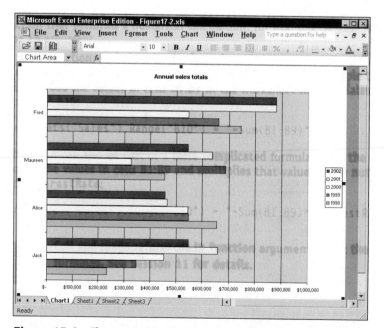

Figure 17-2   *The same chart as Figure 17-1 on a chart sheet*

In either case, the charts are the same in terms of the properties and methods you use to work with them; however, there are a few differences in the way to refer to and create embedded charts and chart sheets.

Embedded Charts

An embedded chart is the better choice when you want the chart displayed as part of a worksheet along with the data and/or other charts. Each embedded chart is represented by a `Chart` object. This `Chart` object is contained within a `ChartObject` object. This seemingly confusing arrangement is necessary because the `Chart` object itself does not have any provision for specifying the size or the position of the chart — these tasks are taken care of by the `ChartObject` object.

Each Excel worksheet has a `ChartObjects` collection that contains one entry for each embedded chart on the worksheet. To add a new embedded chart to a worksheet, you add a `ChartObject` to this collection. The syntax is:

```
SomeWorksheet.ChartObjects.Add(Left, Top, Width, Height)
```

Left and Top specify the position of the chart's top left corner, and Width and Height specify its size. All four arguments are measured in points, a unit equal to $\frac{1}{72}$ inch. The method returns a reference to the newly created `ChartObject`. You then use the `Chart` property to reference the contained chart. For example:

```
Dim co As ChartObject
Dim ch As Chart
Set co = Worksheets("Sheet1").ChartObjects.Add(50, 50, 250, 165)
Set ch = co.Chart
```

After this code executes, a new blank embedded chart exists on Sheet1. You would use the variable ch to refer to it.

More information on the `ChartObject` object is presented later in this session.

If a chart overlaps worksheet data, the data is still there but is not visible. You can show the data by moving the chart or by hiding it.

Chart Sheets

Use a Chart Sheet when you want a chart displayed at the maximum size without distraction from data or other charts. A chart sheet is represented by a `Chart` object, just like an embedded chart is. Unlike an embedded chart, no `ChartObject` is required because the position of a chart on a chart sheet is fixed, and its size is dependent on the size of the sheet. Each workbook has a `Charts` collection that contains all of the chart sheets in that workbook.

Note The workbook's `Charts` collection does not refer to embedded charts — only to chart sheets. Likewise, a worksheet's `ChartObjects` collection refers only to embedded charts and not to chart sheets that may exist in the workbook. To add a new chart sheet to a workbook, call the `Add` method:

```
Charts.Add
```

This method returns a reference to the new chart. The following code adds a new chart sheet to the active workbook and obtains a reference to the new chart (which, of course, is blank):

```
Dim ch As Chart
Set ch = ActiveWorkbook.Charts.Add
```

After this code executes, use the variable `ch` to manipulate the chart.

The Chart Object

The methods you have seen so far for creating a new chart result in a blank chart. The next step is to define the details of the charts so that it displays the correct data in the desired manner. At its most basic, there are two parts to this: identifying the data to be plotted, and specifying the chart type.

Identifying Data to Be Plotted

When identifying the data to be plotted, you need to be aware of how Excel treats data for charts. The concepts of *data series* and *categories* are integral to most Excel chart types. Look at Figure 17-3 for an example. In this worksheet, the data for each flavor is a data series, and there are three data series with each containing four values. The data for each quarter is a category, and there are four categories with each containing three values.

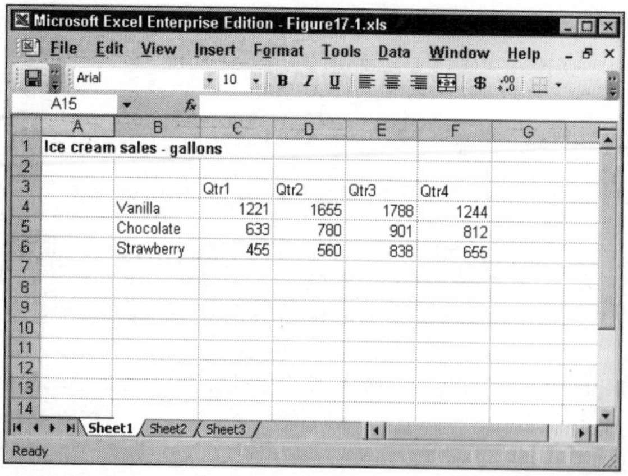

	A	B	C	D	E	F	G
1	Ice cream sales - gallons						
2							
3			Qtr1	Qtr2	Qtr3	Qtr4	
4		Vanilla	1221	1655	1788	1244	
5		Chocolate	633	780	901	812	
6		Strawberry	455	560	838	655	
7							

Microsoft Excel Enterprise Edition - Figure17-1.xls

Figure 17-3 *Excel plots data by data series and categories.*

There's no rule that says data series must be in rows and categories in columns. The same data from Figure 17-3 could just as well be plotted the other way, with each column representing a data series and each row a category. The important thing is that you know how your data is arranged when creating a chart from it.

To specify the data for a chart, call the Chart object's SetSourceData method. The syntax is:

```
SetSourceData(Source, PlotBy)
```

Source is the worksheet range that contains the data. You can refer to it by row and column identifiers, or as a named range if a name has been assigned to the range. PlotBy is a constant specifying whether the data series are in the rows of the range (xlRows) or the columns of the range (xlColumns). Using the worksheet data in Figure 17-3 as an example, the code to set the source data for a chart would be as follows (assuming that ch is a reference to a Chart object):

```
ch.SetSourceData Source:=Worksheets("Sheet1").Range("B3:F6"),
PlotBy:=xlRows
```

Combining this with the other required code, Listing 17-1 shows a procedure to create an embedded chart based on the data in Figure 17-3. The resulting chart is shown in Figure 17-4.

Listing 17-1 *A procedure to create an embedded chart from the data in Figure 17-3*

```
Public Sub CreateEmbeddedChart()

Dim co As ChartObject
Dim ch As Chart

Set co = Worksheets("Sheet1").ChartObjects.Add(50, 100, 250, 165)
Set ch = co.Chart
ch.SetSourceData Source:=Worksheets("Sheet1").Range("B3:F6"),
PlotBy:=xlRows

End Sub
```

There are a few aspects of this example that you should be aware of:

- The labels for the data series and the categories are automatically incorporated into the chart.
- Categories are plotted on the horizontal axis; values are plotted on the vertical axis.
- A chart legend is automatically created and contains a key for identification of the data series.
- The vertical axis of the chart is automatically scaled according to the range of data values.
- When a chart type is not specified, the default clustered column chart is used.

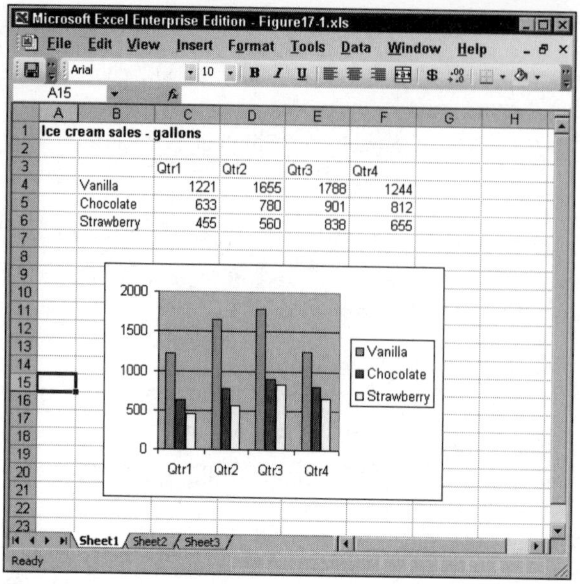

Figure 17-4 *The chart created by the procedure in Listing 17-1*

Specifying Chart Type

The type of a chart is controlled by the Chart object's ChartType property. Excel provides a set of predefined constants for specifying this property. Each constant specifies not only a base type (such as bar, column, or line), but also variations on each type. The variations include whether the chart is displayed as a two- or three-dimensional perspective. There are too many different chart type constants to present here. Table 17-1 describes some of the types that are used most frequently, and you can refer to online help for information on the others.

> To get a feel for the types of charts available in Excel, use the Chart Wizard in Excel to explore the various types and variations.

Table 17-1 *Commonly Used Constants for the ChartType Property*

Constant	Description
xlBar	A bar chart
xlLine	A line chart
xlArea	An area chart
xlPie	A pie chart
xlColumn	A column chart
xlPyramid	A pyramid chart

Most chart types come in 2-D and 3-D versions. The constants have the "3D" characters included. For example, xlArea creates a 2-D area chart, and xl3DArea creates a 3-D area chart.

Setting the chart type is demonstrated in the procedure in Listing 17-2. This code creates a chart sheet for the data in Figure 17-3, specifying a line chart with markers. The result is shown in Figure 17-5.

Listing 17-2 *A procedure to create a chart sheet line chart from the data in Figure 17-3*

```
Public Sub CreateChartSheet()

Dim ch As Chart

Set ch = ActiveWorkbook.Charts.Add
ch.SetSourceData Source:=Worksheets("Sheet1").Range("B3:F6"),
PlotBy:=xlRows
ch.ChartType = xlLineMarkers

End Sub
```

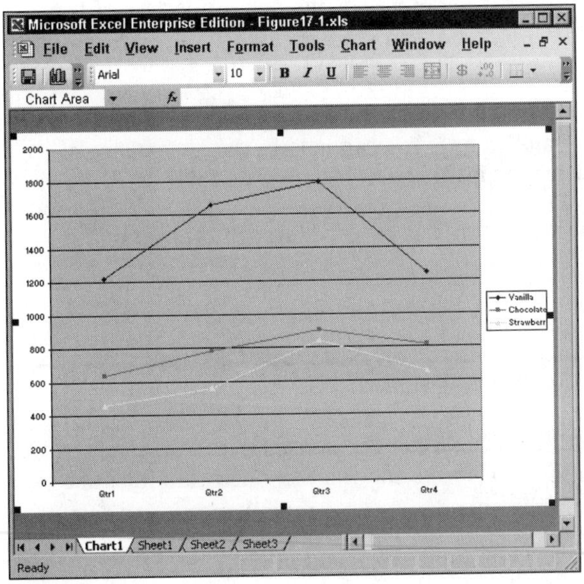

Figure 17-5 *A line chart created as a chart sheet by the procedure in Listing 17-2*

You can change a chart's type at any time — when it is first being created or afterwards.

Controlling Chart Appearance

Aside from the type of chart, there are many other options for controlling how a chart looks. Some of these options are for appearance purposes only, while others pertain to the information the chart conveys to the viewer.

Displaying Chart Titles

Every chart can have a title displayed above the chart. The title is controlled by two properties of the `Chart` object:

- `HasTitle`. A True/False value specifying whether the title is displayed.
- `ChartTitle`. A ChartTitle object that controls the details of the title.

To display a title on a chart, you must set the properties of its `ChartTitle` object and then set `HasTitle` to True. The following is an example that displays the title "Annual Sales" on a chart (assuming that the chart referenced by ch already exists):

```
ch.HasTitle = True
ch.ChartTitle.Text = "Annual Sales"
```

You must set `HasTitle` to True before setting any properties of the `ChartTitle` object. If you do not, an error occurs.

Simply setting the text of the chart title, as in this example, results in a title with the default appearance (font, position, and so on). You can modify the appearance of a chart title using the `ChartTitle` object properties that are described in Table 17-2.

Changing the font of a chart title is covered later in this session.

Table 17-2 *Properties of the ChartTitle Object*

Property	Description
AutoScaleFont	True/False value specifying whether the title's font size changes automatically when the chart size is changed. The default is True.
HorizontalAlignment	Specifies the left-right alignment of the title. Set to xlLeft, xlCenter (the default), or xlRight.
Left	The distance in points from the left edge of the title to the left edge of the chart area

Property	Description
Top	The distance in points from the top edge of the title to the top edge of the chart area
Text	The text of the title. By default this is blank.

For an example of adding a title to a chart, see Listing 17-3 later in this session.

Chart Axis Titles

Most Excel charts have two axes (the pie chart is one exception). The horizontal axis is the category axis, and the vertical axis is the value axis. By default, neither axis is given a title, but you can add titles as required by your application.

A chart's axes are referenced by means of the Chart object's Axes collection. You identify which axis, value, or category you are referring to by using the constants xlCategory and xlValue. Thus, the code

```
SomeChart.Axes(xlCategory)
```

references the chart's category axis, while

```
SomeChart.Axes(xlValue)
```

references its value axis. To add a title to an axis, set its HasTitle property to True; then use the AxisTitle.Text property to set the title. For example, assuming that ch refers to an existing chart:

```
ch.Axes(xlValue).HasTitle = True
ch.Axes(xlValue).AxisTitle.Text = "Sales by region"
```

To remove a title from an axis, set the HasTitle property to False. To modify an existing axis title, change the AxisTitle.Text property. (Changing the font of an axis title is covered later in this session.)

Removing an axis title by setting HasTitle to False does not simply hide the title, but destroys it. To later add a title, you must recreate it from scratch.

Be sure to set HasTitle to True before trying to work with the AxisTitle object. If you do not, an error occurs.

The program in Listing 17-3 is an improvement on the program presented earlier in this session. It creates a chart from the worksheet data presented earlier (see Figure 17-3), with the addition of a chart title and axis titles on both the value and category axes. The resulting chart is shown in Figure 17-6.

Listing 17-3 *Creating an embedded chart with titles*

```
Public Sub CreateEmbeddedChartWithTitles()

Dim co As ChartObject
Dim ch As Chart

Set co = Worksheets("Sheet1").ChartObjects.Add(50, 100, 250, 165)
Set ch = co.Chart
ch.SetSourceData Source:=Worksheets("Sheet1").Range("B3:F6"),
PlotBy:=xlRows
' Add a chart title.
ch.HasTitle = True
ch.ChartTitle.Text = "Ice Cream Sales"
' Add a category axis title.
ch.Axes(xlCategory).HasTitle = True
ch.Axes(xlCategory).AxisTitle.Text = "Period"
' Add a value axis title.
ch.Axes(xlValue).HasTitle = True
ch.Axes(xlValue).AxisTitle.Text = "Sales in Gallons"

End Sub
```

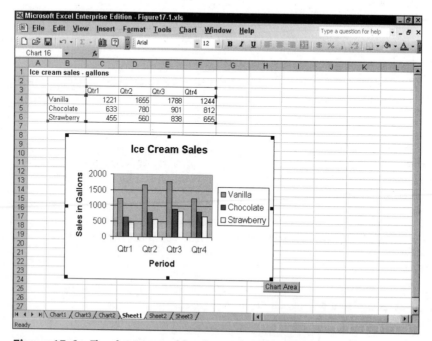

Figure 17-6 *The chart created by the program in Listing 17-3*

Working with Fonts in a Chart

10 Min.
To Go

You can write VBA code to change the font of any text in a chart. All aspects of text appearance are controlled by a Font object that is associated with the particular item (chart title, axis title, and so on). The text items in a chart and the associated Font object are described in Table 17-3.

Table 17-3 *Font Objects Associated with Charts*

To change the font of . . .	Use this Font object
The chart title	Chart.ChartTitle.Font
The category axis title	Chart.Axes(xlCategory).AxisTitle.Font
The value axis title	Chart.Axes(xlValue).AxisTitle.Font
The legend text	Chart.Legend.Font
The category axis tick mark labels	Chart.Axes(xlCategory).TickLabels.Font
The value axis tick mark labels	Chart.Axes(xlValue).TickLabels.Font

 All of the objects listed in Table 17-3 have an AutoScaleFont **property. When this property is True, which is the default, the font size automatically changes when the chart size changes. Setting the font size, therefore, is only setting the initial font size relative to the size of the chart at the time. The actual font size changes if the chart itself is resized.**

 Tick mark labels on an axis are distinct from the axis title. For example on the category axis in Figure 17-6, "Period" is the title while "Qtr1," "Qtr2," and so on are the tick mark labels.

Table 17-4 describes the properties of the Font object that you will probably need to change most often. Here are some examples.

This code changes the chart title to 14-point Arial boldface.

```
With SomeChart.ChartTitle.Font
  .Name = "Arial"
  .Bold = True
  .Size = 14
End With
```

The following code changes the chart legend text to 10-point, red Times New Roman.

```
With SomeChart.Legend.Font
  .Name = "Times New Roman"
  .Color = RGB(255, 0, 0)
  .Size = 10
End With
```

Table 17-4   *Commonly Used Properties of the Font Object*

Property	Description
Bold	True/False value specifying whether the font is boldface.
Color	The color of the font, as an RGB value.
Italic	True/False value specifying whether the font is italics.
Name	The name of the font (its typeface).

Refer to Session 14 for details on using the RGB **function to specify colors.**

The program in Listing 17-4 presents a further improvement on the program from earlier in the session. In addition to creating an embedded chart from the data shown in Figure 17-3, and adding chart and axis titles, this program manipulates the fonts used in the chart to give what is, at least to me, a better appearance.

Listing 17-4   *Program to create an embedded chart with titles and font modifications*

```
Public Sub CreateEmbeddedChart()

Dim co As ChartObject
Dim ch As Chart

Set co = Worksheets("Sheet1").ChartObjects.Add(50, 100, 250, 165)
Set ch = co.Chart
ch.SetSourceData Source:=Worksheets("Sheet1").Range("B3:F6"),
PlotBy:=xlRows

' Add a chart title.
ch.HasTitle = True
ch.ChartTitle.Text = "Ice Cream Sales"
' Change its font.
With ch.ChartTitle.Font
    .Name = "Arial"
    .Size = 14
    .Color = RGB(0, 0, 255)
End With

' Add a category axis title and set its font.
' Also change tick labels.
With ch.Axes(xlCategory)
    .HasTitle = True
    .AxisTitle.Text = "Period"
    .AxisTitle.Font.Name = "Arial"
    .AxisTitle.Font.Size = 10
```

```
        .TickLabels.Font.Name = Arial
        .TickLabels.Font.Size = 8
End With

' Add a value axis title and set its font.
' Also change font of tick labels
With ch.Axes(xlValue)
    .HasTitle = True
    .AxisTitle.Text = "Sales in Gallons"
    .AxisTitle.Font.Name = "Arial"
    .AxisTitle.Font.Size = 10
    .TickLabels.Font.Name = Arial
    .TickLabels.Font.Size = 8
End With

' Change the font in the legend.
With ch.Legend.Font
    .Name = Arial
    .Size = 10
    .Color = RGB(255, 0, 0)
End With

End Sub
```

The resulting chart is shown in Figure 17-7. You can see some of the font changes by comparing this with Figure 17-4, although some changes are not visible in the figure because it does not show color (the chart title is blue, and the legend text is red).

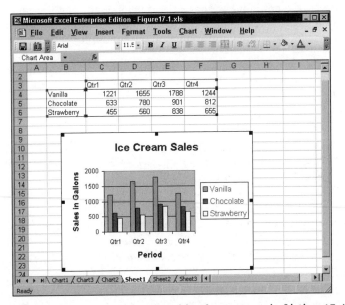

Figure 17-7   *The chart created by the program in Listing 17-4*

The ChartWizard Method

If you have created charts in Excel, you have probably used the Chart Wizard. Similar to other Microsoft wizards, this tool walks you though a series of steps, asking questions about the chart you want to create, and then creates the chart based on your answers. Figure 17-8 shows the first step of the Chart Wizard, in which you select the type of chart to create.

Figure 17-8 *Excel's ChartWizard simplifies the task of creating a chart in Excel.*

VBA programmers have something similar available to them in the `ChartWizard` method. After you have created a blank chart (as explained earlier in this session), you can use the `ChartWizard` method to specify the data for the chart, the type of chart, and several other aspects of the chart's appearance, all in a single call. Sometimes this is easier than setting all of the `Chart` object's individual properties one at a time. The syntax for the `ChartWizard` method is:

```
SomeChart.ChartWizard(Source, Gallery, Format, PlotBy, _
    CategoryLabels, SeriesLabels, HasLegend, Title, ValueTitle)
```

- `Source`. A Range object referencing the data to be plotted.
- `Gallery`. An `xlChartType` constant specifying the type of chart: `xlArea`, `xlBar`, `xlColumn`, `xlLine`, `xlPie`, `xlRadar`, `xlXYScatter`, `xlCombination`, `xl3DArea`, `xl3DBar`, `xl3DColumn`, `xl3DLine`, `xl3DPie`, `xl3DSurface`, `xlDoughnut`, or `xlDefaultAutoFormat`.
- `Format`. A numerical value in the range 1-*n* specifying the built-in autoformat, or chart subtype. The type and number of autoformats, and hence the maximum value of *n*, depends on the `Gallery` argument.
- `PlotBy`. Either `xlRows` (the default) or `xlColumns` specifying whether data series are in rows or columns.
- `CategoryLabels`. The number of columns (if `PlotBy = xlRows`) or the number of rows (if `PlotBy = xlColumns`) containing category labels.

- SeriesLabels. The number of rows (if PlotBy = xlRows) or the number of columns (if PlotBy = xlColumns) containing data series labels.
- HasLegend. True to include a legend; otherwise False. The default is True.
- Title. The text of the chart's title. Optional; the default is no title.
- CategoryTitle. The text of the category axis title. Optional; the default is no title.
- ValueTitle. The text of the value axis title. Optional; the default is no title.

REVIEW

Done!

This was the first of two sessions on creating Excel charts from your VBA programs.

- An Excel chart can be by itself on a chart sheet or embedded as part of a regular worksheet.
- Data to be charted is arranged in data series and categories.
- A chart can be any one of many types supported by Excel.
- You can add titles to the chart itself and to the chart axes.
- The font of all text in a chart can be modified.
- The ChartWizard method combines several steps of creating a chart into a single call.

QUIZ YOURSELF

1. How many charts can you place on a chart sheet? (See the "Embedded Charts and Chart Sheets" section.)
2. What happens if an embedded chart is placed on top of data in a worksheet? (See the "Embedded Charts" section.)
3. What text does Excel use as the default chart title? (See the "Displaying Chart Titles" section.)
4. What is plotted on the horizontal axis of most Excel charts — the data series or the categories? (See the "The Chart Object" section.)
5. What property would you use to change the font of the chart title? (See the "Working with Fonts in a Chart" section.)

Advanced Charting Techniques

Session Checklist

✔ Naming and referencing charts

✔ Preventing user changes by locking charts

✔ Working with the `ChartObject` object

✔ Using scatter charts

✔ Printing charts

**30 Min.
To Go**

The previous session provided an introduction to Excel charts and techniques for creating and manipulating them from VBA programs. More advanced chart programming techniques are covered in this session.

Naming and Referencing Charts

A chart sheet is automatically assigned a name when created. These default names take the form of Chart1, Chart2, and so on. Likewise, embedded charts are assigned names, but the situation is a bit more complicated:

The differences between embedded charts and chart sheets are covered in Session 17.

- The `ChartObject` is assigned a name in the form of Chart 1, Chart 2, and so on. Note that there is a space before the number.

- The `Chart` object is assigned a name that combines the name of the worksheet it is on with the name of the `ChartObject` in which it is contained — for example, Sheet1 Chart 13).

You can rename a `ChartObject` by assigning the new name to the `Name` property. You cannot rename a `Chart` object that is an embedded chart, even though the Microsoft documentation claims you can. That's not a problem because embedded charts are accessed by means of the `ChartObject.Name` property, not the `Chart.Name` property. If you will need to refer to a chart later in code, it is a good idea to assign a meaningful name to `ChartObject.Name`.

To refer to an existing chart sheet, you use the `Workbook` object's `Charts` property. This property returns a collection containing every chart sheet in the workbook. You can reference a chart sheet by its position in the collection, but this is not particularly useful because you usually do not know what a chart's position is. It is better to reference by the chart sheet's name:

```
Charts(ChartName)
```

 If you try to reference an element that does not exist in a collection, an error occurs.

For example, this line of code prints the specified chart sheet:

```
Charts("Sales Summary").PrintOut
```

To reference a specific embedded chart, you must access it by means of its `ChartObject`. This is done using the worksheet's `ChartObjects` collection. As with other collections, you can access individual items by index or name. This code deletes the specified `ChartObject` (and its contained chart) on Sheet1:

```
Worksheets("Sheet1").ChartObjects("Summary").Delete
```

There is no way to directly access all of the embedded charts in a workbook — you must look for embedded charts on each worksheet separately. An example of this is presented later in this session in Listing 18-3.

Locking Charts

By default, a chart in Excel can be modified by the user; however, there may be times when you do not want to permit any modifications. You can lock or protect a chart so that the user can view and print it, but cannot make any changes to the chart. To lock and protect a chart, call the `Protect` method on the `Chart` object:

```
SomeChart.Protect(password)
```

Password is an optional argument that specifies a case-sensitive password for unprotecting the chart. If omitted, the user (or another program) can remove protection from the chart and then modify the chart without restrictions. If included, the password must be provided to unprotect the chart. This is done with the `Unprotect` method:

```
SomeChart.UnProtect(password)
```

The `password` argument is required only if the chart was password-protected.

You learn more about worksheet security and protection in Session 24.

Never lose track of a password used to protect a chart. There's no way to unprotect the chart without it.

The ChartObject Object

20 Min. To Go

As mentioned previously in this session, an embedded chart is contained within a `ChartObject` object. The `ChartObject` controls certain aspects of chart display that are independent of the chart itself, such as its position in the worksheet and its size. These properties and methods are described in Tables 18-1 and 18-2. An example program using some of these properties and methods is presented in Listing 18-1.

Table 18-1　*ChartObject Properties*

Property	Description
BottomRightCell	Returns a Range object referencing the single worksheet cell under the lower right corner of the chart. Read-only.
Chart	Returns a reference to the contained chart.
Height	The height of the chart in points.
Left	The position of the left side of the chart with respect to the left edge of the worksheet; in points.
Placement	Specifies how the `ChartObject` is attached to the worksheet cell under it. Permitted settings are xlMoveAndSize, xlMove, and xlFreeFloating.
PrintObject	If True (the default), the chart is printed when the worksheet is printed. If False, the chart is not printed.
Top	The position of the top the chart with respect to the top of the worksheet; in points.
TopLeftCell	Returns a Range object referencing the single worksheet cell under the top left corner of the chart. Read-only.
Visible	True/False value specifying if the chart is visible.
Width	The width of the chart; in points.

Table 18-2 *ChartObject Methods*

Method	Description
BringToFront	Displays the chart on top of any overlapping charts.
Copy	Copies the ChartObject to the Windows Clipboard.
CopyPicture	Copies an image of the chart to the Windows Clipboard.
Cut	Cuts the ChartObject to the Windows Clipboard.
Delete	Deletes the ChartObject.
SendToBack	Displays the chart behind any overlapping charts.

The Placement property comes into play when cells are added or deleted in the area under an embedded chart. For example, suppose a chart spans columns B through F, and two new columns are inserted in this range. The result depends on the setting of the Placement property:

- xlMoveAndSize. The size and position of the chart are changed to accommodate added or deleted rows/columns.
- xlMove. The position of the chart is changed to accommodate added or deleted rows/columns, but the size remains fixed.
- xlFreeFloating. Neither the size nor the position is changed.

The program in Listing 18-1 illustrates using some of the ChartObject properties and methods. This program goes through all worksheets in the current workbook. All embedded charts are copied to a new worksheet. The name of this new worksheet, as well as the size of the copied charts, are specified in arguments to the procedure. The program logic operates as follows:

1. Use the Worksheets.Add method to add a new worksheet to the workbook.
2. Set the new worksheet's Name property.
3. Loop through the workbook's Worksheets collection.
4. Check each worksheet's Name property to avoid processing the new worksheet.
5. Loop through each worksheet's ChartObjects collection.
6. Use the Copy method to copy each ChartObject to the Clipboard.
7. Use the Worksheet.Paste method to paste the ChartObject into the new worksheet.

Listing 18-1 *A program to copy embedded charts to a new worksheet*

```
Public Sub CopyEmbeddedChartsToNewSheet(name As String, width As Integer, _
    height As Integer)
```

```
' Copies all embedded charts in the current
' workbook to a new worksheet with the
' specified name. The copied charts have
' the specified width and height
' and are arranged in a single column.

' The vertical space between charts.
Const SPACE_BETWEEN_CHARTS = 20

Dim newWS As Worksheet
Dim oldWS As Worksheet
Dim co As ChartObject
Dim yPos As Integer
Dim count As Integer

' Turn screen updating off so screen does
' not flicker as charts are copied.
Application.ScreenUpdating = False

' Add and name the new worksheet.
Set newWS = Worksheets.Add
newWS.name = name

For Each oldWS In Worksheets
    ' Do not copy from the new worksheet.
    If oldWS.name <> name Then
        ' Loop thru the ChartObjects on
        ' this worksheet.
        For Each co In oldWS.ChartObjects
            ' Copy to the clipboard.
            co.Copy
            newWS.Range("A1").Select
            ' Paste into new sheet.
            newWS.Paste
        Next
    End If
Next

' Position and size the charts.
count = 0
For Each co In newWS.ChartObjects
    co.width = width
    co.height = height
    ' Distance from left edge of sheet.
    co.Left = 30
```

Continued

Listing 18-1

```
    co.Top = count * (height + SPACE_BETWEEN_CHARTS) +
SPACE_BETWEEN_CHARTS
    count = count + 1
Next

' Turn screen updating back on.
Application.ScreenUpdating = True

End Sub

Public Sub TestCopyEmbeddedCharts()

CopyEmbeddedChartsToNewSheet "All Charts", 240, 140

End Sub
```

Note that the program sets the ScreenUpdating property to False to prevent flickering while the charts are being copied and resized. Of course, this property must be set back to True at the end of the program so the changes become visible.

You may be wondering why the code selects cell A1 in the new workbook before each paste operation. This is because when you paste a chart into a workbook, the just-pasted chart is selected. When you then try to paste the next chart, Excel thinks you are trying to paste it into the selected chart and generates an error message. By selecting a worksheet cell, the paste operation has the worksheet as its target and works without a problem.

Because the CopyEmbeddedChartsToNewSheet procedure takes arguments, you cannot run it directly but must call it from another procedure. Listing 18-1 includes this procedure, named TestCopyEmbeddedCharts. You may want to modify the arguments to the procedure call — as written, it names the new worksheet All Charts and sizes the copied charts at 240 × 140 points. To try out this program:

1. Copy the code from Listing 18-1 to a module in the VBA Editor.
2. Edit the code in the TestCopyEmbeddedCharts procedure if desired (to change the arguments).
3. Open or create a workbook that contains several embedded charts, ideally on two or more worksheets.
4. Press Alt+F8 to open the Macros dialog box.
5. Select the macro TestCopyEmbeddedCharts and then click Run.

Figure 18-1 shows an example of a worksheet created by this program, showing several copied charts.

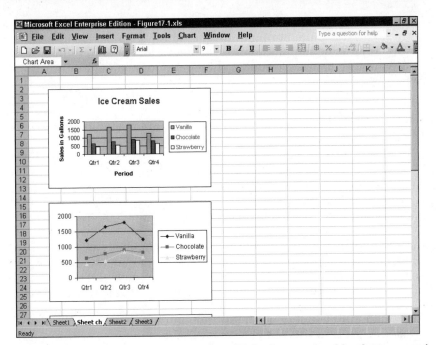

Figure 18-1 *A worksheet containing multiple charts created by the program in Listing 18-1*

Using Scatter Charts

A scatter chart (sometimes called an XY chart) is fundamentally different from other types of Excel charts. Most charts plot values against categories. If you look back at Figure 17-7 in the previous session, for example, you see that Sales in Gallons is a value, plotted on the vertical axis, and Period is a category, plotted on the horizontal axis.

In contrast, a scatter chart plots values versus values; therefore, both the horizontal and vertical axes have values on them. There are numerous kinds of data for which a scatter chart is appropriate. Some examples are:

- Comparing average annual salary with years of experience.
- Charting height versus weight for a diet study.
- Comparing number of units sold with processor speed for computer sales.

Each point in a scatter chart has both an X and a Y value. The X value determines the point's horizontal position, and the Y value determines its vertical position. This is illustrated in Figure 18-2 for a data point where X=2 and Y=3.

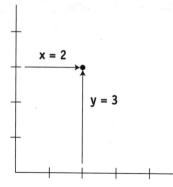

Figure 18-2 *The position of a data point on a scatter chart depends on its X value and a Y value.*

Data for a scatter chart is organized similarly to the data for other chart types. The one difference is that the category labels are replaced by X values. Figure 18-3 shows worksheet data arranged for plotting on a scatter chart. The first column contains the X values for the data. The other two columns contain the Y values for the two data series.

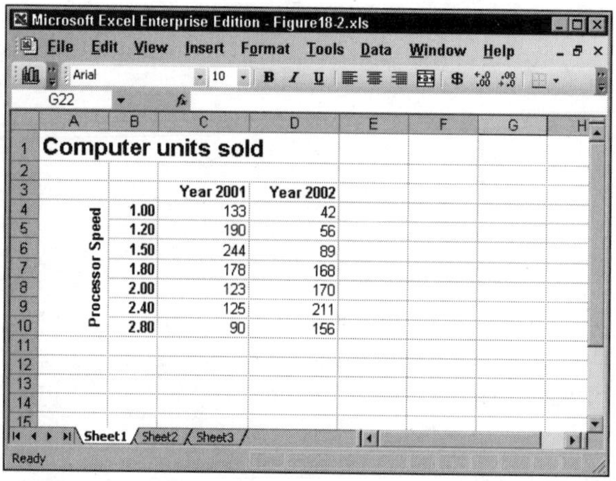

Figure 18-3 *Data organized for plotting on a scatter chart*

Creating a scatter chart in VBA code is not any different from creating other kinds of charts. You must specify the source data range and the chart type; you can then apply optional formatting such as chart and axis labels (as was covered in Session 17). Listing 18-2 shows a VBA program used to create an embedded scatter chart from the data in Figure 18-3. The resulting chart is shown in Figure 18-4.

Listing 18-2 *A program to create a scatter chart from the data in Figure 18-3*

```
Public Sub CreateScatterChart()

Dim co As ChartObject
```

```
Dim ch As Chart

Set co = Worksheets("Sheet1").ChartObjects.Add(50, 200, 250, 165)
Set ch = co.Chart
ch.SetSourceData Source:=Worksheets("Sheet1").Range("B3:D10"),
PlotBy:=xlColumns
ch.ChartType = xlXYScatterLines

' Add a chart title.
ch.HasTitle = True
ch.ChartTitle.Text = Worksheets("Sheet1").Range("A1").Value

' Add a category axis title.
With ch.Axes(xlCategory)
    .HasTitle = True
    .AxisTitle.Text = "Processor Speed (GHz)"
End With

' Add a value axis title.
With ch.Axes(xlValue)
    .HasTitle = True
    .AxisTitle.Text = "Units Sold"
End With

End Sub
```

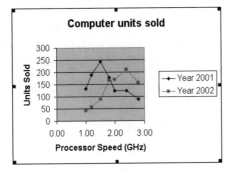

Figure 18-4 *The scatter chart created by the program in Listing 18-2*

Scatter Chart Types

**10 Min.
To Go**

The scatter chart shown in Figure 18-4 plots each data point as a symbol, or marker, and then connects the data points in each series with straight lines. Excel supports several types of scatter charts. The associated `ChartType` constants and descriptions are presented in Table 18-3. You can see how these different types of scatter charts look by plugging the corresponding constant into the program in the listing.

Table 18-3 *Constants for Different Types of Scatter Charts*

ChartType constant	Description
xlXYScatter	Data points as markers, no lines.
xlXYScatterLines	Data points as markers, connected by straight lines.
xlXYScatterLinesNoMarkers	No markers, straight lines.
xlXYScatterSmooth	Data points as markers, connected by smoothed lines (lines curved to obtain a smooth plot).
xlXYScatterSmoothNoMarkers	No markers, data points connected by smoothed lines.

Changing Axis Range

If you examine the scatter chart in Figure 18-4, you may notice that the X (horizontal) axis is not scaled properly. It ranges from 0 to 3 while the data being plotted ranges from 1 to 3. The result is that fully one third of the chart area is empty and wasted. This is because Excel's default is, when all the data values are positive, to scale an axis from 0 to a maximum value that depends on the data. You can change the scaling of an axis (vertical or horizontal) as needed to suit the data being plotted.

For more details on referencing individual axes in a chart please refer to Session 17.

The maximum and minimum values on an axis are controlled by the MaximumScale and MinimumScale properties of the Axis object. For example, to set the scale values for the value (vertical) axis on a chart, you would write the following code:

```
With SomeChart.Axes("xlValue")
    .MinimumScale = 5
    .MaximumScale = 20
End With
```

For the program in Listing 18-2, you need only to change the minimum value on the horizontal axis to 1 (you can let Excel choose the maximum value). The required line of code is:

```
ch.Axes(xlCategory).MinimumScale = 1
```

You should insert this line of code into the program, immediately after the line that sets the ChartType property. Now the resulting chart is much better, as shown in Figure 18-5.

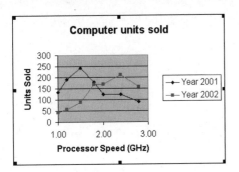

Figure 18-5 *The new chart with the horizontal axis scale set for the data*

 Even though the horizontal axis in a scatter chart is not really a category axis, it is still referred to using the `xlCategory` constant.

 Be careful when setting axis scale manually. If the minimum is too large, or the maximum too small, some of the data will not be plotted.

Printing Charts

You use the `PrintOut` method to print Excel charts as well as worksheets and workbooks. You can use it with various objects to print the desired chart(s). These are summarized in Table 18-4.

Table 18-4 *Using the PrintOut Method to Print Charts*

To print this	Call
A single embedded chart or chart sheet	The `PrintOut` method on the corresponding `Chart` object
All embedded charts on a worksheet (along with other worksheet contents)	The `PrintOut` method on the `Worksheet` object
All embedded charts on the active worksheet (along with other worksheet contents)	The `PrintOut` method on the `ActiveSheet` object
All chart sheets in a workbook	The `PrintOut` method on the workbook's `Charts` collection

Refer to Session 3 for more details on using the PrintOut **method.**

You may have noticed that there is no direct way to print all of the embedded charts on a worksheet without also printing the other worksheet contents. This oversight is easily remedied with a short VBA program, shown in Listing 18-3. This procedure takes a worksheet reference as its one argument. It then loops through the worksheet's ChartObjects collection, calling the PrintOut method on each contained chart. If the worksheet contains no embedded charts, nothing happens.

Listing 18-3   *Printing all embedded charts in a worksheet*

```
Public Sub PrintAllEmbeddedChartsOnSheet(ws As Worksheet)

' Prints all embedded charts on the specified
' worksheet.

Dim co As ChartObject

For Each co In ws.ChartObjects
    co.Chart.PrintOut
Next

End Sub

Public Sub TestPrintAllCharts()

PrintAllEmbeddedChartsOnSheet ActiveSheet

End Sub
```

When printing a worksheet, remember that the ChartObject's PrintObject **property determines whether that specific embedded chart is printed along with the other worksheet contents.**

To test this procedure, you need another procedure containing a single line of code to call it and pass a reference to the correct worksheet. Such a testing procedure is shown in Listing 18-3 as well, printing the charts in the active workbook.

When individual embedded charts are printed using the default settings, they are automatically scaled to fill the printed page regardless of the size of the chart in the worksheet.

Done!

REVIEW

Excel's charting capabilities are powerful, and you can access all this power from your VBA programs.

- You can assign names to charts and then later refer to the chart by this name.
- By protecting or locking a chart, you can prevent the user from modifying it.
- You use the `ChartObject` object to control certain aspects of embedded charts, including their size and position.
- The scatter chart is specialized for plotting values versus values.
- Use the `PrintOut` method to print charts.

QUIZ YOURSELF

1. How is the default name assigned by Excel constructed for an embedded `Chart` object? (See the "Naming and Referencing Charts" section.)

2. Suppose you have password-protected a chart and then realize you have lost or forgotten the password. What can you do to modify the chart? (See the "Locking Charts" section.)

3. How would you determine the range of worksheet cells over which an embedded chart is displayed? (See the "The ChartObject Object" section.)

4. Some scatter chart types are *smoothed*. What does this mean? (See the "Scatter Chart Types" section.)

5. Is there a direct way to access all of the embedded charts in a workbook? (See the "Naming and Referencing Charts" section.)

Creating Custom Dialog Boxes with User Forms

Session Checklist

✔ Overview of user forms

✔ Adding user forms to a project

✔ Basics of user form design

✔ Form properties and methods

✔ Displaying and hiding user forms

✔ A user form example

**30 Min.
To Go**

The Excel programmer can create custom dialog boxes for use in a VBA application. These dialog boxes, called *user forms* in Office, can contain all of the elements that you see in dialog boxes belonging to the Excel application itself as well as other Windows applications. They provide an extremely powerful programming tool, allowing you to provide a custom visual interface for your Excel applications. This session and the next three sessions show you how to create and use user forms.

Overview of User Forms

A user form is composed of three closely related parts:

- The form itself that represents the screen window with its title bar and other components common to all windows in the Windows operating system. The form is represented by a UserForm object.
- The controls on the form that comprise the visual and functional interface of the form. Each type of control is represented by its own class.
- VBA code that is part of the user form. Strictly speaking, a user form does not always have to include code, but in most cases it does.

User Form Limitations

While a user form is a regular window, it lacks some of the features that many program windows have. Specifically:

- The window cannot be resized by the user (although it can be resized in VBA code).
- The window does not have minimize and maximize buttons.
- The window does not have a control menu.

The window can, however, be moved by the user by dragging its title bar.

The UserForm object, as well as the controls that can be placed on a form, have properties and methods that determine the appearance and behavior of the object and also any data that is associated with the object. Most objects also can detect events, which for the most part are user actions such as clicking something with the mouse. By tying these three elements together — properties, methods, and events — your VBA code can customize the appearance and behavior of a user form to suit the specific needs of your application.

The task of creating a user form is made fairly simple by the VBA editor. Specifically, the form designer lets you design a form visually using a WYSIWYG (What You See Is What You Get) editor. All these topics are covered in this session and the following two sessions.

Form Designer Basics

To add a new user form to an Excel project, be sure that the correct project is selected in the Project window. Select Insert ➪ User Form from the VBA Editor menu. The editor opens a new, blank user form. This and other screen components involved in creating user forms are shown in Figure 19-1 and explained here:

- The user form itself (blank in this figure) is where you place controls to create the visual interface.
- Displayed while the user form is active, the toolbox contains icons for the various controls that can be placed on a form, as well as an arrow icon, which you select when you want to work with existing controls on the form.
- The Properties window displays the properties for the currently selected object. This may be the user form itself or a control on the form.
- The Project window lists all forms that are part of each project under the Forms node.
- The View Code and View Object buttons let you switch between viewing the user form's visual interface or its VBA code-editing window.

Properties window

View code   Project window

View object   User form   Tool box

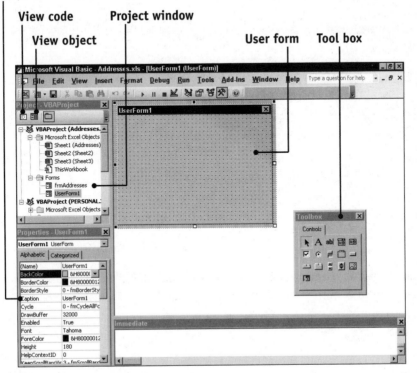

Figure 19-1   *Elements of the user form designer*

A VBA project can contain as many user forms as you want, as long as each one has a unique name.

Designing the Interface

Before designing your user form, it helps to have some idea of what the various controls do and how the finished user form should appear. Controls are covered later in this session, but the following are the basics of designing a form.

To work with controls that are already on the form, be sure the arrow icon in the toolbox is selected. The mouse cursor displays as an arrow in this mode.

- To place a control on the form, click the control's icon in the toolbox; then drag the icon onto the form to place the control.
- Click a control that's already on the form to select it. A selected control displays a thick stippled border with eight square handles on it, as shown in Figure 19-2.

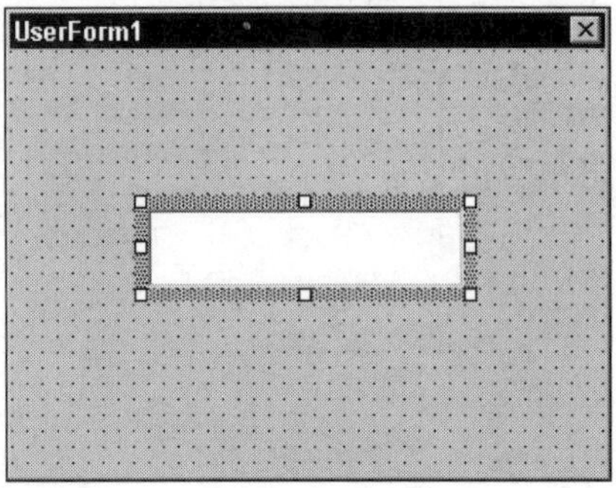

UserForm1   ☒

Figure 19-2   A selected control displays a border and handles.

- To resize a control, select it, point at one of its handles, and drag to the new size.
- To move a control, select it, point at its border, and drag to the new position.
- To delete a control, select it and then press Del.
- To select the form, click its title bar or anywhere between controls.
- To resize the form, select it and then drag one of its white handles to the new size.

To determine what control corresponds to an icon in the toolbox, rest the mouse cursor over the icon for a moment. A tool tip displays the name of the control.

You do not specify the position of a form by dragging it, but rather by setting its Top **and** Left **properties or its** StartUpPosition **property.**

More fine points of user form interface design are presented in Sessions 20 and 21.

Setting Properties

When the user form designer is open and an object (form or control) is selected, that object's properties are displayed in the Properties window. There are three parts to this window:

- The drop-down list at the top displays the object type and name of the selected object (the name is in bold type). You can select another object from this list.
- The Alphabetic tab lists all the object's properties in alphabetical order.
- The Categorized tab lists all the object's properties organized by category, such as Appearance, Data, Font, and so on.

There are two columns on each tab. The left column lists the property name, and the right column displays the current property setting. To change a property, click its name. The way you then make changes depends on the specific property:

- For an enumerated property (one that can take any of a set of predefined values), use the drop-down list in the right column to select the value.
- For a True/False property, double-click to toggle the value between True and False.
- For a property with a text or numeric value, click in the right column and enter or edit the property value.
- For more complex properties, the right column displays a button with ellipses (...). Click the button to display the property's dialog box. Make changes to the settings as needed; then close the dialog box to return to the properties window.

To get online help for a property, select the property in the Property window and press F1.

Form Properties

**20 Min.
To Go**

Each user form has a set of properties that control its appearance and behavior. There are over 30 form properties, some of which are used infrequently. Remember that all properties can be set using the Properties window, and can also be read and (except for read-only properties) set in VBA code. The syntax for referring to properties is the same as for other objects:

```
UserFormName.PropertyName
```

Each user form is assigned a name when created: UserForm1, UserForm2, and so on. This name (the Name property) is what you use to refer to the form in VBA code. Assign a descriptive name to each user form as soon as you create it to avoid having to use the default name.

Generally, you set all of the user form's properties at the design stage. Setting form properties in code is usually reserved for situations where you need to change the appearance or behavior of the form during program execution.

Appearance Properties

The following user form properties are related to its appearance:

- BackColor. The color of the form background. When setting this property in the Property window, select from palettes of predefined colors. In code, set this property with an RGB value using the RGB function.
- BorderColor. The color of the form border (if one is displayed). In code, set this property with an RGB value.

- BorderStyle. Set to fmBorderStyleSingle or fmBorderStyleNone.
- Caption. The text displayed in the form's title bar.
- Font. The default for text on the form. See Session 14 for more details on working with fonts.
- ForeColor. The color used for text and drawing on the form. In code, set this property with an RGB value.
- SpecialEffect. Controls the overall look of the form's interior. See Table 19-1 for permitted settings.

Table 19-1   *Settings for the UserForm Object's SpecialEffect Property*

Constant	Form Interior Appearance
fmSpecialEffectFlat	Flat
fmSpecialEffectRaised	Raised
frmSpecialEffectSunken	Sunken (recessed)
fromSpecialEffectEtched	Carved border
frmSpecialEffectBump	Ridge on the bottom and right edges, flat on other edges.

Behavior and Position Properties

These form properties control behavior, size, and position:

- Height. The form height in points.
- Left. The distance from the left edge of the screen to the left edge of the form, in points.
- ShowModal. If True (the default), the user must close the user form before any other code is executed and before using any other part of the application. If False, the user can switch away from the form while it is still displayed and use other parts of the application (such as another form).
- StartUpPosition. The position of the form when first displayed. See Table 19-2 for permitted settings.
- Top. The distance from the top of the screen to the top of the form, in points.
- Width. The form width in points.

Note that the Top and Left properties affect the initial position of the form only when the StartUpPosition property is set to Manual; however, after the form is displayed, changing these properties in code moves the form.

Table 19-2   *Settings for the UserForm Object's StartUpPosition Property*

Constant	Effect
Manual	Position is determined by the Top and Left properties.
CenterOwner	If Excel is displayed, the form is centered with respect to the Excel window. If Excel is not displayed, the form is centered on-screen.
CenterScreen	The form is centered on-screen.
WindowsDefault	The form is positioned at the top left of the screen.

The ShowModal property is usually left at its default value of True. This is appropriate for most user forms because it would not make sense for the program to continue operating until the form is closed (for example, when the form is used to accept input of data from the user). In some special cases, however, you would want to set this property to False. One example is when you create a user form to display instructions on program use to the user. It is then desirable to keep that user form displayed while the user works in another form.

Form Methods

The UserForm object has several methods. The ones that you are likely to need are described in Table 19-3.

Table 19-3   *Selected methods of the UserForm Object*

Method	Description
Hide	Hides the form if it is displayed; otherwise, it has no effect.
Move(Left, Top, Width, Height)	Moves the form and changes its size according to the arguments. Arguments are optional; any that are omitted are left at the current values.
PrintForm	Prints the form on the default printer
Show	Displays the form (and loads it if it is not already loaded)

Calling the Move **method on the user form has the same effect as setting its** Top, Left, Width, **and** Height **properties.**

Displaying, Using, and Hiding Forms

The sequence of steps involved in using a form in your application is summarized here. These steps assume that the form design has been completed (or at least has progressed enough to permit testing). This code assumes that the Name property of the user form is MyUserForm.

1. Create an instance of the user form, at the same time declaring a variable that references the form.

   ```
   Dim frm As New MyUserForm
   ```

2. If necessary, use the form reference to set values of properties for the form and its controls.

   ```
   frm.Backcolor = RGB(210, 210, 210)
   frm.TextBox1.Value = "Some text"
   ```

3. Display the form to the user.

   ```
   frm.Show
   ```

4. At this point the user interacts with the form by entering data, selecting options, and performing other actions for which the form was designed.

5. When finished, the user takes some action to close the form, typically by clicking a button on the form. Code in the form executes the Hide method to hide the form.

   ```
   Me.Hide
   ```

6. Code in your program can now retrieve information from the form's controls as needed.

   ```
   Response = frm.TextBox1.Value
   ```

7. Unless you want to use the form again, destroy it by setting its reference to Nothing in order to free up the memory that the form used.

   ```
   Set frm = Nothing
   ```

In code that is part of a form, the Me keyword is used to refer to the form (see step 5 above). Because the form reference is implicit within the form's code, you can also use property and method names without the Me qualifier. Thus, the code in step 5 above could simply say Hide.

Be aware that only the line of code in step 5 above is part of the form. All the remaining code is in your program, which is part of a VBA module.

A Simple User Form Example

10 Min. To Go

The user form presented in this section is intended to illustrate some of the basic procedures involved in creating and using forms in your Excel applications. It does not perform any useful tasks; real-world examples of useful forms are presented in Session 21.

The form contains three controls:

- A text box in which the user can enter information to be returned to the program.
- A button that moves the form to the top left of the screen.
- A button that closes the form.

The first part of creating this demonstration is to design the form.

1. In the VBA Editor, select Insert ⇨ User Form to add a new user form to the current project.
2. In the Property window, change the form's Name property to TestForm and its Caption property to User Form Demo.
3. Click the form to activate it. Then in the toolbox, click the Command Button icon.
4. Place the button at the desired location by dragging on the form.
5. In the Property window, change the button's Name property to cmdMove and its Caption property to Move.
6. Click the form again, and add another Command Button. Change its Name property to cmdClose and its Caption property to Close.
7. Return to the form again, and add a TextBox control to the form. Leave this control's properties at their default values.
8. Click the Save button on the toolbar to save the project.

At this point the form design is complete, although you still must add some code. The form should look something like Figure 19-3.

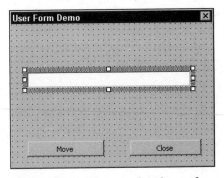

Figure 19-3   *The completed user form*

The next step is to add the required code to the form. This code is placed in event procedures and is executed automatically when the user takes certain actions (in this case, when the command buttons are clicked). You learn more about events and event procedures later; for now, however, follow the directions to complete the demonstration project.

With the user form still selected, click the View Code button in the Project window. The code-editing window for the user form opens. Note that there are two drop-down lists at the top of this window. You use these lists as follows:

- The list on the left contains all the controls on the form, and an entry for the user form itself, as shown in Figure 19-4. It also contains an entry (General). To edit code for a control or for the form, select the item in this list.

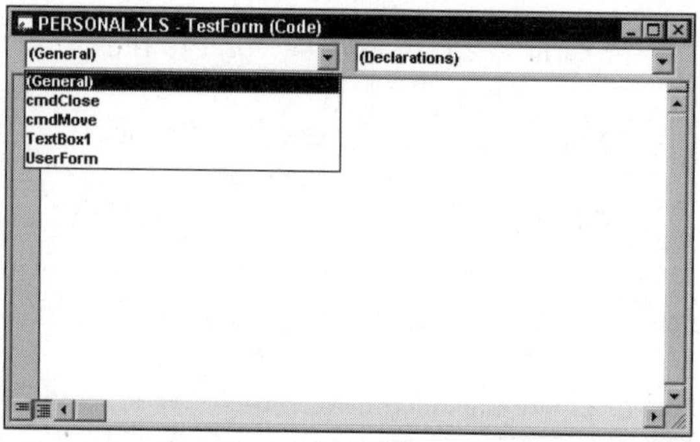

Figure 19-4   *Selecting the object whose code you want to edit*

- The list on the right lists all of the available event procedures for the item selected in the first list. Select the desired event, and the editor automatically enters the outline of the event procedure. Select (Declarations) to enter/edit code outside of any procedure.

If you double-click a control on the form during design or the form itself, the code editing window opens and displays the default event procedure for that control. The default event procedure — the one that the Microsoft people think will be used most often — is the Click event for many controls.

To add the event code to the demonstration project, follow these steps:

1. In the left list in the editing window, select cmdClose.

2. The list on the right automatically selects the Click event because this is the most commonly used event for the Command Button control. The outline of the event procedure is entered in the window, as shown in Figure 19-5.

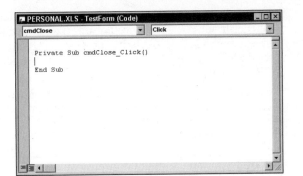

Figure 19-5 *The editor automatically enters the outline of the event procedure in the editing window.*

3. Enter the single line of code Me.Hide in the procedure, between the opening and closing lines.

4. Select cmdMove in the left list.

5. In the event procedure for the cmdMove button, enter the single line of code Me.Move 10, 10.

6. Click the Save button to save the project.

At this point the user form is complete. The next and final step is to add the code to the project to display and retrieve data from the form.

1. In the Project window, double-click the name of a code module to open its editing window.

2. Select Insert ⇨ Procedure to display the Add Procedure dialog box.

3. Enter TestUserForm as the procedure name and then click OK. The blank procedure is entered into the editing window.

4. Enter the code shown in Listing 19-1 into the procedure.

Listing 19-1 *A procedure to display and test the user form*

```
Public Sub TestUserForm()

Dim s As String
Dim frm As New TestForm

frm.Show
s = frm.TextBox1.Value
MsgBox "You entered " & s

End Sub
```

The user form demonstration is complete, and you can test it by running the TestUserForm procedure. When you do, the form is displayed. If you click the Move button, the form shifts to the top right corner of the screen. Click the text box to activate it, enter some text in the text box, and click the Close button. The program displays a message box with the text you entered, showing how the VBA code can retrieve data from a user form.

This is a simple demonstration. Sessions 20 and 21 provide more information about user forms, along with examples, and Session 22 presents a couple of complete, real-world user form programs.

Done!

REVIEW

This session introduced you to creating custom dialog boxes with Excel's user forms. Some of the things you learned are

- A user form can contain the same controls that are used in many other Windows applications.
- A VBA project can contain as many user forms as it needs.
- Forms and controls have properties that specify their appearance and behavior.
- The VBA editor provides a visual design tool that lets you create the visual interface of your user forms.
- You display a form to the user by calling its Show method in VBA code.
- In a form's code, you can use the Me keyword to refer to the form.

QUIZ YOURSELF

1. Two of the three main components of a user form are the form itself and the controls on the form. What is the third main component? (See the "Overview of User Forms" section.)
2. What property determines the text that is displayed in the title bar of a user form? (See the "Appearance Properties" section.)
3. The position of a user form on the screen is measured in relation to what point? (See the "Behavior and Position Properties" section.)
4. What's the difference between a modal form and a non-modal form? (See the "Behavior and Position Properties" section.)
5. When your program is finished using a form, how does it destroy the form? (See the "Displaying, Using, and Hiding Forms" section.)

Controls for User Forms

At the heart of any user form is its controls. There are over a dozen controls available to the programmer for user forms, and they cover a wide range of data display and entry needs. This session describes these controls and their properties, and shows examples of how to use them.

**30 Min.
To Go**

A Summary of Controls

Excel provides 15 controls for you to place on user forms. Each control serves a specific purpose and has its own set of properties, methods, and events. Table 20-1 provides a brief summary of the available controls. The following sections cover some of the controls in more detail. Space limitations preclude covering all of the controls in detail; those controls not discussed are marked with an asterisk in the table. You can refer to the online help for information on using these controls.

Table 20-1 *Summary of Excel's User Form Controls*

Control	Function
CheckBox	Displays an option that can be turned on or off
ComboBox	Combines the function of a TextBox and a ListBox

Continued

Table 20-1   *Continued*

Control	Function
CommandButton	Displays a button that is selected by the user to carry out some action
Frame	Used to group other controls, such as OptionButtons
Image*	Displays an image
Label	Displays text that cannot be edited by the user
ListBox*	Displays a list of items from which the user can select
MultiPage*	Displays two or more tabs at the edge of the user form, permitting the user to select from multiple pages on the form
OptionButton	Similar to a CheckBox, but only one OptionButton in a group can be selected at one time. To create a group of OptionButton controls, place a Frame control on the user form; then draw the OptionButton controls on the frame.
RefEdit	Enables the user to select range in a worksheet
ScrollBar*	Displays a vertical or horizontal scroll bar on the user form
SpinButton*	Increments and decrements numbers by clicking with the mouse
TabStrip*	Performs essentially the same function as a MultiPage but is more flexible and correspondingly harder to use
TextBox	Displays text that the user can edit
ToggleButton	A button that can be either up or down, permitting the user to select and deselect items.

Common Control Properties

While each User Form control has its own set of properties, there are several properties that are common to all or most controls. Rather than repeating this information for each control, a compilation of common properties is shown in Table 20-2. Other properties for individual controls are covered in the following sections.

Table 20-2 *Common Properties of User Form Controls*

Property	Description
BackColor	An RGB value specifying the control's background color
ControlTipText	The text that is displayed when the user hovers the mouse cursor over the control; blank by default.

Property	Description
Enabled	If True, the control is enabled, and the user can interact with it. If False, the control is visible but "grayed out," and the user cannot interact with it.
Font	A Font object controlling the font used to display text in the control. See Session 14 for more information on using the Font object.
ForeColor	An RGB value specifying the control's foreground color
Locked	If True, the control cannot be edited or changed. The default is False.
Visible	True to display the control; False to hide it.

User Form Control Details

This section presents detailed information on what each type of control can be used for and how it works.

The CheckBox Control

The CheckBox control provides an option or setting that the user can turn on or off by clicking. It consists of a small box with an adjacent label. When on, the box displays a check mark; when off, the box is empty. The Caption property determines the label displayed next to the box; the Value property returns True if the box is checked, False if not. You can set the control's state by assigning True or False to the Value property in code.

The ComboBox Control

The ComboBox control combines the capabilities of a TextBox control and a ListBox control. It displays a list of text items from which the user can select as well as an editing box for exiting or entering data. A ComboBox can operate in one of two modes, controlled by its Style property. Settings for this property are described in Table 20-3.

Table 20-3 *Settings for the ComboBox Control's Style Property*

Constant	Description
frmStyleDropDownCombo	The user can select an item from the list or type a value in the edit region. This is the default style.
frmStyleDropDownList	The user is restricted to selecting an item from the list.

Items are added to a ComboBox using its AddItem method. The syntax is:

```
ComboBox.AddItem Item
```

For example, the following code adds four items to a ComboBox:

```
ComboBox1.AddItem "West"
ComboBox1.AddItem "East"
ComboBox1.AddItem "North"
ComboBox1.AddItem "South"
```

You cannot add items to a ComboBox at design time, but only in code. The form's `Initialize` **event procedure (covered later in this session) is usually the best place to put this code.**

Each item you add to a ComboBox is assigned a numerical index. The first item added has index equal to 0, the second item has index equal to 1, and so on. When the user selects an item in the ComboBox or enters text in the edit area, the control's `Value` property returns the text (or an empty string if no item is selected). The value returned by the `ListIndex` property is as follows:

- If the user has selected an item in the ComboBox's list, the item's index number is returned.
- If the user has not selected and item or has entered text in the edit area, -1 is returned.

By default, a ComboBox is blank when the form is first displayed — the user must open the form and select from the list, or enter some text. If you want the control to display an initial value, do one of the following (after loading the control with data):

- Set the control's `ListIndex` property to the index of an item that has been added to the list.
- Set the control's `Value` property to a string.

For example, this code loads the ComboBox and sets it to initially display Red:

```
ComboBox1.AddItem "Blue"
ComboBox1.AddItem "Red"
ComboBox1.AddItem "Green"
ComboBox1.AddItem "Brown"
ComboBox1.ListIndex = 1
```

The following program demonstrates using a ComboBox in a VBA program. Follow these steps to create and run the program.

1. In the VBA Editor, select Insert ⇨ UserForm to add a new user form to the project.
2. Change the form's `Name` property to ComboBoxDemo and its `Caption` property to ComboBox Demo.
3. Add a ComboBox control to the form; leave its properties as the default values.
4. Add a CommandButton control to the form and change its `Caption` property to Close.
5. In the Project window, click the View Code button to display the code-editing window for the form.

6. From the list at the top left of the editing window, select CommandButton1.

7. The editor may automatically enter the Click event procedure (because it is the control's default event). If not, select Click from the list at the top right of the editing window.

8. Enter the single line of code Me.Hide in the Click event procedure.

9. From the list at the top left of the editing window, select UserForm.

10. From the list at the top right of the editing window, select Initialize.

11. Enter the code from Listing 20-1 in the Initialize event procedure.

12. Save the project.

Listing 20-1   *Code for the user form's Initialize event procedure*

```
Private Sub UserForm_Initialize()

ComboBox1.AddItem "Vanilla"
ComboBox1.AddItem "Chocolate"
ComboBox1.AddItem "Coffee"
ComboBox1.AddItem "Strawberry"
ComboBox1.AddItem "Cherry"
ComboBox1.ListIndex = 0

End Sub
```

This completes designing the form for the demonstration. You must now create the program to display the form and retrieve the selected value from the ComboBox:

1. Open the code-editing window for a module in your project (or, if necessary, select Insert ⇨ Module to add a new module).

2. Select Insert ⇨ Procedure to add a new procedure. Name the procedure TestComboBoxDemo.

3. Add the code from Listing 20-2 to the new procedure.

Listing 20-2   *A procedure to test the user form and ComboBox control*

```
Public Sub TestComboBoxDemo()

Dim frm As New ComboBoxDemo
frm.Show
MsgBox "You selected " & frm.ComboBox1.Value

End Sub
```

When you run the TestComboBoxDemo procedure, the user form displays. Make a selection in the ComboBox (see Figure 20-1) and click Close. The program pops up a Message Box with the selection you made.

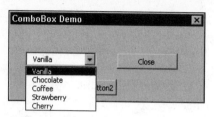

Figure 20-1   *Making a selection from a ComboBox*

**20 Min.
To Go**

The CommandButton Control

The CommandButton control displays a button on a form. The main use for this control is to carry out some action when the user clicks the button. To perform an action, put the required code in the Click event procedure for the control. An example of this was presented earlier in this session in the section on the ComboBox control.

It is sometimes desirable to have default and cancel buttons on a form. The default button is automatically selected (as if it had been clicked) when the user presses Enter (as long as no other command button has the focus), and the cancel button is automatically selected when the user presses Esc.

- To make a command button the default, set its Default property to True.
- To make a command button the cancel button, set its Cancel property to True.

A user form can have only one default button and one cancel button on it.

In many cases, a dialog box has a command button with the caption OK or something similar. This button closes the form and tells the calling program to accept the data from the form. Likewise, the cancel button (usually with the Cancel caption) also closes the form, but tells the program to ignore data from the form. But how does the calling program know which button was selected to close the form?

The trick lies in creating a global Boolean variable within the form. This is a variable declared outside of any event procedure, and is therefore accessible to code outside the form. To create such a variable, open the code-editing window for the user form and then select (General) in the list at the top left of the window. Enter the variable declaration, using the Public keyword in place of Dim:

```
Public Cancelled As Boolean
```

Here's how to use this variable:

1. Code in the Click event procedure for the form's OK button sets this variable to False and then hides the form.

2. Code in the Click event procedure for the form's Cancel button sets this variable to True and then hides the form.

3. Code in the calling program checks the value of this variable and retrieves data from the form only if it is False. If it is True, data from the form is ignored.

The following program demonstrates this technique. Here are the steps required:

1. Add a new user form to a project.
2. Change its Name property to CommandButtonDemo and its Caption property to CommandButton Demo.
3. Add a CommandButton to the form. Change its Name property to cmdOK, its Caption property to OK, and its Default property to True.
4. Add a second CommandButton to the form. Change its Name property to cmdCancel, its Caption property to Cancel, and its Cancel property to True.
5. Open the code-editing window for the form, and select (General) from the list at the top left of the window.
6. Enter this single line of code: Public Cancelled As Boolean.
7. Add Click event procedures for each CommandButton, and add the code shown in Listing 20-3.

Listing 20-3   *Code for the two CommandButton controls' Click event procedures*

```
Private Sub cmdCancel_Click()

Cancelled = True
Me.Hide

End Sub

Private Sub cmdOK_Click()

Cancelled = False
Me.Hide

End Sub
```

Now that the form is complete, create the procedure that displays the form. In a code module in your project, add a new procedure named TestCommandButtonDemo and insert the code shown in Listing 20-4.

Listing 20-4   *Code to run the CommandButton demo form*

```
Public Sub TestCommandButtonDemo()

Dim frm As New CommandButtonDemo
frm.Show
If frm.Cancelled = True Then
    MsgBox "You closed the form with the Cancel button"
Else
    MsgBox "You closed the form with the OK button"
End If

End Sub
```

The Frame Control

The Frame control is used to group other controls; it has no functionality of its own, although it can detect Click events. A Frame control displays as a rectangular bordered box with a caption. After placing a Frame control on a form, you can place other controls on it. This provides the following capabilities:

- If you move the Frame control (either while designing the form or in code), the contained controls move along with it.
- If you set the Visible property of the Frame control to False, all of its contained controls are hidden as well.

The most common use for a Frame control is to create groups of OptionButton controls. An example of this is presented in the section on the OptionButton control later in this session.

The Label Control

The Label control displays text that the user cannot edit. It is used to provide information or instructions on a form. For example, you can place a Label control next to a TextBox control to identify the TextBox and specify what data it contains. While the user cannot edit a Label control, its text can be changed in code (via the Caption property). Furthermore, it can detect Click events so it can be used as an alternative to the CommandButton control as a way of initiating actions in response to user input.

The OptionButton Control

The OptionButton is similar to a CheckBox control in that it permits the display and selection of a True/False, yes/no option, usually as a small circle that is empty when the option is off and filled when the option is on; the user toggles it by clicking. The OptionButton is different in that one and only one of a group of OptionButton controls can be selected at a time.

A group of OptionButtons can be defined by placing them all within a Frame control. The technique is to first place the Frame control on the form and then place the OptionButton controls on the frame. You must place the OptionButton directly on the Frame control to make it part of the group — you cannot drag an existing OptionButton from another part of the form onto the frame.

Another way to define a group of OptionButtons is by means of the GroupName property. All OptionButton controls with the same GroupName are considered to be part of a group, and are mutually exclusive even if they are not together in a Frame control.

Setting an OptionButton's Value property to True automatically sets other buttons in the same group to False. To determine which OptionButton in a group is selected, your code must go through all the OptionButton controls looking for one whose Value property is True. This is demonstrated in the demo program.

**You can have two or more groups of OptionButton controls on a form by plac-
ing each group within its own Frame control or by assigning different
GroupName properties.**

The following program demonstrates the use of OptionButton controls. Follow these steps
to create the user form.

1. In the VBA Editor, select Insert ➪ UserForm to add a new user form to the project.

2. Change the form's Name property to OptionButtonDemo, and its Caption property
to Option Button Demo.

3. Add a Frame control to the form, and change its Caption property to Choose a
Color.

4. Add an OptionButton in the Frame control. Change its Caption property to Blue
and its Name property to optBlue.

5. Add two more OptionButton controls on the frame, setting the Name and Caption
properties to optRed and red for the first one and optGreen and Green for the second one.

6. Change the Value property of one of the OptionButton controls to True (it does
not matter which one).

7. Add a CommandButton to the form but not on the frame. Change its Caption
property to OK.

8. Double-click the CommandButton control to edit its Click event procedure. Enter
the single line of code Me.Hide in the procedure.

9. Save the project.

The completed form should look similar to Figure 20-2. The next step is to write the VBA
procedure that displays this user form and retrieves the user's data.

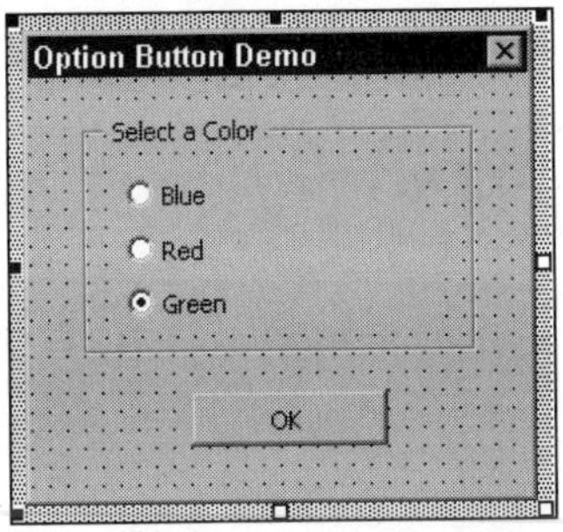

Option Button Demo ☒

┌─ Select a Color ──────────────
│   ○ Blue
│
│   ○ Red
│   ● Green
│
│   ┌────────────┐
│   │   OK   │
│   └────────────┘

Figure 20-2 *The complete Option Button Demo form*

1. Open a code module in your project.

2. Use the Insert ➪ Procedure command to add a procedure named
TestOptionButtonDemo.

3. Add the code from Listing 20-5 to the procedure.

Listing 20-5   *A procedure to test the OptionButtonDemo form*

```
Public Sub TestOptionButtonDemo()

Dim frm As New OptionButtonDemo
Dim s As String

frm.Show

' Determine which option button is selected.
If frm.optBlue.Value = True Then
    s = "Blue"
ElseIf frm.optRed.Value = True Then
    s = "Red"
ElseIf frm.optGreen.Value = True Then
    s = "Green"
End If

MsgBox "You selected " & s

End Sub
```

Run the TestOptionButtonDemo program, and the form that you designed is displayed. Select a color, noting how you can select only one at a time. When you click OK, the program displays your choice in a Message Box.

The RefEdit Control

The RefEdit control enables the user to select a range of cells in a worksheet. After the range has been selected, the control returns the address of the range as a string containing the name of the sheet and absolute references to the cells. The RefEdit control can be used only on forms that are shown modally (that is, they have the ShowModal property set to True).

The RefEdit control displays as a text entry box adjacent to a button. When the user clicks the button, the user form collapses to a small size. The user can then use the mouse to drag over a range in the worksheet. When the desired range has been selected, the user clicks the button displayed on the collapsed user form. The user form expands to its original size, with the sheet and cell address of the selected range displayed in the text entry box. This text is available in code via the control's Value property. If the user has not selected a range, this property returns a blank string.

To see the RefEdit control in action, create and build this demonstration program. The program displays a form with a RefEdit control and a button labeled Format. The user clicks the RefEdit control and then selects a range in a worksheet. Upon returning to the user form, clicking the Format button changes the font in the range to red and displays a message box with the range address in it. Finally, the form is closed.

To create the user form, follow these steps:

1. Select Insert ➪ User Form to add a new user form to the project.
2. Change the form's Name property to RefEditDemo and its Caption property to RefEdit Demo.

10 Min. To Go

3. Add a RefEdit control to the form, leaving all of its properties at their default values.
4. Add a CommandButton to the form. Change its `Caption` property to Format.
5. Double-click the CommandButton to open its Click event procedure in the editing window.
6. Add the code from Listing 20-6 to this procedure.

Listing 20-6   *Code in the RefEditDemo form*

```
Private Sub CommandButton1_Click()

Dim s As String
Dim r As Range

s = RefEdit1.Value
' Check for no selection.
If s = "" Then
    MsgBox "Please make a selection"
Else
    ' Format the range.
    Set r = Range(s)
    r.Font.Color = RGB(255, 0, 0)
    ' Display the range address.
    MsgBox "You formatted the range " & s
    ' Close the form.
    Me.Hide
End If

End Sub
```

All the code for this program is in the user form itself, so all you need is a procedure to display the form. Create a new procedure in a VBA module (you might call the procedure TestRefEditDemo) and put the following code in the procedure:

```
Dim frm As New RefEditDemo
frm.Show
```

To test the program, follow these steps:

1. Run the procedure to display the form.
2. Click the RefEdit control to collapse the form and select a range in the worksheet. It's a good idea to select a range that contains data so you can see the effect of the formatting. Figure 20-3 shows the worksheet with the collapsed user form and a range selected.
3. Click the button on the collapsed form to return to the user form.
4. Click the Format button to format the range and display the message box.
5. Close the message box, which also closes the user form.

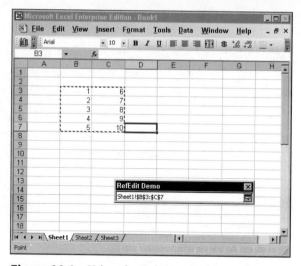

Figure 20-3   *Using the RefEdit control to select a range*

The TextBox Control

The TextBox control is one of the most useful controls available to the Excel programmer. It can display text to the user for editing and can also be displayed as blank to permit the user to enter data.

With its default settings, a TextBox control displays a single line of text. If the text it contains is too wide for the size of the control, it scrolls out of view off to the right. The user can move around in a text box with the usual text-editing keys (including the arrow and End and Home keys). This is the case even if the text box's height is sufficient to display multiple lines of text.

If you want to display more than one line of text in a TextBox control, set its MultiLine property to True. The user can then start a new line of text by pressing Shift+Enter (or just Enter, depending on the setting of the EnterKeyBehavior property as explained in Table 20-4). Also, text automatically wraps to a new line when it reaches the right edge of the text box. If you do not want text to wrap, so that new lines start only when the user presses Shift+Enter, set the control's WordWrap property to False.

If a multiline TextBox control contains more lines of text than can be displayed, the extra lines scroll out of view at the top and/or bottom of the text box. You can display scroll bars in a text box, permitting scrolling vertically and horizontally to bring text into view. This is done by setting the ScrollBars property to one of the following values:

- fmScrollBarsNone (the default)
- fmScrollBarsHorizontal
- fmScrollBarsVertical
- fmScrollBarsBoth

Table 20-4 describes some other properties of the TextBox control.

Table 20-4 *Some Properties of the TextBox Control*

Property	Description
EnterKeyBehavior	If False (the default), pressing Enter moves the focus to the next control and the user must press Shift+Enter to start a new line in the text box. If True, pressing Enter starts a new line.
MaxLength	The maximum number of characters that the text box can hold. If 0 (the default), there is no limit.
PasswordChar	Specifies the placeholder character used to display text in the text box. For example, set this property to "*" to display all asterisks. Used for password entry to prevent accidental viewing of the password by an unauthorized person. The default blank setting displays all characters as themselves.
TabKeyBehavior	If True, pressing Tab inserts a tab into the text (but only if the MutliLine property is also True). If False (the default), pressing Tab moves the focus to the next control.
TextLength	Returns the number of characters in the text box

To retrieve or set the data in a TextBox control, use either its Text or Value property. These two properties are exactly equivalent, with the older Text property being retained for compatibility with earlier versions of Excel.

 Turn to Session 22 for an example of using the TextBox control.

The ToggleButton Control

The ToggleButton control is used to select and display True/False values. Functionally it is essentially identical to the CheckBox control but displays its state as either up or down (for False and True, respectively). The control's Value property returns True or False depending on its state. Changing the Value property changes the control's appearance.

Done!

REVIEW

This session covered the controls that are available for user forms in Excel programs.

- There are 15 different controls available.
- The Enabled property determines whether a control can be modified by the user.
- The Visible property determines if a control is shown on the form.
- The TextBox control is used for the display and entry of text data.

- Both the ComboBox and ListBox controls display a list of items from which the user can select.
- Use the CheckBox, OptionButton, or ToggleButton control for on/off options.
- The RefEdit control enables the user to select a range of cells in a worksheet.

QUIZ YOURSELF

1. What's the main difference between the CheckBox control and the OptionButton control? (See the "A Summary of Controls" section.)

2. How do you configure a TextBox control so it can contain multiple lines of text? (See the "The TextBox Control" section.)

3. How do you add items to the list of a ComboBox control? (See the "The ComboBox Control" section.)

4. What does it mean to set the Default property of a CommandButton to True? (See the "The CommandButton Control" section.)

5. Describe two ways to create a group of OptionButton controls. (See the "The OptionButton Control" section.)

PART
IV

Saturday Evening Part Review

1. What's the main difference between an embedded chart and a chart sheet?
2. How do you control the size and position of a chart sheet?
3. How do you add a new chart sheet to a workbook?
4. How do you specify the data to be plotted in a chart?
5. Suppose that Ch references a chart. How would you italicize the chart's title?
6. Your workbook contains a chart sheet named "Sales Summary." What VBA statement would print this chart to the default printer?
7. How would you prevent a chart from being modified by the user?
8. Suppose a worksheet contains several embedded charts that overlap each other. How would you make sure that a specific chart is not hidden by the others?
9. How is a scatter chart fundamentally different from most other Excel charts?
10. How would you print all chart sheets in a workbook?
11. Suppose you do not want a particular embedded chart to be printed when the worksheet is printed. How is this accomplished?
12. What are the three components of a user form?
13. How do you specify that a user form is centered on-screen when initially displayed?
14. How do you close a user form?
15. How do the OptionButton and CheckBox controls differ?
16. How do you create a group of OptionButton controls?
17. Suppose you are editing the visual interface of a user form. What's the quickest way to display the code for a control's default event?
18. You want the user to be able to select a command button by pressing Enter. How is this done?

19. Which control lets the user select a range in a worksheet?

20. Which control would you use to let the user select zero, one, or more yes/no options?

21. Which control property determines whether a control can be accessed/modified by the user?

☑ Friday

☑ Saturday

 Sunday

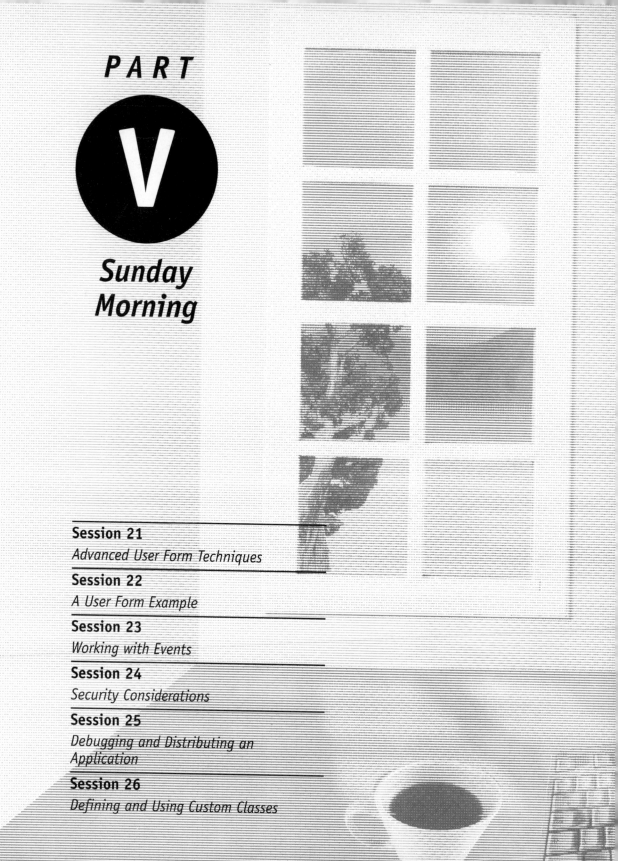

PART

V

Sunday Morning

Advanced User Form Techniques

Session Checklist

✔ Using control events

✔ Tools for aligning and sizing controls

✔ Working with the z-order

✔ Controls and the tab order

In the previous two sessions, you learned the fundamentals of user form design and some details about the controls available for user forms. This session goes a bit further, covering some of the more advanced aspects of user form design and use.

**30 Min.
To Go**

Using Control Events

The controls that are used on user forms can detect certain types of events. These events are, for the most part, the result of user actions, such as clicking a control or pressing keys. You have already seen one of these events, Click, used in some sample programs. Other events for forms and controls are described in Table 21-1. These are not all the events that are available to a programmer, but they are the ones you'll need most often.

Table 21-1 *Events Available for User Forms and Controls*

Event	Available for	Occurs
Click	Forms; most controls	When the user clicks the object
DblClick	Forms; most controls	When the user double-clicks the object

Continued

Table 21-1

Continued

Event	Available for	Occurs
Change	CheckBox, OptionButton, ComboBox, TextBox, and some other controls	When the control's data changes
Enter	Most controls	Just before the control receives the focus
Exit	Most controls	Just before the control loses the focus
KeyDown	TextBox and other controls	When a key is pressed while the control has the focus; the event procedure receives information identifying the key.
MouseMove	Form, controls	When the mouse cursor moves over the object

If you do not place code in the event procedure for an event, that event is ignored.

Events are connected to your VBA program by *event procedures*. An event procedure is a section of code that executes automatically when the event occurs, and it is identified by two pieces of information:

- The name of the object (a control or the form) that receives the event.
- The name of the event.

The convention for naming event procedures is *objectname_eventname*. For example, for a CommandButton control named cmdOK, the event procedure for the Click event is named cmdOK_Click. This name is all that is required to connect the procedure to the event.

The interval that is required for a double click (as opposed to two separate clicks) is set in the Windows Control Panel under the Mouse heading.

The KeyDown event deserves special mention because it can be handy when used in conjunction with a TextBox control. Specifically, it enables you to intercept keystrokes before they reach the TextBox, seeing what character was entered and then either accepting it or discarding it according to the function of the control. For example, you can use this event to create a TextBox that accepts only numeric input.

The KeyDown event procedure receives two arguments when the event occurs:

- KeyCode. An integer value specifying the key that was pressed.
- Shift. An integer value identifying which shift keys (Shift, Alt, and Ctrl) were down when the key was pressed.

To work with the KeyCode argument in the event procedure, you usually use the constants that are defined by VBA for each key. These constants take the form vbKey*XX* where *XX* identifies the key. For example, vbKeyA is the A key, vbKeyDown is the down key, and vbKeyNumpad5 is the 5 key on the numeric keypad. You can find a complete list of the KeyCode values in the VBA online help.

The Shift argument identifies which shift keys, if any, were down. In this context the term *shift keys* refers to the Shift, Ctrl, and Alt keys. There are three constants you can use for this purpose:

- fmShiftMask refers to the Shift key.
- fmCtrlMask refers to the Ctrl key.
- fmAltMask refers to the Alt key.

If no shift key was down, the Shift argument is 0. If one of the keys was down, the Shift argument is equal to the corresponding constant. If two or three of the shift keys are down, the argument is the logical AND of the corresponding arguments. For example:

```
If Shift = fmShiftMask And fmCtrlMask Then
    ' Shift and Ctrl keys were down.
End If
```

It's important to note that the KeyCode argument identifies the key that was pressed and that's all. For example, if KeyCode is equal to vbKey7, you know that the 7 key along the top of the keyboard was pressed; however, only by examining the Shift argument can you determine if the user was entering 7 or was pressing the Shift key at the same time in order to enter an ampersand (&).

After checking the key, you can do two things with the code in the KeyDown event procedure:

- Set the KeyCode argument to 0, which cancels the keystroke.
- Leave the KeyCode argument as is, which allows the keystroke to get through to the control.

You learn how to use the KeyDown **event procedure to restrict input to a text box in Session 22.**

20 Min.
To Go

Advanced Form Design

You have already learned the fundamentals of user form design in Session 19. These basics serve you well for designing relatively simple forms, but at some point you want greater control over the appearance of your forms. These techniques are covered in this section.

The Form Grid

You may have already noticed when placing or resizing controls on a form that you cannot select just any position or size. Rather, the position and size of any control is constrained by the grid of dots that is displayed on the form. In other words, the corners of any control must fall on this grid, not in between two grids. This feature is valuable because it makes it easier for you to precisely align controls with each other and make controls the same size. You can turn off the grid or change its size by selecting Tools ⇨ Options from the VBA Editor menu to display the Options dialog box, and then clicking the General tab (see Figure 21-1). The Form Grid Settings part of the dialog box has the following settings:

- **Show Grid.** If this option is checked, the grid is displayed. Note that the grid can be displayed without being active, and can also be active without being displayed.
- **Width, Height.** This controls the spacing between grid points. The default is 6 points, or 1/12 inch.
- **Align Controls to Grid.** If this option is checked, the position and size of controls are forced to align with the grid.

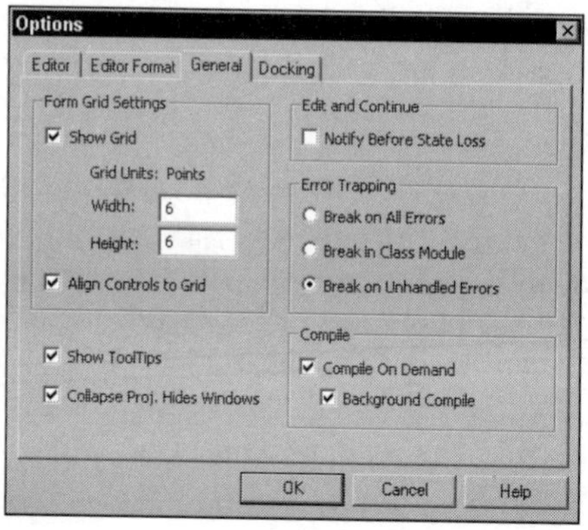

Figure 21-1 *Setting options for the design form grid*

Changing the grid size, or turning it on after it has been off, does not affect controls that are already on the form. Only controls added subsequently are affected.

Control Placement and Alignment Tools

The form designed provides some handy tools that aid you in placing controls on a form and setting the sizes. These tools let you place and size controls with a precision that is difficult to achieve manually. To use most of these tools, you need to select multiple controls on a form as follows:

1. Click the first control to select it. This will serve as the guide control (explained later in this session).
2. Hold down the Shift key and then click the second control.
3. Repeat step 2 until all the desired controls are selected.

When you select multiple controls, the first control selected displays white handles while the other selected controls display black handles. This is shown in Figure 21-2. The white handles mark the guide control — the one used as the reference for the formatting commands. For example, if you are using a command to align controls, they will be aligned at the position of the guide control.

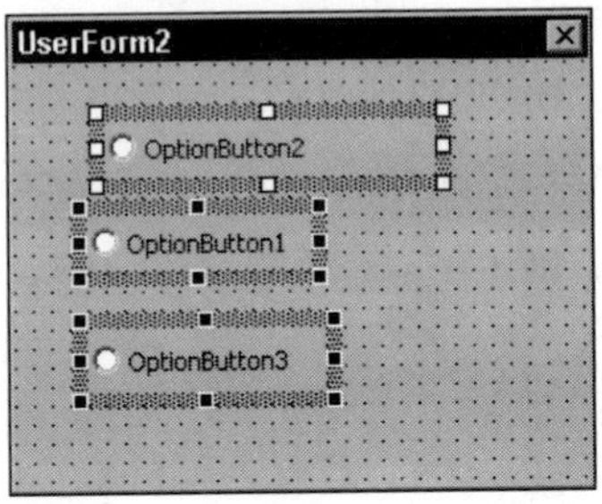

Figure 21-2   *When multiple controls are selected, the guide control has white handles.*

When multiple controls are selected, click anywhere on the form to deselect them.

Multiple selected controls can be moved as a group by dragging and can also be deleted as a group by pressing Delete. More useful, however, are the commands found on the Format menu. These commands are described in Table 21-2.

Table 21-2   *Format Menu Commands*

Command	Action
Align ⇨ Lefts, Centers, or Rights	Aligns the left edge, center, or right edge of selected controls to the horizontal position of the guide control
Align ⇨ Tops, Middles, or Bottom	Aligns the top edge, middle, or bottom edge of selected controls to the vertical position of the guide control
Align ⇨ To Grid	Aligns the position and sizes of controls to the current form grid
Make Same Size ⇨ Width, Height, or Both	Sizes the controls to match the guide control
Horizontal Spacing ⇨ Make Equal	Equalizes the horizontal space between selected controls

Continued

Table 21-2

Continued

Command	Action
Horizontal Spacing ⇨ Increase or Decrease	Increases or decreases the horizontal space between selected controls
Horizontal Spacing ⇨ Remove	Removes horizontal space between selected controls
Vertical Spacing ⇨ Make Equal	Equalizes the vertical space between selected controls
Vertical Spacing ⇨ Increase or Decrease	Increases or decreases the vertical space between selected controls
Vertical Spacing ⇨ Remove	Removes vertical space between selected controls
Center in Form ⇨ Horizontally or Vertically	Centers the control(s) in the form either horizontally or vertically
Arrange Buttons ⇨ Bottom	Arranges selected CommandButton controls along the bottom of the form
Arrange Buttons ⇨ Right	Arranges selected CommandButton controls along the right edge of the form

The following exercise shows you how you might use some of these commands. It is not a real project, but it does use a user form to demonstrate some of these design commands.

1. Select Insert ⇨ UserForm to add a new user form to a project.

2. Add the following controls to the form: four CheckBox controls, one TextBox control, one Label control, and two CommandButton controls. Your form should look something like Figure 21-3. Do not be concerned with control captions and other properties.

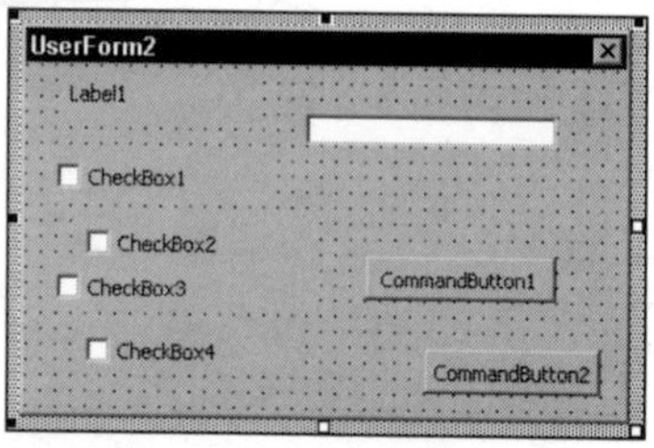

Figure 21-3   *The form before arranging the controls*

3. Change the size and position of the Label control, placing it in the top left corner of the form.

4. With the Label control still selected, hold down the Shift key and then click the TextBox control.

5. Select Format ⇨ Align ⇨ Tops to vertically align the Label and TextBox controls.

6. Select Format ⇨ Make Same Size ⇨ Height to make the text box the same height as the label.

7. Select Format ⇨ Horizontal Spacing ⇨ Remove to bring the controls together.

8. Move one of the CheckBox controls to the desired location, below the Label control. Change its size, if necessary.

9. With the first CheckBox control still selected, press Shift and then click the other three CheckBox controls. The first CheckBox control has white handles, and the others have black handles.

10. Select Align ⇨ Lefts to align all CheckBox controls with the first one.

11. Select Format ⇨ Make Same Size ⇨ Both to make all CheckBox controls the same size.

12. Select Format ⇨ Vertical Spacing ⇨ Make Equal to make the vertical space between the controls equal.

13. Select one of the CommandButton controls and then change its size as needed.

14. Press Shift and then click the other CommandButton control.

15. Select Format ⇨ Make Same Size ⇨ Both to make the two CommandButton controls the same size.

16. Select Format ⇨ Arrange Buttons ⇨ Right to position the two CommandButton controls along the right side of the form.

17. If necessary, drag the two controls (still both selected) to the final position.

The final appearance of the form is shown in Figure 21-4. Achieving this nice, neat appearance manually would have been a lot more work.

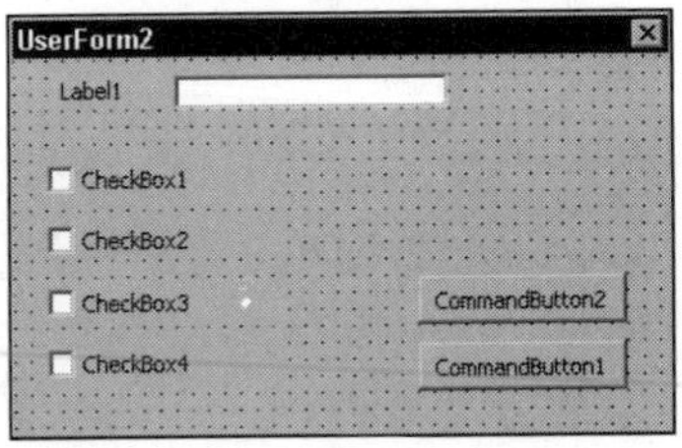

Figure 21-4 *The form after arranging the controls*

**10 Min.
To Go**

Overlapping Controls and the Z-Order

Most of the time, the controls on your user forms don't overlap each other, so there's no problem with one control hiding another. (Using a `Frame` control to group other controls is the one common exception to this rule.) For some forms, however, it may be desirable to overlap controls to achieve the layout you want. When controls overlap, how do you determine which one is on top?

The layering of overlapping controls is determined by the *z-order*. The control that is on top, hiding all or part of other controls, is said to be at the top of the z-order. Likewise, the control that is under all other overlapping controls is at the bottom of the z-order. You can control the z-order at design time and in code.

To change the z-order position of a control, select the control and then select Format ⇨ Order. There are four commands available on the submenu:

- **Bring to Front** puts the control at the top of the z-order.
- **Send to Back** puts the control at the back of the z-order.
- **Bring Forward** moves the control up one position in the z-order.
- **Send Backward** moves the control back one position in the z-order.

In code, you are limited to moving a control to the top or the back of the z-order using the `ZOrder` method. The syntax is

```
ControlName.ZOrder(position)
```

Set the `Position` argument to `fmTop` or `fmBottom`.

Focus and the Tab Order

When a form is displayed during program execution, one control has the focus. This is indicated in various ways for different controls, the most common being the display of a dotted outline on or around the control. In Figure 21-5, for example, CheckBox2 has the focus.

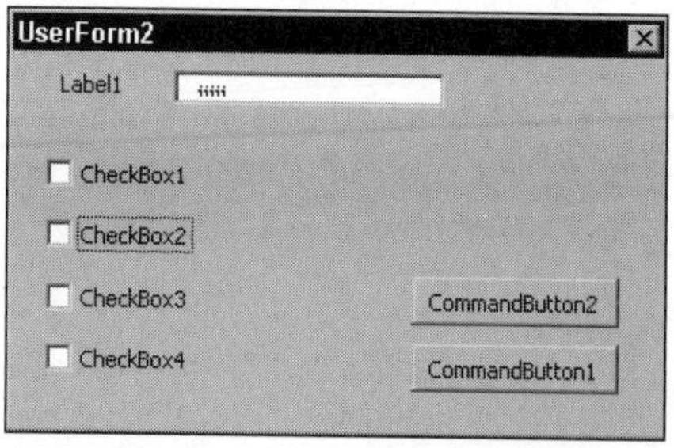

Figure 21-5 *The control with the focus is usually indicated by a dotted outline.*

When a control has the focus, it receives user input as dictated by the nature of the control. For example

- A TextBox with the focus accepts characters and editing commands from the keyboard.
- A CheckBox or OptionButton with the focus is toggled between True and False by the Spacebar.
- A CommandButton with the focus is selected.
- The items in a ComboBox or ListBox with the focus can be scrolled through using the Up and Down arrow keys.

When the form is displayed, the user can move the focus to a control by clicking it (clicking also selects CommandButton controls). The user can also move the focus by pressing Tab or Shift+Tab. The order in which the focus moves between controls is called the *tab order*, with Tab moving forward in the order and Shift+Tab moving backwards.

 If you want clicking to select a CommandButton **control without moving the focus to it, set the control's** TakeFocusOnClick **property to False. This is useful when you want a** CommandButton **to carry out some action, but leave the form displayed while leaving the focus unchanged.**

For some forms, having the correct tab order can make a difference in how usable the form is. In a data entry form, for example, the tab order should follow the natural order of data entry, with the last tab taking the focus to the OK button. There are two control properties that relate to the tab order:

- TabStop. If True, the control can receive the focus by tabbing. If False, the control can receive the focus only by clicking with the mouse. The default is True for all controls.
- TabIndex. A numeric value specifying the position of the control within the tab order. The first control has TabIndex equal to zero.

When you place controls on a form, the TabIndex property is assigned in order. Often this does not result in the tab order that is suitable for the form. There are three ways to change the tab order. You can manually edit the TabIndex property of all the controls on the form, but this is time-consuming. You can also use the View ⇨ Tab Order command, which displays the Tab Order dialog box as shown in Figure 21-6. To change the tab order, select a control in the list and use the Move Up and Move Down buttons to change its position in the tab order.

The last way to change the tab order is in code, by calling the UserForm object's SetDefaultTabOrder method. This method creates a tab order beginning with the control in the top left corner of the form and then moving across and down. You can also call this method on a Frame control to set the tab order for controls on the frame. This method of setting the tab order is appropriate only when the controls on the form are arranged according to the desired tab order.

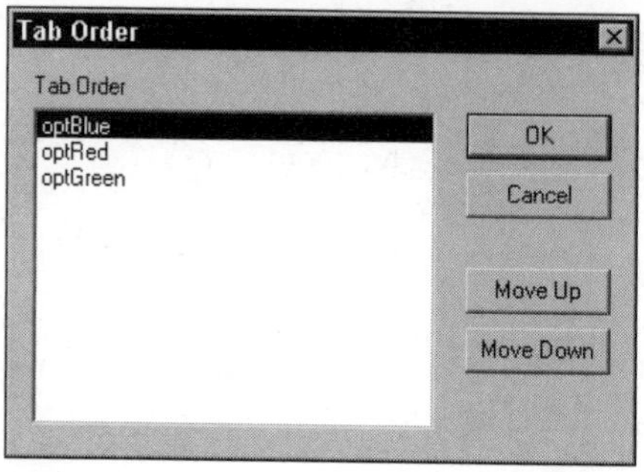

Figure 21-6   You can set the tab order in the Tab Order dialog box.

The Label **control has a** TabIndex **property, but it cannot receive the focus and has no** TabStop **property. When tabbing, the focus moves to the control that follows the** Label **in the tab order, or the control that precedes it when pressing Shift+Tab.**

When a user form is displayed, the focus is by default set to the control with TabIndex = 0. To set the focus to another control, call that control's SetFocus method. You can use this method at any time to move the focus as required by the program.

Tab Order and the Frame Control

When a form includes a Frame control that has other controls on it, two independent tab orders exist:

- The form itself has a tab order that includes all control on the form, including the Frame control, but not the control on the Frame control.
- The Frame control has its own tab order for the controls it contains.

When tabbing through such a form, the focus moves through the form's tab order until it reaches the frame. The focus then moves through the control on the Frame in order. Finally, the focus moves back to the next control (the one following the Frame) in the form's tab order.

These separate tab orders are reflected in the Tab Order dialog box. When the form or a control on it is selected, the Tab Order dialog box displays the tab order for the controls on the form (including any Frame controls) but not the controls on the Frame. If the Frame control or any control on it is selected, the Tab Order dialog box displays the tab order for the controls on the Frame.

Done!

REVIEW

In this session you learned some of the more advanced aspects of designing and using user forms.

- Each control responds to certain user events, and you can write code that is executed when an event occurs.
- Controls on the form are by default aligned with a grid. You can change the size of the grid or turn it off.
- The VBA Editor's Format menu contains many commands that assist you in placing, aligning, and sizing controls.
- When two or more controls overlap, the one that is displayed on top is controlled by the z-order.
- When a form is displayed, pressing Tab moves the focus from control to control in an order determined by the tab order.

QUIZ YOURSELF

1. What event occurs when the data in a control changes? (See the "Using Control Events" section.)
2. How do you change the spacing of the form design grid? (See the "The Form Grid" section.)
3. When selecting multiple controls to align, to which control are the others aligned? (See the "Control Placement and Alignment Tools" section.)
4. At runtime, how do you bring a control to the top of the z-order? (See the "Overlapping Controls and the Z-Order" section.)
5. What property determines whether a control can receive the focus by tabbing? (See the "Focus and the Tab Order" section.)

A User Form Example

Session Checklist

✔ Planning the sample project

✔ Creating the workbook

✔ Designing the form

✔ Writing the code

✔ Validating data

✔ Testing the project

**30 Min.
To Go**

Planning the Project

This example of an Excel program that uses a user form to assist the user in entering data is something that you might want to do in the real world. Of course, the user could always enter data directly into a worksheet, so why bother creating a program and a user form for the purpose? There are several reasons:

- **User fatigue.** Staring at a grid of worksheet rows and columns for extended periods can induce fatigue and increase the chance of errors. A nicely designed user form is much easier on the eyes.

- **Greater accuracy.** You can write code to ensure that each item of data is placed in the proper location in the worksheet. Manual entry is much more prone to mistakes.

- **Data validation.** Code in a user form can validate the data that was entered and perform checks, such as verifying that a zip code, for example, contains five digits and nothing more (or, in the case of the newer codes, nine digits and a dash). It's much easier to catch bad data before it is entered than to deal with it later.

Here's the scenario for the project. A workbook is being used to maintain name and address data for a group of people. The workbook is named Addresses.xls, and the worksheet that the data is on is also called Addresses. This worksheet contains column headings for the various items of data, as shown in Figure 22-1. For simplicity's sake, let's assume that all addresses are in the United States.

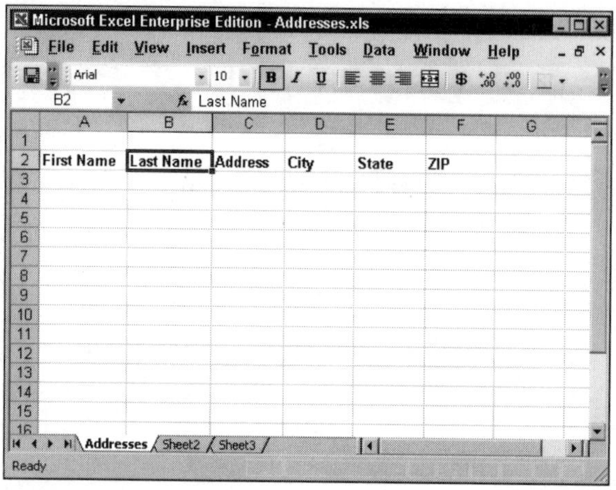

Figure 22-1   *The template for the Addresses worksheet*

When the program runs, it performs the following tasks:

1. Makes the Addresses worksheet active.
2. Locates the first blank row of data. The workbook may contain existing data, or it may be blank as shown in Figure 22-1.
3. Displays a user form that enables the user to enter the data for one person.
4. Continues displaying the user form until all data has been entered.
5. Saves the workbook and then closes the program.

The user form itself has the following functionality:

- Provides TextBox controls for entry of first name, last name, address, city, and five-digit zip code.
- Provides a ListBox control for selection of state.
- Displays a Next command button that saves the current data in the worksheet and displays the form again for more data entry.
- Displays a Done command button that saves the current data, saves the workbook, and closes the form.
- Displays a Cancel command button that discards the current data and closes the form.
- Verifies that no field is left blank.
- Verifies that the zip code entry is a valid zip code.

Part 1: Creating the Workbook

The first task to complete is creating the Addresses workbook. Follow these steps:

1. Start Excel to open a new, blank workbook.
2. Rename Sheet1 to Addresses by double-clicking the name tab on the worksheet and then entering the new name.
3. Enter the data column headings as shown in Figure 22-1. You can format these any way you want, but be sure they are in cells A2 through F2.
4. Save the workbook as Addresses.

At this point the workbook template is complete, and you can proceed with designing the user form.

Part 2: Designing the Form

To create the new, blank user form and set its properties:

1. Press Alt+F11 to open the VBA Editor.
2. In the Project window, click the entry labeled VBAProject (Addresses).
3. Select Insert ⇨ UserForm to add a new user form to the project.
4. Use the Properties window to change the form's Name property to frmAddresses and its Caption property to Address Entry.

The next steps add the TextBox controls for data entry, a ComboBox control for the states, CommandButton controls for the actions, and Label controls to identify each text box and the list box.

1. Add a TextBox control to the form, and change its Name property to txtFirstName.
2. Add a Label control next to the TextBox, and change its Caption property to First Name:.
3. Add four more TextBox controls, changing the Name properties to txtLastName, txtAddress, txtCity, and txtZip.
4. Put a Label control next to each of the new TextBox controls, and set the Caption properties to Last Name:, Address:, City:, and Zip Code:.
5. Add a ComboBox control to the form and change its Name property to cmbStates. Change its Style property to fmStyleDropDownList.
6. Put a Label control next to the ComboBox with the Caption property set to State:.
7. Add a CommandButton control. Change its Name property to cmdDone and its Caption property to Done.
8. Add another CommandButton control. Change its Name property to cmdNext, its Caption property to Next, and its Default property to True.
9. Add a third CommandButton control. Change its Name property to cmdCancel, its Caption property to Cancel, and its Cancel property to True.

All of the required controls are now on the form. Use the form designer's formatting commands and tools to arrange and size the controls as you want. Your finished design should look similar to Figure 22-2.

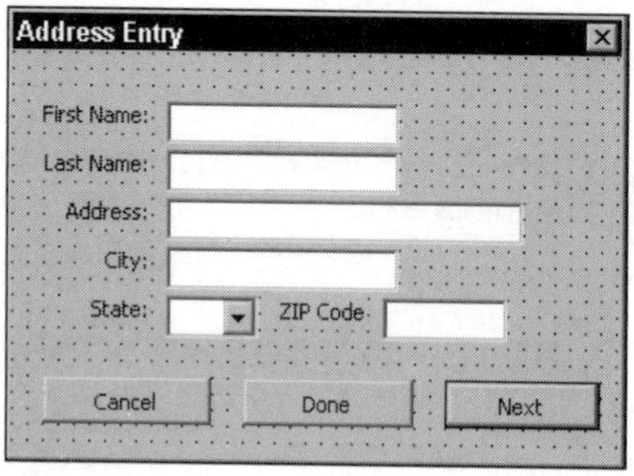

Figure 22-2 *The form after placing all of the controls*

This is a good time to check the tab order of the controls on the form. The desired order is to have the six data entry controls at the top of the tab order, in the correct sequence, followed by the three CommandButton controls.

Part 3: Writing the Initialization Code

The initialization code for this form needs to do only one thing: load the ComboBox control with abbreviations for all the states. For the sake of brevity, the code in this example loads only some states into the control; a real application would, of course, need to have all states in the ComboBox.

To add this code:

1. Click the View Code button in the Project window to open the code-editing window for the user form.
2. From the list at the top left of the window, select UserForm.
3. From the list at the top right of the window, select Initialize.
4. Enter the code from Listing 22-1 into this event procedure.

Listing 22-1 *User form initialization code that loads state abbreviations into the ComboBox*

```
Private Sub UserForm_Initialize()

'Load the combobox with states.
cmbStates.AddItem "AL"
cmbStates.AddItem "AR"
cmbStates.AddItem "CA"
cmbStates.AddItem "CO"
cmbStates.AddItem "FL"
cmbStates.AddItem "LA"
```

```
cmbStates.AddItem "MD"
cmbStates.AddItem "NC"
cmbStates.AddItem "NY"
cmbStates.AddItem "WV"

End Sub
```

Part 4: Restricting Zip Code Entry to Digits

A nice touch for this project is to restrict data entry in the zip code field to digits. This can be considered a form of data verification. Rather than checking data after it is entered (as will be done for some fields in the next section), it is sometimes more efficient to simply prevent improper data from being entered in the first place.

The way to examine keyboard input before it reaches a control is with the KeyDown event. As you learned in Session 21, this event receives an argument that identifies the key that was pressed. If the key is acceptable, it is passed through; if not, it is cancelled.

From the list of KeyCode values in the VBA online help, you can see the code values for the keys 0 through 9 are 48 though 57; therefore, if the KeyDown event procedure receives a KeyCode argument in the range 48 through 57, a digit was entered and can be passed through. Any other values must be cancelled.

You can restrict the data in the txtZip **TextBox to five characters by setting its** MaxLength **property, although that is not done in this project.**

To add this code to the form, open the code-editing window for the form and then add the KeyDown event procedure for the txtZip control. Add the code from Listing 22-2 to the procedure. Note the use of the Beep statement, which causes the system to make a sound if an incorrect key is pressed.

Listing 22-2   *The KeyDown event procedure for the TextBox passes through only digits*

```
Private Sub txtZip_KeyDown(ByVal KeyCode As MSForms.ReturnInteger, _
    ByVal Shift As Integer)

' Pass through only digits.
If KeyCode < 48 Or KeyCode > 57 Then
    KeyCode = 0
    Beep
End If

End Sub
```

As written in Listing 22-2, the TextBox accepts only digits entered at the top of the keyboard, not those entered using the numeric keypad. It is a good programming exercise for you to modify the code so that keypad input is accepted as well.

Part 5: Writing the Data Validation Code

The verification code checks the data when the user clicks the Next or Done button. The specific items that need to be checked are:

- The First Name, Last Name, Address, and City fields are not blank.
- A state is selected.
- The zip code field contains five characters. Because input to this field has been restricted to digits, this is all the verification that is required.

If the verification is successful, the data is entered in the worksheet, and the form is cleared and displayed again for another entry. Alternatively, if the Done button was selected, the form is closed. You can see that the verification is performed when the user clicks either the Next or Done button. For this reason the verification code should not be placed in the Click event procedure for a button, but rather in its own procedure. This procedure can then be called from both the Done and the Next buttons' Click event procedures.

Follow these steps to create the validation procedure:

1. Display the code-editing window for the user form.
2. Select Insert ⇨ Procedure to open the Add Procedure dialog box.
3. Enter ValidateData as the procedure name; select Function under Type.
4. Click OK.

The validation code is placed in a function (instead of a sub procedure) so it can return a value to the calling program: True if validation succeeds, False if it fails.

The code for the validation procedure is shown in Listing 22-3. Note that in addition to the code within the function, the return specifier As Boolean has been added to the first line of the function. You should add the code in this listing to your program.

Listing 22-3   *The Data Validation function*

```
Public Function ValidateData() As Boolean

' Returns True if the data in the user form
' is complete, False otherwise. Displays a
' message identifying the problem.

If txtFirstName.Value = "" Then
    MsgBox "You must enter a first name."
    ValidateData = False
    Exit Function
End If
If txtLastName.Value = "" Then
    MsgBox "You must enter a last name."
```

```
        ValidateData = False
        Exit Function
    End If
    If txtAddress.Value = "" Then
        MsgBox "You must enter an address."
        ValidateData = False
        Exit Function
    End If
    If txtCity.Value = "" Then
        MsgBox "You must enter a city."
        ValidateData = False
        Exit Function
    End If
    If cmbStates.Value = "" Then
        MsgBox "You must select a state."
        ValidateData = False
        Exit Function
    End If
    If txtZip.TextLength <> 5 Then
        MsgBox "You must enter a 5 digit zip code."
        ValidateData = False
        Exit Function
    End If

    ValidateData = True

End Function
```

Part 6: Completing the Project

**10 Min.
To Go**

To be complete, this project needs only the Click event procedures for the three CommandButton controls. To reiterate, this is what the command buttons should do:

- The Next button validates the data. If validation succeeds, the data is entered in the worksheet, and the form is cleared for entry of the next address. If validation fails, the form retains its data so the user can correct it as needed.

- The Done button performs the same tasks as the Next button with one exception: If validation succeeds, the form closes after the data is entered in the worksheet.

- The Cancel button discards any data currently entered in the form and then closes the form.

You may have noticed that the Done and Next buttons share a task, which is entering the validated data in the worksheet. Whenever a task needs to be performed in more than one situation, a programmer recognizes this as an opportunity for putting the required code in a procedure. If you create a procedure that transfers the data from the form to the worksheet, this procedure can be called by both the Done and the Next button's Click event procedure.

At the same time, the form needs code to clear all data from its controls. This is necessary when the Next button is clicked, of course, but also when the Cancel or Done button is clicked. Even though the form is hidden with the Hide method, it retains any data in its controls the next time it is displayed. For this reason, the controls need to be cleared. This is a simple matter of setting the Value property of each control to a blank string. This code is placed in a procedure named ClearForm, as shown in Listing 22-4. Add this procedure to the form now.

Listing 22-4   *The ClearForm procedure erases all data from the form's controls*

```
Public Sub ClearForm()

' Clears all data from the form.
txtFirstName.Value = ""
txtLastName.Value = ""
txtAddress.Value = ""
txtCity.Value = ""
txtZip.Value = ""
cmbStates.Value = ""

End Sub
```

Entering the data into the worksheet requires that the program locate the first empty data row. You know that the first column heading is in cell A2. This means that the first blank row could start in cell A3 or any cell below it. There are several ways you could identify the first empty row. The one used here is as follows:

1. Start with cell A2 as a reference point.
2. Use the CurrentRegion property to get a range containing the header row plus all existing data.
3. Use the Offset method to get a range offset by the number of rows in the original range. This new range is one row below the original range and contains the six cells in the first empty row.
4. Use the Cells property to access individual cells in this range to insert the data.

The code for the EnterDataInWorksheet procedure is shown in Listing 22-5. Add this procedure to the user form using the techniques you have already learned.

Listing 22-5   *The EnterDataInWorksheet procedure*

```
Public Sub EnterDataInWorksheet()

' Copies data from the user form
' to the next blank row in the worksheet.
```

```
Dim r As Range, r1 As Range

Set r = Worksheets("Addresses").Range("A2").CurrentRegion
Set r1 = r.Offset(r.Rows.Count, 0)
r1.Cells(1).Value = txtFirstName.Value
r1.Cells(2).Value = txtLastName.Value
r1.Cells(3).Value = txtAddress.Value
r1.Cells(4).Value = txtCity.Value
r1.Cells(5).Value = cmbStates.Value
r1.Cells(6).Value = txtZip.Value

End Sub
```

Now that the procedure for data entry has been written, the project needs only the Click event procedures for the three CommandButton controls to be finished. This code is shown in Listing 22-6. Note that each of these three event procedures calls the ClearForm procedure that you created earlier. Enter this code in the user form, and the project is ready to try.

Listing 22-6 *The Click event procedures for the CommandButton controls*

```
Private Sub cmdCancel_Click()

ClearForm
Me.Hide

End Sub

Private Sub cmdDone_Click()

If ValidateData = True Then
    EnterDataInWorksheet
    ClearForm
    Me.Hide
End If

End Sub

Private Sub cmdNext_Click()

If ValidateData = True Then
    EnterDataInWorksheet
    ClearForm
End If

End Sub
```

Part 7: Testing the Project

You can test the project by pressing F5 while the user form is open in the VBA Editor. You can also write a macro that displays the form using the Show method. Figure 22-3 shows the program in action. When you try it out, you'll see that this program and user form makes data entry much easier than it would be to enter the data directly in the workbook.

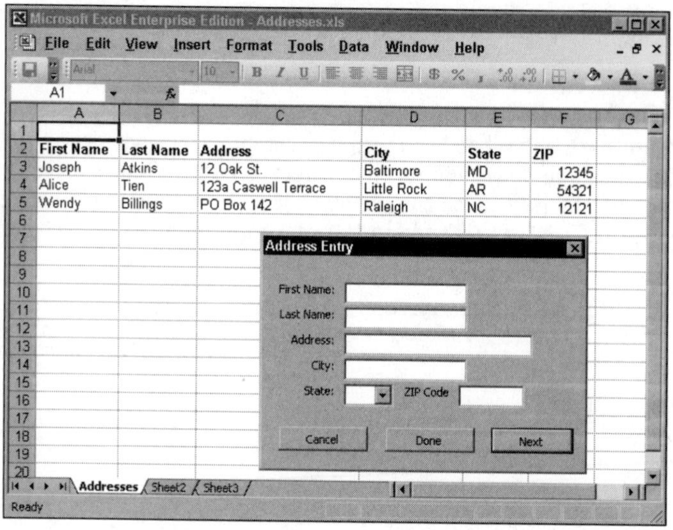

Figure 22-3   *Running the program to enter addresses*

REVIEW

Done!

This session walked you through the complete process of creating a real-world program that uses a user form for data entry.

- It's always a good idea to plan your project before you start programming.
- Data validation is an important part of any program for data entry.
- Data validation can be performed after the data is entered, or while it is being entered.
- When you have code that will be used in more than one location in a program, place it in a procedure.

QUIZ YOURSELF

1. Give two advantages to using a user form for data entry. (See the "Planning the Project" section.)

2. Name one task that a form's initialization code might perform. (See the "Writing the Initialization Code" section.)

3. In which event would you place code that restricts entry into a TextBox control to certain characters? (See the "Restricting Zip Code Entry to Digits" section.)

Working with Events

Session Checklist

✔ The categories of Excel events

✔ Writing event handler code

✔ Enabling and disabling events

✔ Workbook, worksheet, and application-level events

✔ How to use events not related to an object

**30 Min.
To Go**

E vents are an important part of Excel programming. You had an introduction to events in Session 21 where user form controls and some of the events they can respond to were covered. That's only part of the picture, however. Understanding and working with Excel events is an important tool for creating easy-to-use, responsive applications.

Event Categories

The events to which an Excel program can respond can be categorized in two ways. One method organizes events in terms of the object that receives the event, as follows:

- Application events
- Workbook events
- Worksheet events
- User form and control events
- Nonobject events

Nonobject events is a special category that contains events not associated with a specific object.

Events for user form controls were covered in Session 21.

The other way to categorize events is by the event itself, such as what happens to trigger the event. This results in three categories of events:

- Events that are always the result of user actions, such as clicking a control on a user form or pressing a key
- Events that can be caused either by user action or by VBA code, such as opening a workbook or activating a chart
- Events that have no relation to user actions, such as the occurrence of a particular time of day

Overall, the assortment of events offered by Excel should meet just about any programming need.

Event Handler Code

Your program responds to events by placing code in *event handlers*. An event handler is a special kind of VBA procedure that is automatically executed when the related event occurs. There's a strict rule you must follow when naming these procedures; the name must be in the form of *objectname_eventname*. For example, the TextBox control has the Click event; for a TextBox whose name is txtAddress, the event handler procedure must be named txtAddress_Click. This is essential because the procedure name connects the procedure to the event.

In most situations, the VBA Editor creates the outline (the first and last lines) of the event procedure for you. When a code-editing window is open, there are two drop-down lists at the top of the window (see Figure 23-1). The object list, at the top left, shows those objects for which event-handing code can be placed in the current window. The event list at the top right lists the events for the object selected in the first list. When you select an event, the Editor automatically enters the outline of the procedure in the window. You can enter event procedures manually, but this auto-entry feature saves time and reduces errors.

If you do not create an event procedure for an event or if the event procedure contains no code, Excel ignores the event.

Where should you place event-handling procedures in your project? If the procedure is placed in the wrong location, it does not respond to its event even though it is named properly. The following sections provide some specific advice on the placement of events; here are some guidelines:

- Event procedures for a user form (and its controls) should always go in the user form module itself.
- Event procedures for a workbook, worksheet, or chart should always be placed in the project associated with the workbook.

- If the object and the event can be found in the object and event list at the top of the editing window, it is all right to place the procedure in the current module.
- Never place event procedures in a code module (those project modules listed under the Modules node in the Project window).

The object list   **The event list**

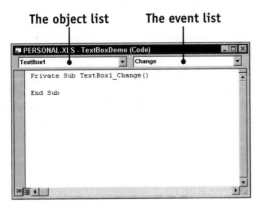

Figure 23-1 *Entering event procedures in a code-editing window*

Event Sequences

When working with events, you need to understand that some actions result in more than one event being triggered in Excel. In these situations, the multiple events occur in a specific order. In some situations you need to be aware of this order when deciding which event procedure to use for your code. Here's an example: When a new worksheet is added to a workbook, the following three application-level events are triggered in this order:

- WorkbookNewSheet occurs when you add a new worksheet.
- SheetDeactivate occurs when the previously active worksheet is deactivated.
- SheetActivate occurs when the new worksheet is activated.

A similar situation exists when the user clicks a control on a user form: the MouseDown, MouseUp, and Click events occur in that order.

Using the Debug.Print statement in event procedures, you can determine which events occur and in what order.

**20 Min.
To Go**

Enabling and Disabling Events

Excel's default is for all events to be enabled. You can disable most events by setting the Application object's EnableEvents property to False. Doing this disables all events except those for user forms and controls. When would you need to disable events? This situation arises when the code in an event procedure would cause the same event to be triggered again, either directly or indirectly.

Here's an example. The Worksheet_Change event is triggered whenever data in the worksheet is modified. You can use this event for data validation, such as verifying that the value entered in a certain cell is always within a specified range. If the data falls outside this range, your code displays a message and clears the cell so the user can re-enter the data. The problem is that the act of clearing the cell triggers the Worksheet_Change event again, resulting in a never-ending cycle of Worksheet_Change events. To avoid this problem, you would alter the code in the event procedure so that the code does the following:

1. Set the EnableEvents property to False.
2. Clear the worksheet cell.
3. Set the EnableEvents property to True.

Because it is a property of the Application **object, the** EnableEvents **property applies to all open workbooks. You cannot selectively disable events for one workbook.**

Workbook Events

There are several Excel events that happen at the level of a workbook. Those workbook-level events that are used most often are summarized in Table 23-1.

Table 23-1 *Workbook-Level Events*

Event	Occurs when
Activate	A workbook is activated
BeforeClose	A workbook is about to be closed
BeforePrint	All or part of the workbook is about to be printed
BeforeSave	A workbook is about to be saved
Deactivate	A workbook is deactivated
NewSheet	A new workbook is created
Open	A workbook is opened
SheetActivate	Any worksheet is activated
SheetChange	Any worksheet is changed by the user or code
SheetDeactivate	Any worksheet is deactivated
SheetSelectionChange	The selection on any worksheet is changed

To work with workbook-level events, open the `ThisWorkbook` module for the project. Select Workbook in the object list; the event list contains all of these events plus some not covered here. The following sections provide more details and examples on two of the workbook-level events.

The Open Event

The `Open` event is perhaps the most widely used of the workbook-level events. Triggered when a workbook is opened, it can be used for a variety of tasks that include:

- Opening other required workbooks
- Activating a specific worksheet
- Defining custom toolbars
- Displaying welcome messages, reminders, or program instructions

Be aware that if the user holds down the Shift key when opening a workbook, the `Open` event is not triggered.

Excel's security settings may prevent macros from being executed. See Session 24 for more details on macro security.

The event procedure in Listing 23-1 shows how to use the `Open` event to perform a weekly backup of a workbook. When the workbook is opened, the `Open` event procedure checks to see if today is Friday (because Friday is the day on which you want the backup performed). If so, the `SaveCopyAs` method is used to back the workbook up to a network drive. In this example, it is assumed that G: is a network drive.

Listing 23-1 *Using the Open event procedure to perform weekly backups*

```
Private Sub Workbook_Open()

' If today is Friday, back up
' the workbook to a network drive.

If Weekday(Now) = vbFriday Then
    ThisWorkbook.SaveCopyAs "g:\backups\" & ThisWorkbook.Name
End If

End Sub
```

You could also use the `Workbook_Close` event procedure to perform a backup, which would have the added advantage of including the latest changes in the backed up file.

The NewSheet Event

The NewSheet event is triggered whenever a new worksheet is added to the workbook. An argument that identifies the new sheet is passed to this event procedure. The syntax is

```
Private Sub Workbook_NewSheet(ByVal sh As Object)
...
End Sub
```

Code in the procedure can make use of the reference to the new sheet to perform various actions, such as inserting row and column headings into the worksheet. In the following example, the NewSheet procedure is used to prompt the user for a name for the sheet, which is then assigned to the worksheet's Name property. This ensures that no new worksheets keep the default name that is assigned by Excel. The code is shown in Listing 23-2.

Listing 23-2   *Using the NewSheet event to prompt the user for a sheet name*

```
Private Sub Workbook_NewSheet(ByVal Sh As Object)

Dim sheetname As String

Do
    sheetname = InputBox("Enter a name for the new worksheet")
Loop Until sheetname <> ""
Sh.Name = sheetname

End Sub
```

Worksheet Events

The events that are detected by a worksheet are summarized in Table 23-2.

Table 23-2   *Frequently Used Worksheet-Level Events*

Event	Occurs when
Activate	The worksheet is activated
Calculate	The worksheet is recalculated
Change	Data in the worksheet is changed
Deactivate	The worksheet is deactivated
SelectionChange	The selection in the worksheet is changed

The event procedures for a worksheet-level event must be placed in the module for that specific worksheet. To enter the outline of the event procedure, select Worksheet from the object list at the top left of the code-editing window and then select the specific event from the events list.

The Change Event

The Change event is triggered whenever cells in the worksheet are changed. This occurs when the change is initiated by the user as well as when the change is made by VBA code. Not every kind of change is registered, however, as follows:

- Changing cell comments does not trigger the Change event.
- Changing cell formatting does not trigger the event, but clearing all formatting with the Edit ⇨ Clear Formats command does.
- Pressing Delete to delete cell contents triggers the event even if the cell was empty.
- Some Excel commands trigger this event (for example, Tools ⇨ Spelling) while others do not (for example, Data ⇨ Sort).

One possible use for the Change event is to keep track of changes in a worksheet; however, Excel's own Track Changes command (on the Tools menu) does an excellent job of tracking worksheet changes without the bother of programming. One area where this event can really be useful is with data validation. While Excel has a built-in data validation feature, it has limitations that can be overcome by using the Change event. This is shown in the following demonstration.

Using the Change Event for Data Validation

For this demonstration, I return to the Loan Calculator worksheet that was last visited in Session 14. This worksheet calculated monthly payments for an installment loan, with the user entering values for the loan amount, the interest rate, and the loan term. An additional degree of safety could be achieved for this application by validating the amount entered for the interest rate. While loan interest rates vary, they do tend to fall within a certain range. Interest rates in the range of 2 to 10 percent, for example, are common, while a rate of 50 percent would be very unlikely — unless you are borrowing from your local loan shark!

The goal of this project is to validate the data in the Interest Rate cell. Whenever this data is changed, the program checks to see if it falls in the range of 2 to 10 percent. If not, the program displays a message to the user and asks him to verify the value that was entered. The Loan Calculator program is shown in Figure 23-2. The interest rate is entered in cell C5.

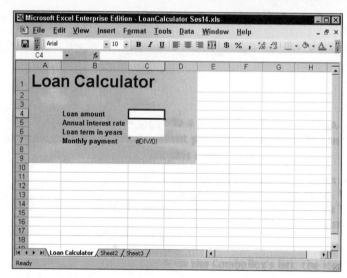

Figure 23-2　The Loan Calculator worksheet

If you did not save a copy of the Loan Calculator worksheet, return to Session 14 and run the program in Listing 14-2 to create it.

When the Change event procedure is called, it is passed an argument containing a Range object for the range that was changed. By checking the Address property of this Range object, the program can determine which cell was changed. When cell C5 has been changed, this property returns the value $C$5. It is then easy to check the value in this cell and, if it is out of range, display a message and select the cell.

To add the data validation code, follow these steps:

1. Open the Loan Calculator worksheet.
2. Press Alt+F11 to open the VBA Editor.
3. In the Project window, double-click the Sheet1 (Loan Calculator) item to open the code-editing window for the worksheet.
4. At the top of the editing window, select Worksheet from the object list and Change from the event list.
5. Add the code from Listing 23-3 to the Worksheet_Change event procedure.

Listing 23-3　*Data validation code for the Loan Calculator worksheet*

```
Private Sub Worksheet_Change(ByVal Target As Range)

With Target
    If .Address = "$C$5" Then
        If .Value < 0.02 Or .Value > 0.1 Then
            MsgBox "Please verify the interest rate you just entered."
```

```
            .Select
        End If
    End If
End With

End Sub
```

When the code has been added, return to the worksheet and enter some data. If you enter an interest rate that is less than 2 percent (0.02) or greater then 10 percent (0.10), you get the warning message shown in Figure 23-3.

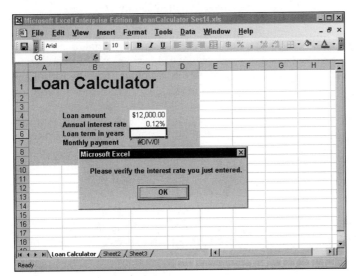

Figure 23-3 *Validating data in the Loan Calculator worksheet*

Application Events

Application-level events are not restricted to a single workbook or worksheet, but respond to events in any workbook or worksheet. The application events that are used most often are summarized in Table 23-3.

Table 23-3 *Frequently Used Application-Level Events*

Event	Occurs when
NewWorkbook	A new workbook is created
SheetActivate	Any worksheet is activated
SheetChange	Any worksheet is modified (by the user or code)

Continued

Table 2-3

Continued

Event	Occurs when
SheetDeactivate	Any worksheet is deactivated
WorkbookActivate	Any workbook is activated
WorkbookBeforeClose	Before any workbook is closed
WorkbookDeactivate	Any workbook is deactivated
WorkbookNewSheet	A new worksheet is added to any workbook

Note that some of these same events are also detected at the workbook or worksheet level. For example, when a workbook is activated, the Application.WorkbookActivate event is fired, and the event procedure receives an argument identifying the workbook. The individual workbook's Activate event is then fired. Because this second event procedure is associated with a specific workbook (the one that was activated), there is no need for an argument to the event procedure identifying the workbook. Whether your program uses the more global event at the application level or the more local event at the workbook or worksheet level depends entirely on the needs of the program and the task the event procedure is to carry out.

Writing Application Event Procedures

Application-level event procedures require some special programming techniques. Because all of the modules in a VBA project are associated with either a specific workbook or a specific worksheet, you cannot use them to create code for the entire Excel application. Rather, you must follow these steps:

1. Select Insert ⇨ Class Module to add a new class module to the form.
2. If desired, change the Name property of the class module from the default Class1 to something else, such as AppEvents.
3. In the code-editing window for the new module, add the following line of code (you can replace the name xlApp with any legal VBA name):

   ```
   Public WithEvents xlApp As Application
   ```

4. Select Insert ⇨ Module to add a new code module to the project. Alternatively, you can open an existing code module, if you prefer.
5. At the module level (outside any procedures), add the following line of code. You can replace XL with any legal VBA name. AppEvents is the name that you assigned to the class module in step 2.

   ```
   Dim XL As New AppEvents
   ```

6. Connect the declared object with the existing Application object. This code can be placed in any module, but is commonly placed in the Workbook_Open event procedure in the ThisWorkbook module:

   ```
   Set XL.xlApp = Application
   ```

7. Return to the class module to write your application-level event procedures. When you select the object name (xlApp in this example) in the objects list at the top of the code-editing window, the events for the Application object are available in the events list.

The following example walks you through the steps of using an application-level event procedure.

The WorkbookBeforeClose Event

**10 Min.
To Go**

This example program makes use of the WorkbookBeforeClose event to query the user each time she tries to close a workbook. This event procedure has the following syntax:

```
Private Sub object_WorkbookBeforeClose(ByVal Wb As Workbook, _
    Cancel As Boolean)
```

When the event occurs and the procedure is called, the Wb argument contains a reference to the workbook that is being closed. If the Cancel argument is set to True by code in the procedure, the close is aborted; therefore, this event procedure is the place to put code that queries the user for confirmation before closing any workbook.

1. Open the workbook that you want to use for this project, or you can use a new, blank workbook.
2. Press Alt+F11 to open the VBA Editor.
3. Select Insert ➪ Class Module to add a new class module to the project. Change its Name property to AppEvents.
4. Add the following line of code to the class module:
   ```
   Public WithEvents xlApp As Application
   ```
5. Select Insert ➪ Class Module to add a new code module to the project or open an existing code module.
6. In the code module at the module level (outside any procedures), add the following line of code:
   ```
   Public XL As AppEvents
   ```
7. Double-click the ThisWorkbook node in the Project window to open its code-editing window.
8. Insert the Open event procedure for the Workbook object and then add the following line of code to it:
   ```
   Set XL.xlApp = Application
   ```
9. Return to the code-editing window for the class module.
10. Insert the WorkbookBeforeClose event procedure for the xlApp object.
11. Add the code from Listing 23-4 to this event procedure.

Listing 23-4 *Code in the WorkbookBeforeClose event procedure verifies the closing of any workbook*

```
Private Sub xlApp_WorkbookBeforeClose(ByVal Wb As Workbook, Cancel As
Boolean)

Dim reply As Integer
reply = MsgBox("Close " & Wb.Name & "?", vbYesNo)
If reply = vbNo Then
    Cancel = True
End If

End Sub
```

After completing the project, you must close the workbook and then re-open it. This is necessary because an essential part of the code is in the workbook's Open event procedure, and it is not executed until the workbook is opened. At this point, you can open and then try to close any other workbook, or try to close the original workbook. A confirmation dialog box pops up, and you can select to close the workbook or not. Here's how this works:

1. The workbook contains a class named AppEvents. This class contains a variable named xlApp that is of type Application — in other words, it can hold a reference to the Excel application itself.

2. The code module declares a variable named XL that refers to a new instance of the class AppEvents. This means that the object AppEvents actually exists and the variable xlApp (from step 1) also exists.

3. When the original workbook (containing the program) is opened, its Open event procedure is triggered. The code in this procedure assigns a reference to the Application object to the variable xlApp. At this point the variable xlApp references the running Excel application.

4. When an attempt is made to close a workbook, the WorkbookBeforeClose event is triggered and identified by its name. The xlApp part of the name refers to the Excel application (from step 3), and the remainder of its name identifies the specific event.

As long as the original workbook is open, an attempt to close any workbook triggers the confirmation message.

Other Events

The final events discussed in this session are those that are not associated with a specific object. There are two such events: the OnTime and OnKey events.

The OnTime Event

The OnTime event is trigged at a specific time of day. To define an OnTime event, use the Application object's OnTime method:

```
OnTime(EarliestTime, Procedure, LatestTime, Schedule)
```

- EarliestTime is a required argument specifying the time of day when the event is to be triggered.
- Procedure is a required argument specifying the name of the procedure to be run. This procedure should be placed in a code module.
- LatestTime is an optional argument that specifies the latest time when the event can be triggered.
- Schedule is an optional True/False argument. Set to True (the default) to schedule a new event; set to False to clear a previously scheduled event.

The LatestTime argument is used because Excel triggers an OnTime event only when it is in Ready mode. If another procedure is executing when the time for an OnTime event comes, the OnTime procedure is postponed until the running procedure terminates. If the LatestTime argument is omitted, Excel waits as long as needed to run the OnTime procedure. If this argument is included, Excel waits only until that time, after which the OnTime event does not occur.

The following code tells Excel to run the specified procedure at 5:00 p.m.

```
Application.OnTime TimeValue("5:00PM"), "SomeProcedure"
```

This code cancels the event defined in the previous example:

```
Application.OnTime TimeValue("5:00PM"), "SomeProcedure", , False
```

This code schedules the procedure to run 10 minutes from the current time:

```
Application.OnTime Now + TimeValue("00:10:00"), "SomeProcedure"
```

The following program illustrates a real-world example of using this event. The purpose is to remind workers to take their coffee breaks at 10:00 a.m. and 3:00 p.m. You can create this project in any workbook, as follows:

1. Open the workbook and then open the VBA Editor.
2. Open the code-editing window for the ThisWorkbook module.
3. Insert the code from Listing 23-5 into the Workbook_Open event procedure.
4. Open a code module for the workbook, or create a new one (select Insert ⇨ Module), if necessary.
5. Add the procedure shown in Listing 23-6 to add the break reminder message to the code module.

Listing 23-5   *Code for the Workbook_Open event procedure*

```
Private Sub Workbook_Open()

Application.OnTime TimeValue("10:00AM"), "BreakReminder"
Application.OnTime TimeValue("3:00PM"), "BreakReminder"

End Sub
```

Listing 23-6   *TheBreakReminder procedure is displayed at 10:00 a.m. and 3:00 p.m.*

```
Public Sub BreakReminder()

MsgBox "It's time for your break!"

End Sub
```

After creating the project, save and close the workbook; then reopen it so the Workbook_Open event procedure is triggered. At the appointed times according to the system clock, the reminder message box pops up.

The OnKey Event

The OnKey event is triggered when a specific key (or key combination) is pressed. This event can respond to any keystrokes in Excel and has higher priority than keyboard events related to user form controls, such as KeyDown. You can define OnKey procedures that execute when the specified key or key combination is pressed. To do so, use the Application object's OnKey method, as follows:

```
Application.OnKey(key, Procedure)
```

Key is the key or key combination to detect, and Procedure is the name of the procedure to execute. The Key argument is a string and is constructed as follows:

- For a letter or other character key, use that character.
- For a noncharacter key, use the codes in Table 23-4.
- To specify a key combination, use the + (for Shift), ^ (for Ctrl) and/or % (for Alt) symbols in front of the keycode.

Table 23-4   *Key Codes for the OnKey Method*

Key	Code
BACKSPACE	{BACKSPACE} or {BS}
BREAK	{BREAK}
CAPS LOCK	{CAPSLOCK}

Key	Code
CLEAR	{CLEAR}
DELETE or DEL	{DELETE} or {DEL}
DOWN ARROW	{DOWN}
END	{END}
ENTER (numeric keypad)	{ENTER}
ENTER	~ (tilde)
ESC	{ESCAPE} or {ESC}
HELP	{HELP}
HOME	{HOME}
INS	{INSERT}
LEFT ARROW	{LEFT}
NUM LOCK	{NUMLOCK}
PAGE DOWN	{PGDN}
PAGE UP	{PGUP}
RETURN	{RETURN}
RIGHT ARROW	{RIGHT}
SCROLL LOCK	{SCROLLLOCK}
TAB	{TAB}
UP ARROW	{UP}
F1 through F15	{F1} through {F15}

The following code specifies that the procedure named BackUp is to be executed whenever the user presses Ctrl+B:

```
Application.OnKey("^b", "BackUp")
```

To cancel an OnKey event and return the key to its normal function, call the OnKey method without the Procedure argument. For example, if you had assigned a procedure to the PgUp key, the following code cancels that assignment and returns PgUp to its default function in Excel:

```
Application.OnKey("{PgUp)")
```

Use care when assigning OnKey events. If you reassign key combinations that are used in Excel, such as Ctrl+P for Print or Ctrl+1 for Format Cells, you are likely to confuse and frustrate the user.

If you want to assign a Ctrl+*key* combination to a procedure, it is better to use the Macro dialog box instead of the OnKey method. Refer to Session 2 for information on this option.

Done!

REVIEW

This session showed you how to use Excel's events in your VBA applications.

- Events can be detected at the application, workbook, or worksheet level.
- For a program to respond to an event, you must place the code in the corresponding event handler.
- To disable all events in Excel, set the Application.EnableEvents property to False.
- Some events trigger event procedures at more than one level — for example, at the workbook and worksheet levels.
- Use the OnTime event to execute a procedure at a specific time of day.

QUIZ YOURSELF

1. Are all events triggered by user actions? Explain. (See the "Event Categories" section.)
2. How do the Workbook.SheetChange and the Worksheet.Change events differ? (See the "Workbook Events" and "Worksheet Events" sections.)
3. Is the Change event triggered for any and all changes in a worksheet? (See the "The Change Event" section.)
4. Where must event procedures for worksheet-level events be placed? (See the "Workbook Events" section.)
5. What event would you use to detect when a new worksheet is added to any open workbook? (See the "Workbook Events" section.)

Security Considerations

Session Checklist

✔ Protecting entire workbooks

✔ Preventing changes to worksheet ranges

✔ Preventing users from viewing and modifying VBA code

✔ Using macro security to protect against malicious macro code

✔ Using digital certificates to sign your projects

**30 Min.
To Go**

S ecurity is an important consideration for almost every Excel project. One aspect of security deals with the contents of workbooks, such as preventing users from modifying all or part of a workbook. The other aspect concerns VBA code, including using digital signatures to validate VBA code. These topics are covered in this session.

Workbook Protection

You can protect an entire workbook in two ways. You can require a password for opening and viewing the workbook, and you can also require a password for modifying and saving the workbook. To assign one or both of these passwords to a workbook in Excel, follow these steps:

1. Select File ⇨ Save As.
2. In the Save As dialog box, open the Tools menu (at the top right) and select General Options. Excel displays the Save Options dialog box, as shown in Figure 24-1.

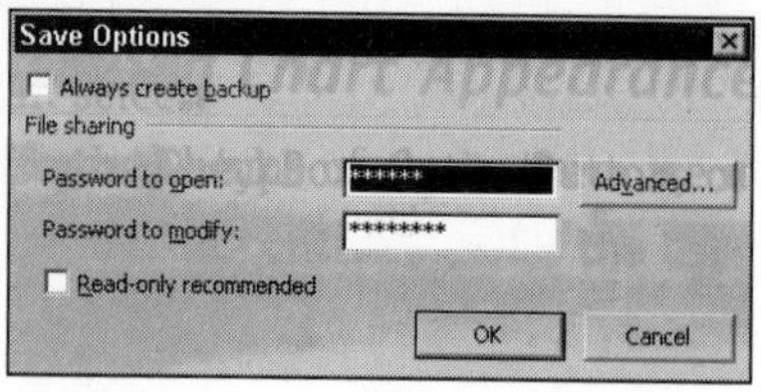

Figure 24-1 *Assigning open and modify passwords for a workbook*

3. Enter a password in the Password to open and/or the Password to modify text boxes, and click OK.

4. When requested, re-enter the password(s) to verify.

5. Back in the Save As dialog box, enter a file name and then click Save.

To save a workbook with password protection from a VBA program, use the SaveAs method. The Password argument specifies the password required to open the file, and the WriteResPassword argument specifies the modify/save password.

The SaveAs **method was explained in detail in Session 3.**

For example, the following code saves the active workbook with "redwine" as the password to open and view, and "rowboat" as the password to modify and save:

```
ActiveWorkbook.SaveAs Filename:= _
    "PWProtected.xls", FileFormat:=xlNormal, Password:="redwine", _
    WriteResPassword:="rowboat",  ReadOnlyRecommended:=False
```

20 Min.
To Go

Worksheet Protection

Workbook protection is a tool that lets you lock selected areas of a worksheet. Its primary use is to prevent unauthorized changes to worksheet cells, ensuring that users are limited to making changes in those cells where it is appropriate. For example, think back to the Loan Calculator worksheet that was developed in Session 14. There are three cells in the worksheet in which the user entered information; other cells are labels and formulas that the user should not change. By using worksheet protection, user changes could be restricted to those three cells (as will be demonstrated soon).

When using worksheet protection, it's a good idea to use some type of formatting to differentiate cells that a user can change from those he or she cannot change. Most often, the cell background color is used for this purpose.

There are two levels to worksheet protection. At the first level, individual cells are either locked or unlocked, with all cells being locked by default. A cell being locked has no effect unless the entire worksheet is protected, which is the second level. Worksheet protection is off by default; therefore, to allow users to enter data only in selected worksheet cells, you must follow these steps:

1. Select the cell(s) that the user will be permitted to edit.
2. Select Format ⇨ Cells to display the Format Cells dialog box, and display the Protection tab (see Figure 24-2).

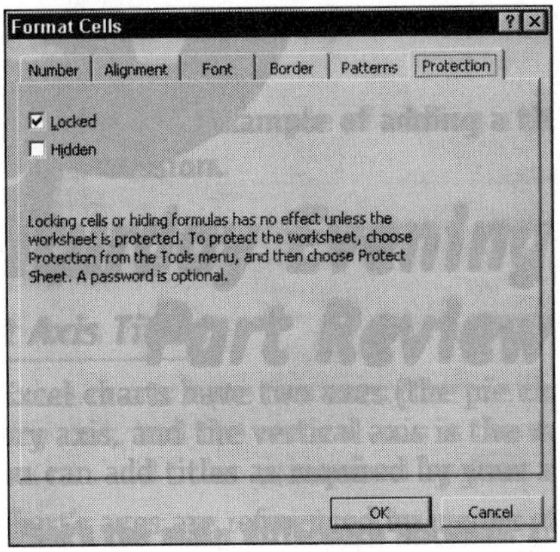

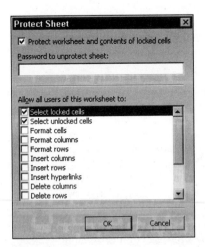

Figure 24-2 *Setting the Locked property for worksheet cells*

3. Turn off the Locked option; then click OK.
4. Repeat steps 1 through 3 to unlock addition cells, if needed.
5. Select Tools ⇨ Protection ⇨ Protect Sheet to display the Protect Sheet dialog box (see Figure 24-3).

Figure 24-3 *Turning worksheet protection on*

6. To ensure that users are not able to remove protection, enter a password in the designated field. If this is not a concern, leave this field blank.
7. Click OK.

To remove protection from a worksheet, select Tools ⇨ Protection ⇨ Unprotect sheet. You have to enter the password if one was assigned.

You should always use worksheet protection in workbooks that will be distributed. You may think you can trust your users not to make changes where they shouldn't, but it's best to be safe.

If you password-protect a worksheet's protection, be sure to keep a record of the password. I know of no way to remove protection if the password is forgotten.

VBA Code and Worksheet Protection

Worksheet protection can be assigned in a VBA program. The procedure to follow is:

1. Define a range for the cell or cells that will not be locked.
2. Set the Range object's Locked property to False.
3. Repeat steps 1 and 2 to unlock additional cells, if required.
4. Call the Worksheet object's Protect method with the appropriate arguments.

The Protect method has no required arguments. When called with no arguments, it applies default protection with no password. If you want to assign a password, use the Password argument. The other arguments specify details of the protection, providing the same options that are available in the Protect Sheet dialog box (see Figure 24-3). You can refer to the online VBA help for more information on these arguments.

If you are using VBA code to assign protection with a password, be sure to protect the code itself (as explained later in this session). Otherwise, the user can learn the password by viewing the code.

Protection Options

If you look again at Figure 24-3, you can see that there is a variety of protection options displayed in the lower part of the dialog box. These options control exactly what the user can and cannot do when protection is on. By default, the user can select locked or unlocked cells and enter data in unlocked cells. All other worksheet changes are prohibited throughout the entire worksheet, not just in locked cells. This includes deleting or adding rows and columns, formatting cells, and changing formatting. This strict protection is perfectly appropriate in many situations, when all the user should be able to do is enter and/or edit data in selected worksheet cells. At other times, however, you may want to provide greater freedom to the user. If so, check the desired options in the Protect Sheet dialog box.

Protecting the Loan Calculator Worksheet

To demonstrate using VBA code to apply worksheet protection, let's return to the Loan Calculator application that was last visited in Session 23. You'll recall that this is a program that creates a worksheet for calculating loan payments. The user enters information about the loan (amount, interest rate, and term), and the program calculates and displays the monthly payment. There are three cells in this worksheet into which the user enters data (cells C4:C6); all other cells should be locked to prevent changes.

To modify this program, add the code in Listing 24-1 to the original code from Listing 14-2. The new code should be placed near the end of the procedure, just before the code that saves the workbook.

Listing 24-1 *Adding worksheet protection to the Loan Calculator worksheet*

```
' Protect the worksheet.
ws.Range("C4:C6").Locked = False
ws.Protect Password:="frogbreath"
```

When the program is run to create the worksheet, the user will not be able to make any changes to the worksheet except for entering data in cells C4:C6.

Protecting Your VBA Code

When you have finished and distributed a VBA project, you certainly do not want users modifying your code. You may also want to prevent users from viewing your code to ensure that the results of all your programming efforts are not "borrowed." You can lock a VBA project and assign a password to it; then, users can run your programs, but they can't view or modify their code.

To protect a VBA project, follow these steps:

1. In the VBA Editor, make sure the correct project is active.
2. Select Tools ⇨ *XXXX* Project Properties (where *XXXX* is the name of the project).
3. In the Project Properties dialog box, select the Protection tab (see Figure 24-4).
4. Select the Lock Project for Viewing option; then enter and confirm the password.
5. Click OK.

When a project is protected, users are prompted for the password if they try to open the project in the VBA Editor.

> **Note** **I recommend that you make it a habit to always protect the VBA code in projects you distribute. There is rarely if ever any valid reason for users to be able to access the code.**

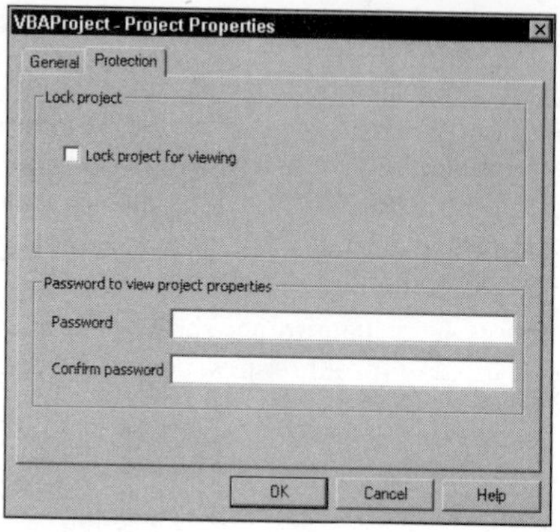

Figure 24-4 *Preventing users from viewing and modifying VBA code*

Macro Security

**10 Min.
To Go**

Because VBA is such a powerful language, it has the potential for serious mischief. A malicious programmer could create macros that could do anything from create a minor annoyance on the user's system to causing major damage by deleting data or operating system files. Given that Excel can execute a macro automatically when a workbook is opened, this problem is even more acute. Clearly, it is not a good idea to let any macro run without restrictions.

Execution of macros is controlled by Excel's Macro Security settings. These settings rely in part on the fact that macros can be digitally signed, as explained later in the session. When a macro has been signed, you know where it comes from and can choose to run it or not depending on the source. To set Excel's macro security level, follow these steps:

1. In Excel, select Tools ➪ Macro ➪ Security to display the Security dialog box.
2. Select the Security Level tab (see Figure 24-5).

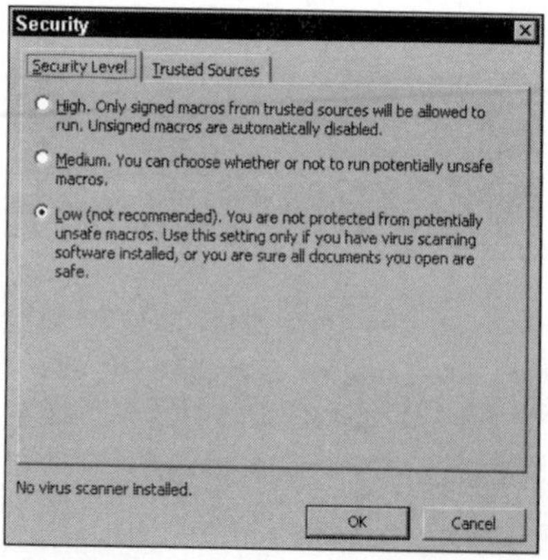

Figure 24-5 *Setting Excel's macro security level*

3. Select the desired security level (see the following list) and then click OK.

The available security levels are

- **High.** Only macros signed by trusted sources are run.
- **Medium.** Macros from trusted sources are run. The user is prompted to run other macros (those signed by sources not on the trusted list or not signed at all).
- **Low.** All macros are run without restriction.

> **Some computer viruses come packaged as Excel macros and can be detected by commercial virus-scanning software. For security in Excel, other Office applications, and for your system in general, you should have one of these products installed and be sure to keep it updated. (The Security Level dialog box displays a message indicating whether a virus scanner is installed.)**

Adding a Trusted Source

When your macro security level is set to Medium or High and you open a workbook or add-in that contains digitally signed macros, Excel compares the digital signature to your current list of trusted sources. If a match is not found, Excel prompts you with details on the source. If you check the Always Trust Macros from this Source option, the source is added to your Trusted Sources list.

Removing a Trusted Source

If you need to remove a source from the Trusted Sources list, follow these steps:

1. In Excel, select Tools ⇨ Macro ⇨ Security to display the Security dialog box.
2. Select the Trusted Sources tab.
3. Select the source and then click the Remove button.
4. Click OK.

Using Digital Certificates to Sign Macros

If you want to sign your macros with a digital certificate, you must first obtain a certificate and install it on your system (see the "Digital Certificates" sidebar); then follow these steps:

1. With the project open and active in the VBA Editor, select Tools ⇨ Digital Signature to display the Digital Signature dialog box (see Figure 24-6). This dialog box displays the certificate that the project is currently signed with, or [No certificate] if it is not signed.

Digital Certificates

A digital certificate can be thought of as an online identity card. Certificates are issued by a certification authority (a commercial firm or other organization), and they contain information about you or your organization as well as the issuing authority. Various encryption techniques are used to prevent counterfeiting of certificates. The information contained in a certificate can be verified via the Internet with the issuing authority. You can perform a Web search for "digital certificate" to find more information and locate certification authorities.

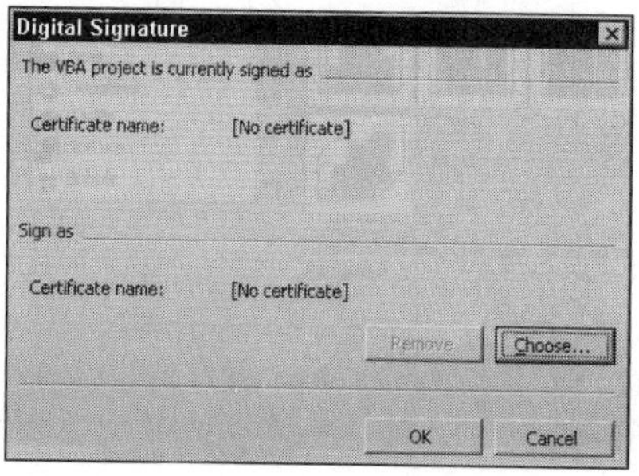

Figure 24-6   *Assigning a digital signature to macros*

2. Click the Choose button to display a list of available certificates.

3. Select the desired certificate and then click OK to return to the Digital Signature dialog box. The selected certificate is now displayed.

4. Click OK.

> **You should always protect the VBA code in a project that will be digitally signed and distributed; otherwise, a user could modify your code and then redistribute the project along with its digital signature.**

Done!

REVIEW

This session explained the various tools that Excel and VBA provide to enhance the security of your projects.

- An entire workbook can be password-protected for opening, viewing, and modifying.
- Range locking and worksheet protection enable you to limit user input to specified cells in the worksheet.
- You can protect a project's VBA code from viewing and modification.
- Excel's macro security settings help protect the user from malicious macros.
- You can validate your VBA code by digitally signing it.

QUIZ YOURSELF

1. How can you let users open and view a workbook, but prevent them from making any changes? (See the "Workbook Protection" section.)

2. When you turn on protection for a worksheet, what cells are locked by default? (See the "Worksheet Protection" section.)

3. How do you turn on worksheet protection in VBA code? (See the "VBA Code and Worksheet Protection" section.)

4. When you are distributing a VBA project to end-users, when should you apply protection to the VBA code? (See the "Protecting Your VBA Code" section.)

5. When Excel's macro security level is set to High, how can you run unsigned macros? (See the "Macro Security" section.)

Debugging and Distributing
an Application

Session Checklist

✔ Understanding program bugs

✔ Avoiding program bugs

✔ Using VBA's debugging tools

✔ Distributing an Excel application

**30 Min.
To Go**

It's a rare program that does not turn up at least a couple of bugs, but VBA provides some excellent tools that help you track them down and fix them. This session explains what bugs are and shows you how to deal with them, as well as covering some of the factors involved in distributing an application.

Debugging an Application

It is important that an Excel application be thoroughly debugged before you distribute it. Even so, some bugs may slip past your testing only to be found and reported by users; therefore, it is important for you to know how to use VBA's debugging tools to locate and fix bugs.

What Are Bugs?

A bug is an error in code that prevents a program from working properly. You can think of a bug as similar to an error, although these two terms have different meanings in programming circles.

An *error* (sometimes called *runtime error*) is a problem that prevents the program from running. If not handled properly, an error has the potential to stop a program dead in its tracks. You learn about handling runtime errors in Session 27.

In contrast, a bug does not prevent a program from running. Rather, it causes the program to produce incorrect results. For example, a data input program that inserts the data into the wrong part of a worksheet is considered a bug. Likewise, if code for some numerical calculation produces an incorrect result, that is considered a bug, too. There's no way to list or describe the bugs that may crop up in an Excel program because there is an essentially infinite number of potential bugs. Think of it this way — anything that a program is supposed to do can be done incorrectly.

While VBA reports errors to you, there's no such mechanism for bugs. The only way to find bugs is to test your program; then test it again. There are also some programming practices that help reduce bugs, described in the following section.

When testing a program for bugs, it's always a good idea to get some help. Other testers may find bugs that slipped past you.

Avoiding Bugs

The most important step you can take to reduce bugs in your programs is to always use the Option Explicit statement. When this statement is in effect, each and every variable in your program must be explicitly declared. If you try to use an undeclared variable, VBA displays an error message. This prevents misspelled variable names from slipping by. Without Option Explicit, a misspelled variable name is merely considered to be a new variable, and the result is likely to be a bug.

The Option Explicit statement and how to enable it for an entire project were covered in Session 4.

Aside from always using Option Explicit, the following guidelines can help in reducing program bugs:

- If your program contains a lot of code, divide it into relatively small procedures. Large procedures are more prone to bugs and are more difficult to fix when a bug does occur. There's no strict guideline to what constitutes a "large" procedure, but if a procedure exceeds 25-30 lines of code, start thinking about ways to break it down into two or more smaller procedures.

- Use global and public variables only when really necessary. While this type of variable may seem to simplify certain programming tasks, they are prone to problems. Almost all situations that seem to call for a global or public variable can be handled with procedure arguments and function return values.

- Be sure to use a floating-point data type for numeric variables when required. Use of an integer type in certain situations can result in rounding errors and bugs.

Debugging Tools

Almost all bugs are the result of two factors — working alone or in combination:

- Program execution takes an incorrect path.
- One or more variables take on incorrect values.

VBA's debugging tools are designed to track down both causes of bugs.

Breakpoints

In the VBA Editor, you can set a *breakpoint* on any line of code. When execution reaches that line of code, VBA enters break mode, which allows you to perform various debugging tasks (this will be explained soon). To set a breakpoint, put the editing cursor on the line of code and then press F9. You can use this same technique to remove a breakpoint, too. A line with a breakpoint is displayed as light text on a dark background and a circle icon in the adjacent margin, as shown in Figure 25-1. You can set as many breakpoints in a program as you need.

```
PERSONAL.XLS - Module1 (Code)
(General)                              IsLeapYear

Function IsLeapYear(year As String) As Boolean

' The year argument is a string specifying the year
' of interest, for example, "2003".
' Returns True if the year is a leap year, False if not.

Dim d1 As String, d2 As String

d1 = "1/1/" & year
d2 = "12/31/" & year

If DateDiff("d", d1, d2) = 365 Then
    IsLeapYear = True
Else
    IsLeapYear = False
End If

End Function
```

Figure 25-1　*A breakpoint is displayed with a dark background and a small circle in the margin.*

You can change the display format for breakpoints and other code elements on the Editor Options tab in the Options dialog box by selecting Tools ⇨ Options.

Breakpoints are useful for tracing program execution. When VBA is in break mode, you can perform other debugging actions, described in the following sections. When VBA has stopped at a breakpoint, the line is highlighted in yellow.

VBA stops just before executing a line that contains a breakpoint. In other words, when VBA stops at a breakpoint, the line containing the breakpoint has not yet been executed. You can also set a breakpoint only on lines that contain executable code. This excludes Dim statements, among others. VBA will not let you set a breakpoint on a nonexecutable line.

Step Commands

After VBA has stopped at a breakpoint, you usually want to continue program execution. You have several options, described in Table 25-1.

Table 25-1 *Execution Commands in Break Mode*

Command	How	Description
Continue	Run ⇨ Continue or F5	Continues execution normally
Reset	Run ⇨ Reset	Stops execution and resets the program
Step Into	Debug ⇨ Step Into or F8	Executes the next statement then pauses again
Step Over	Debug ⇨ Step Over or Shift+F8	If the next statement is a procedure call, the command executes the entire procedure and then pauses at the first statement upon returning from the procedure. If the next statement is not a procedure call, the command executes it and then pauses.
Step Out	Debug ⇨ Step Out or Ctrl+Shift+F8	If execution is currently within a procedure, the command executes the remainder of the procedure and then pauses at the first statement upon returning from the procedure. If execution is not currently within a procedure, the command executes it and then pauses.
Run to Cursor	Debug ⇨ Run to Cursor or Ctrl+F8	Continues execution then pauses at the line containing the editing cursor

The use of VBA's Step commands depends on the details of your debugging session. For example, if you want to track execution of every line of code, you would use Step Into. If you have already determined that a bug is not caused by a certain procedure, use Step Over to execute through the procedure code and pause when it has completed. If you think you have found the bug and want to correct the code to fix it, use Reset to end the program.

Code Editing in Break Mode

VBA enables you to modify your code while in break mode. This can be useful when you think you have spotted the problem and want to fix it right away. With some edits, however, VBA is unable to continue execution from where it was paused and must reset the project to start it again. In this situation, VBA displays a warning dialog box.

Using Watches

A *watch* enables you to determine the value of a program variable during execution. The simplest way to check a variable is in break mode. Simply rest the mouse cursor over the variable's name in your code, and VBA pops up a small window with the current value. When this is not sufficient, VBA offers more sophisticated watch tools.

VBA can monitor the value of any variable or expression during program debugging. A watch expression can be any VBA expression, such as a program variable, an object property, or a function call. By setting a watch, you can keep an eye on the value of the variable or property to see if and when it changes.

There are several ways you can use a watch expression:

- You can monitor its value. Visual Basic displays the expression value in the Watches window (this window opens automatically when you define a watch expression). The displayed value is updated whenever the program enters break mode.
- You can specify that the program enter break mode whenever the value of the expression changes.
- You can specify that the program enter break mode whenever the value of the expression becomes True.

To set a watch expression, select Debug ➪ Add Watch to open the Add Watch dialog box, shown in Figure 25-2.

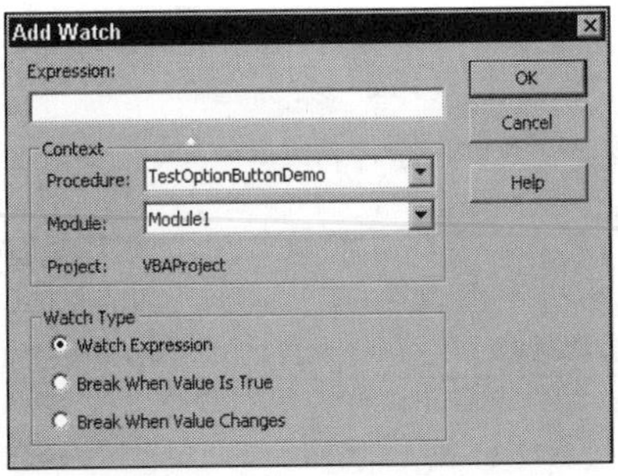

Figure 25-2 The Add Watch dialog box

Then follow these steps:

1. Enter the watch expression in the Expression box. If the cursor was on a variable or property name or if you had selected an expression in code, this would be automatically entered here.

2. Leave the settings under Context at the default values.

3. Under Watch Type, select the desired type of watch.

4. Click OK.

Any watch that you add is displayed in the Watches window, as shown in Figure 25-3. Each watch expression is displayed on its own line; the icon at the left end of the line identifies the type of watch (Watch Expression, Break when Value Changes, or Break when Value is True). The columns in the Watch Window display the following information:

- **Expression.** The expression being watched

- **Value.** The current value of the expression, or <Out of context> if the program is not executing or the variable is out of scope

- **Type.** The data type of the expression, if relevant

- **Context.** The context (part of the project) in which the expression is being evaluated

Watches			
Expression	Value	Type	Context
6d Count	Empty	Variant/Empty	Module1
6d X	<Out of context>	Empty	Module1.testBreak
6d x < 12	<Out of context>	Empty	Module1.testBreak

Figure 25-3   *The Watch window displays all defined watches.*

When you execute a program for which watches are defined, the data in the Watch Window is updated every time the program breaks.

If you cannot see the Watch Window, select View ⇨ Watch Window from the VBA Editor menu.

Table 25-2 lists some sample watches for a variety of debugging situations.

Table 25-2   *Sample Watch Expressions*

Purpose	Type of Watch	Watch Expression
To monitor the value stored in the variable Str1	Watch Expression	Str1
To monitor the length of the text in the TextBox control txtName	Watch Expression	txtName.TextLength

Purpose	Type of Watch	Watch Expression
To break when Count is less than 0	Break when Value is True	Count < 0
To break when the Value property of the ListBox control named List1 changes	Break when Value Changes	List1.Value
To break when X is greater than Y	Break when Value is True	X > Y

10 Min. To Go

Using Quick Watches

You can use a *quick watch* to take a quick look at the value of a variable or expression. While the program is in break mode, position the editing cursor on the variable or property name of interest or highlight the expression you want to evaluate. Press Shift+F9 or select Debug ➪ Quick Watch to display the Quick Watch dialog box, as shown in Figure 25-4. This dialog box displays the variable or expression of interest and its current value. Click the Add button to add the variable or expression as a regular watch expression.

Figure 25-4 *The Quick Watch window*

Distributing an Application

Distributing an Excel application can be a simple or complex process. If your application is for internal use in a small office, distribution may consist only of making the workbook file available on the server and sending an e-mail to your colleagues. For other scenarios, such as a shareware application that is available for general download on the Web or an application that will be distributed throughout a large, multi-office organization, the situation can get more complex. For example, to use an Excel application, you must have Excel installed. There is no runtime version of Excel that allows people to run applications without Excel.

At a minimum, distributing your project requires making the Excel workbook file that contains the project available to your end users. Some projects contain more than one workbook, and others contain related files such as online help. Because you created the project, you are aware of the file or files that it requires.

Some applications are best distributed as add-ins, a topic covered in Session 29. Providing online help for your application is covered in Session 30.

Excel Compatibility Issues

Excel has been through many versions, with the current version being called Excel 2003. Remember that not everyone upgrades to the latest version of software as soon as it is available. For many businesses, it is cost-effective to stay with an earlier version of Excel as long as it does the job. This means that there are still plenty of people using Excel 2002 Excel 2000, and even Excel 97. Some of these people may be potential users of your application.

Microsoft has made a concerted effort to maintain as much compatibility as possible between versions. Particularly relevant to the VBA developer, there have been only minor changes to the Excel object model and the VBA language. This means that many VBA programs created with the latest version of Excel work fine in earlier versions; however, you can be sure only by testing.

Done!

REVIEW

This session showed you how to use VBA's debugging tools and discussed factors involved when distributing an Excel application.

- A program bug is a code error that makes the program run incorrectly.
- Most bugs are due to variables taking incorrect values and/or program execution branching incorrectly.
- You can set a breakpoint anywhere in a program to force the program to pause at that point.
- When a program is paused in break mode, you can single-step through the code to locate bugs.
- VBA's watches let you track the value of program variables during program execution.

QUIZ YOURSELF

1. How does a runtime error differ from a program bug? (See the "What Are Bugs?" section.)
2. How do you set a breakpoint in your code? (See the "Breakpoints" section.)
3. What is the difference between the Step Into command and the Step Over command? (See the "Step Commands" section.)
4. Describe two ways to get a quick look at a variable's value in break mode. (See the "Using Watches" section.)
5. What should you do if you cannot be sure that all users of your application will be running the latest version of Excel? (See the "Excel Compatibility Issues" sidebar.)

Defining and Using Custom Classes

Session Checklist

✔ Fundamentals of VBA classes

✔ Advantages of using classes

✔ Creating class properties

✔ Defining class methods

✔ Class events

**30 Min.
To Go**

E xcel programming is based on the classes provided by the Excel object model. By this time you are probably convinced of the utility of classes. This usefulness is further enhanced by the ability to define your own classes and use them in your VBA programs. These are the topics of this session.

Class Fundamentals

A class that you create in VBA is similar to any other class in most respects. It is a plan, or blueprint, for an object that performs a task needed by your program. After the class is complete, you can use it like any other class or data type in VBA, creating as many instances (objects) from the class as you want. Programmer-defined classes can have properties and methods as well as event procedures for class events. They cannot, however, have a visual interface.

If you need a custom visual interface, you can create a user form, covered in Sessions 19 through 22. While user forms are not classes, strictly speaking, they share some of the same characteristics of classes.

VBA's support of classes has some features of "real" object-oriented programming but lacks others such an inheritance.

A VBA class definition resides in a class module. A module holds only a single class. To add a new class to a VBA project, select Insert ⇨ Class Module from the VBA Editor menu. The class is assigned a default name such as Class1, Class2, and so on. Be sure to change this to something descriptive of the class because this is the name you use in code to create instances of the class. To change a class's name, change the Name property in the Properties window.

When first created, a class is empty — that is, it contains no code. A class's code consists mainly of its properties and methods, as will be explained later in this session.

The Advantages of Classes

Why would you consider creating a class for use in your VBA project? There's nothing a class can do that cannot be done by regular (non-class) VBA code, so what's the big deal? The advantages of using classes fall into three areas:

- **Ease of use.** After a class is defined, using it in a program is easy. Create an instance of the class and call its properties and methods — what could be easier?
- **Reusability.** A properly designed and programmed class is a self-contained unit that performs a specific task. It's a simple matter to use a class in as many VBA projects as needed, with no extra programming effort.
- **Fewer errors and bugs.** A class is by its very nature isolated from the rest of the program except for the properties and methods that you specifically create. As such, it is less prone to program errors and bugs that can be caused by unintended interactions between different sections of code.

As already mentioned, VBA classes do not have visual interfaces. What, then, can they be used for? You can use a class, with its attendant advantages, for just about anything that does not require a visual interface. In practice, however, classes are most often used for maintaining and manipulating data. A class is typically designed around some real-world unit of data. For example, a program that keeps track of donors to a charitable organization might well use a Person class. There would be one instance of the class for each person. Class properties would hold information about the person, such as name, address, and phone number. Class methods would perform actions related to the person, such as printing out a personalized appeal letter. Whenever a new person is added, a new instance of the Person class is created, and all of the class capabilities are instantly available.

Instantiating Classes

A class that you create using VBA is similar to any other class — it is a blueprint that can be used to create an object. You must instantiate the class in your program — that is, create an object based on the class — before you can use it in your program. The syntax is the same as for any of the classes in the Excel object model:

```
Dim varname As New classname
```

Varname is any legal VBA variable name, and classname is the name of the class. For example, suppose you had defined a class named Person. You could then write the following:

```
Dim MyBrother As New Person
Dim MySister As New Person
Dim MyWife As New Person
```

Now you have three instances of the Person class — three objects — for use in your program.

When you are finished using an object, you should destroy it by setting its reference to the special value Nothing.

Class Properties

A property is an individual piece of information stored by the class. A property can be any of VBA's built-in data types. Returning to the Person class mentioned earlier, this class might have type String properties for the person's first name and last name, a type Currency property for the amount of their last contribution, and a type Date property for the date of their last contribution.

Most class properties are read/write properties, meaning that a program can both set the property value as well as read it. For this kind of property, a class module needs three elements:

- A class variable to store the property value. This variable must be declared at the module level (outside of any procedures) using the Private keyword.
- A Property Get procedure that is called when a program retrieves the property value. A Property Get procedure is actually a function that returns a value (the property value).
- A Property Let procedure that is called when a program sets the property value.

Creating Property Procedures

Property procedures (both Let and Get) can be added to a class automatically. Here are the steps to follow:

1. With the class module active, select Insert ⇨ Procedure from the VBA Editor menu to display the Add Procedure dialog box (see Figure 26-1).
2. In the Name field, enter the name of the property.
3. In the Type section, select the Property option.
4. Click OK.

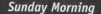

Figure 26-1 Use the Add Procedure dialog box to add property procedures to a class module.

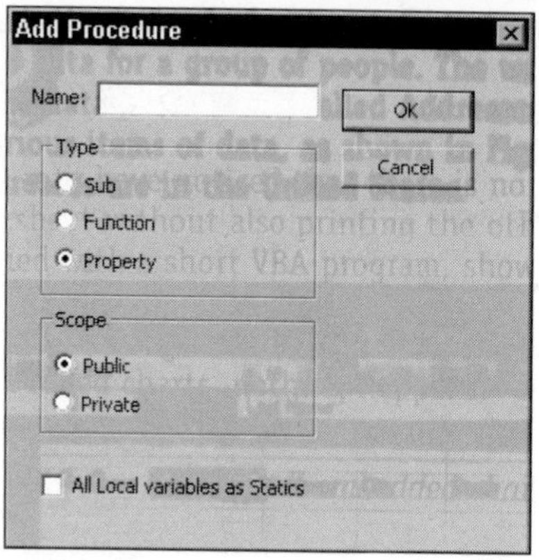

The VBA Editor inserts the outlines of the Get and Let procedures in your class module. The following shows the procedure outlines that are entered if you create a property called FirstName:

```
Public Property Get FirstName() As Variant

End Property

Public Property Let FirstName(ByVal vNewValue As Variant)

End Property
```

Please note several things about these procedures:

- The Get procedure has a return value. The data type of this value is by default Variant, as indicated by the As Variant clause. It is this return value that passes the property value to a program that requests it.
- The Let procedure is passed an argument named vNewValue, which is also type Variant by default. When a program sets the property value, the new value is passed to the object in this argument.
- Both procedures contain no code — they still must be connected to the property. This is explained later in this section.

> **A property should be left with the default Variant type only when it is appropriate for the data being stored. Otherwise you should select another VBA data type to suit the data.**

The Property Variable

20 Min. To Go

A class needs a place to store a property value. The property procedures do not provide this — all they provide is a connection between the property and the program outside the class. In most cases, the property value is stored in a module-level variable. The syntax is as follows:

```
Private varname As datatype
```

This statement must be placed at the module level, outside of any property procedures or methods in the class. The elements of this declaration are:

- The Private keyword limits the variable's scope to the class module. In other words, the variable is not directly accessible to code outside the class.
- Varname is any legal VBA variable name.
- Datatype specifies the type of the property. It can be any of VBA's data types or a user-defined type.

User-defined data types are covered in Session 4.

The data type of a property variable should of course be appropriate for the data that the property holds. For the FirstName property, type String is appropriate, so the variable declaration could be written as follows:

```
Private pFirstName As String
```

A variable that is used for a property is not special in any way except that it is connected to the property procedures (as covered in the next section). Its name can be any legal variable name, but I have found it useful to use the property name with a "p" prefix. This makes it clear that the variable is used for a property and which one.

Connecting the Property to the Property Procedures

The final step in creating a class property is to connect the property variable to the property procedures. Here is what's required:

1. Change the data type of the Let procedure's argument to match the data type of the property variable. If the type is Variant, no change is needed.
2. Change the return type of the Get procedure to match the data type of the property variable. Again, if the type is Variant, no change is needed.
3. Add code to the Get procedure that returns the value of the property variable to the calling program.
4. Add code to the Let procedure that stores the value passed in the procedure argument in the property variable.

For the Firstname property used for this example, the completed property procedures are shown in Listing 26-1 along with the property variable.

Persisting Object Data

Persisting data from an object is no different from persisting any other data from a VBA program. VBA programs most often persist data by saving it in a worksheet or workbook kept hidden from the user, then saving the workbook. You could use the same technique in a class module.

Listing 26-1   *Completed code for the FirstName property*

```
Private pFirstName As String

Public Property Get FirstName() As String
    FirstName = pFirstName
End Property

Public Property Let FirstName(ByVal vNewValue As String)
    pFirstName = vNewValue
End Property
```

Array Properties

In some situations you may need to implement a property that is an array. For example, if you need a property that holds more than one value, you can use this technique. This can be accomplished by adding an extra argument to both the Get and the Let procedures. This argument serves as the index into the array. The property variable itself must of course be an array. For example:

```
Private pArrayProperty(100) As Variant
```

The Get and Let procedures would then look similar to the following. Note that both the Get and the Let procedures check the value of the index variable to ensure that it is within the legal range for the property array.

```
Public Property Get ArrayProperty(ByVal index As Integer) As Variant

If index >= LBound(pArrayProperty) And index <= UBound(pArrayProperty)
Then
    ArrayProperty = pArrayProperty(index)
Else
    ArrayProperty = Null
End If

End Property

Public Property Let ArrayProperty(ByVal index As Integer, _
```

```
      ByVal vNewValue As Variant)

If index >= LBound(pArrayProperty) And index <= UBound(pArrayProperty)
Then
      pArrayProperty(index) = vNewValue
End If

End Property
```

To create the Get **and** Let **procedures for an array property, use the Insert ⇨ Procedure command as described earlier in this session to create the procedure outlines; then edit the procedures to add the required index arguments to the procedures.**

To use an array property, you must specify the array index when setting or reading the property:

```
X = Obj.ArrayProperty(5)
Obj.Property(10) = "Smith"
```

Note that in the previous example, the Get procedure returns the value Null if the program requests a property index that is out of range. This is important because it lets the calling program know that a valid property value was not returned.

Read-Only Properties

A property can be made read-only by deleting its Get procedure. A program can read such a property but cannot set its value. In many situations, a read-only property is not associated with a single property variable in the class module. Rather, the property value is calculated or generated on the fly each time it is read. An example of this is shown later in the session.

The Null Keyword

The Null keyword is a special VBA value that is used to indicate invalid data. When invalid data, as signified by the value Null, is a possibility, the program must test for the Null value. You cannot do this using the usual comparison operators; therefore, the comparison expression

```
If SomeExpression = Null
```

always returns False regardless of the value of the expression. Rather, you must use the IsNull function:

```
If IsNull(SomeExpression)
```

Accessing Properties in Code

Properties of programmer-defined classes are accessed similar to any other properties, using the `ObjectName.PropertyName` syntax. Suppose you create an instance of the Person class as follows:

```
Dim Somebody As New Person
```

You could then set its properties as follows:

```
Somebody.FirstName = "Henry"
Somebody.LastName = "Brinkler"
```

And likewise, read its properties as shown here:

```
str = Somebody.FirstName
```

Class Methods

It may surprise you to hear that you already know all about class methods. This is because a method is nothing more than a procedure inside a class module — it's simply a difference of terminology. Everything you learned about creating VBA procedures in Session 7 applies to methods as well. A method can be a function that returns a value, or a sub procedure that does not. You can use the Insert ⇨ Procedure command to add methods to a class module just like you do to add procedures to a regular code module.

 It is important to define helper methods using the `Private` **keyword. Having a helper method available to code outside the class can cause all sorts of problems.**

By default, class methods are public and can be called from outside the class. You can also create *helper* methods that are not visible outside the class and can be called only by code within the class. To create a helper method, replace the `Public` keyword in the method definition with `Private`. For example:

```
Private Sub HelperMethod()
```

A helper method exists only to perform tasks within the class. If the code in a regular — that is, public — method gets long and complex, consider creating one or more helper methods. Also, if there is a task that is required by two or more public methods in a class, consider putting the code for that task in a helper method and calling it from the public methods as needed.

Property Validation

A property procedure can be used to validate property data. Specifically, the `Let` procedure can include code that verifies the property value passed to the object meets the requirements of the program. For example, a Telephone Number property could include validation to ensure that a valid number in the format *nnn-nnn-nnnn* was passed to the property. If the property value fails validation, the code in the Let procedure can take appropriate action, such as displaying a warning message to the user.

An example of property validation is presented at the end of the session.

Class Events

A VBA class module has two events associated with it. They are

- Initialize. Triggered when the class is instantiated.
- Terminate. Triggered just before the object is destroyed.

The Initialize event procedure can be used to initialize the value of variables in the object or perform other actions that are required. For example, an object may need to read data from a worksheet, and this code can be placed in the Initialize event procedure. The Terminate event procedure can be used to perform any required cleanup, including tasks such as saving object data.

Reusing a Class

After you have defined a class in one VBA project, you can use it in any other VBA project. Here are the steps required:

1. In the VBA Editor, activate the class module.
2. Select File ⇨ Export File to display the Export File dialog box.
3. Select a path for the exported file. The default filename is the class name with the .CLS extension. You can change the name, but not the extension.
4. Click Save.
5. Open the second project; if it is already open, activate it.
6. Select File ⇨ Import File to display the Import File dialog box.
7. Select the file you exported and then click Open.

Changes that you make to the original class are not automatically transferred to projects into which the class has been imported. You must repeat the export/import process to update the other projects with the modified class.

**10 Min.
To Go**

A Class Demonstration

This section shows you how to create a complete Person class that demonstrates the class programming principles you have learned. As always, it is a good idea to begin with a little planning. This class has the following members:

- Read/write properties for FirstName and LastName.
- A read-only property FullName that is created on the fly by concatenating the values of the FirstName and LastName properties, with a space between them.

- An Email property for the person's e-mail address. The Let procedure includes validation code that catches invalid e-mail addresses.
- A method named PutDataInCell that puts all of the person's data together in a single string and puts that string in a specified worksheet cell (passed as a Range object to the method).

The term *members* is sometimes used to refer collectively to all of the properties and methods of a class.

In this class, the String data type could be used for all of the properties. This exercise uses the Variant type instead, and for a good reason. In data-oriented applications, it is common practice to use the special value Null to indicate no valid data. A type String property cannot hold the value Null, while a type Variant can. To make this feature work, the property values need to be set to Null initially. Code for this task is placed in the class module's Initialize event procedure.

The code for the Person class module is shown in Listing 26-2. Rather than walk you through all of the detailed steps for creating this class — you should already know the required procedures by now — the required steps in broad outline are

1. In the VBA Editor, use the Insert ⇨ Class Module command to add a new class module to your project. Change its Name property to Person.

2. Add the Option Explicit statement and the declarations of the three property variables to the module (refer to the listing for the exact syntax).

3. Use the Insert ⇨ Procedure command to add property procedures for the FirstName, LastName, Email, and FullName properties. Remember to delete the Let procedure for the FullName property because it is a read-only property. Add the code from the listing to these property procedures.

4. Use the Insert ⇨ Procedure command to add a sub procedure (method) named PutDataInCell. Add the code, including the argument declaration, as shown in the listing.

Validating an E-Mail Address

In the context of this program, validating an e-mail address does not mean verifying that it is an actual working address. The best that can be done is to verify that the address follows the proper format. For example, aaa@bbb.com has the correct format. The things checked are

- The address must contain an ampersand (@), and it cannot be the first character in the address.
- The address must contain at least one period (.), and it must come at least two character positions after the @.

You'll see how this validation is implemented in the Let procedure for the Email property.

Listing 26-2   *The Person class*

```
Option Explicit

Private pFirstName As Variant
Private pLastName As Variant
Private pEmail As Variant

Public Property Get FirstName() As Variant
    FirstName = pFirstName
End Property

Public Property Let FirstName(ByVal vNewValue As Variant)
    pFirstName = vNewValue
End Property

Public Property Get LastName() As Variant
    LastName = pLastName
End Property

Public Property Let LastName(ByVal vNewValue As Variant)
    pLastName = vNewValue
End Property

Public Property Get Email() As Variant
    Email = pEmail
End Property

Public Property Let Email(ByVal vNewValue As Variant)

    Dim pos As Integer
    ' Validate email address.
    ' Must contain "@" but not in the first position.
    pos = InStr(vNewValue, "@")
    If InStr(vNewValue, "@") < 2 Then
        MsgBox "Invalid email address: " & vNewValue
        Exit Property
    End If
    ' Must also contain at least one period that is
    ' at least 2 characters after the @.
    If InStrRev(vNewValue, ".") < pos + 1 Then
        MsgBox "Invalid email address: " & vNewValue
        Exit Property
    End If
    ' Data is OK - accept property.
    pEmail = vNewValue

End Property
```

Continued

Listing 26-2   *Continued*

```vb
Public Property Get FullName() As Variant

' This is a read-only property.
' Return Null if name data not valid.
If IsNull(pFirstName) Or IsNull(pLastName) Then
    FullName = Null
Else
    FullName = pFirstName & " " & pLastName
End If

End Property

Private Sub Class_Initialize()

pFirstName = Null
pLastName = Null
pEmail = Null

End Sub

Public Sub PutDataInCell(r As Range)

' Writes the person's full name and email
' to the specified worksheet cell. If data
' is not valid, writes "<invalid data>"
' to the cell.

If IsNull(pFirstName) Or IsNull(pLastName) Or IsNull(pEmail) Then
    r.Value = "<invalid data>"
Else
    r.Value = FullName & " - " & pEmail
End If

End Sub
```

After you have entered all the code for the Person class, write a small program that tests the class, such as the one shown in Listing 26-3. This program should be placed in a regular code module. You can see that this program creates two person objects, assigns their data, and calls the PutDataInCell method to insert the data into the active worksheet. Figure 26-2 shows the result.

Listing 26-3   *A program to test the Person class*

```vb
Public Sub TestPersonClass()

Dim p1 As New Person
Dim p2 As New Person
```

```
p1.FirstName = "Sam"
p1.LastName = "Jackson"
p1.Email = "sam@somewhere.com"
p1.PutDataInCell (ActiveSheet.Range("A1"))
p2.FirstName = "Wanda"
p2.LastName = "Wilson"
p2.Email = "wwilson@whatever.com"
p2.PutDataInCell (ActiveSheet.Range("A2"))

End Sub
```

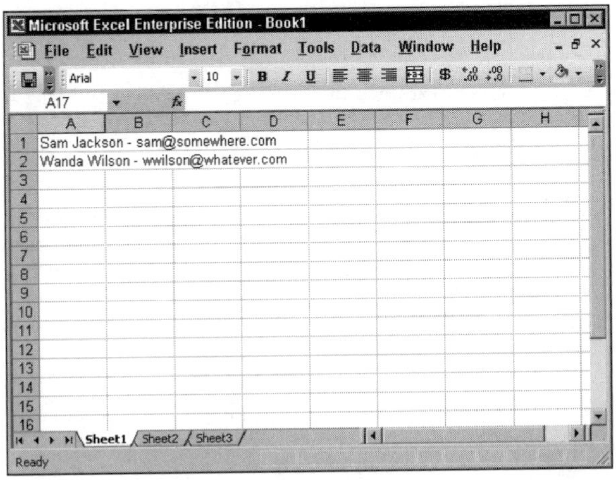

Figure 26-2 The worksheet after testing the Person class

REVIEW

This session showed you how to create your own custom classes in VBA, and how to use them in your programs.

- A class definition is placed in a class module.
- A VBA class does not have a visual interface.
- VBA classes can have properties to hold data and methods to perform actions.
- Similar to any class, a VBA class must be instantiated before you can use it.
- Each class has the Initialize and Terminate events that are fired when the class is instantiated and destroyed, respectively.

Done!

QUIZ YOURSELF

1. How many classes can be defined in a class module? (See the "Class Fundamentals" section.)

2. Name two advantages of using classes. (See the "The Advantages of Classes" section.)

3. How do you define a read-only property? (See the "Read Only Properties" section.)

4. What is the Null keyword used for? (See the "The Null Keyword" sidebar.)

5. How is a class method different from a regular VBA procedure? (See the "Class Methods" section.)

PART

V

Sunday Morning
Part Review

1. When does a control's Exit event occur?
2. How does a VBA program change the double-click interval?
3. True or False: The KeyDown event procedure can tell whether the user entered 4 or $ using the KeyCode argument.
4. How does code in the KeyDown event procedure cancel a keystroke?
5. What's the fastest way to align controls on a form?
6. Suppose one control is being hidden by an overlapping control. At runtime, how would you make the hidden control visible?
7. How would you prevent the user from moving the focus to a control by tabbing?
8. How are event procedures named?
9. Which events are *not* disabled by setting the Application.EnableEvents property to False?
10. Which event is triggered when the user makes a change in any worksheet?
11. How can the user prevent the Open event from triggering when a workbook is opened?
12. What is data validation?
13. Where should you place event procedures for workbook-level events?
14. How can you define code to be executed at a specific time of day?
15. How can you permit users to view a workbook but not modify it?
16. True or False: Password protecting a workbook prevents users from viewing your VBA code.
17. True or False: A bug prevents a program from running.
18. When should a program use the Option Explicit statement?
19. What is a *breakpoint*?
20. What's the difference between the debug commands Step Over and Step Into?

21. When a program is paused at a breakpoint, what's the quickest way to determine the current value of a program variable?

22. True or False: Values in the Watch Window are continuously updated as the program runs.

23. How does VBA report bugs to the programmer?

24. True or False: An end-user must have an installed version of Excel to run your Excel applications.

25. Where do you place code for a custom VBA class?

26. True or False: A custom VBA class can include a visual interface.

27. How do you create a read-only property?

28. True or False: The return value of the Property Get procedure must have the same data type as the argument to the Property Let procedure.

29. How can you validate data for properties that can take only certain values?

30. How do you refer to an object property in code?

31. How is a class method different from a regular VBA procedure?

32. What is a helper method?

33. What event is triggered just before an object is destroyed?

PART

VI

Sunday Afternoon

Handling Runtime Errors

Session Checklist

✔ Understanding runtime errors and their causes

✔ How to enable error trapping in a procedure

✔ Using the Err object

✔ Writing error-handling code

✔ Deferring error handling

✔ Using errors as programming tools

30 Min.
To Go

A runtime error is an error that occurs while the program is running and can stop the program dead in its tracks unless the error is handled. This session explains what runtime errors are and how to handle them in your programs.

What's a Runtime Error?

A program error that occurs while the program is running is called a *runtime error*, and it's important to understand how a runtime error (or simply *error* from now on) differs from two other kinds of problems that can occur in a VBA program:

- A *bug* is a flaw in program logic that causes the program to produce incorrect results. Unlike an error, a bug does not prevent the program from running.

- A *syntax error* is a mistake in VBA syntax. The VBA Editor catches and flags syntax errors as you write your code, so they never have a chance to affect program execution.

When an error occurs and the program does not include code to handle it, the program stops and displays a dialog box with a description of the error, as shown in Figure 27-1. There's usually no way to recover from an unhandled error, which is why they are so nasty. At best you'll have an annoyed user, and at worst you'll suffer data loss.

Figure 27-1   *VBA signals an unhandled error by displaying this dialog box.*

You can see that the error dialog box gives you a brief description of the error as well as the error number. Every VBA error has its own error number. In this example, the error was Subscript out of range, which occurs when code tries to access a nonexistent array element, and its number is 9. You can also see that there are four buttons in this dialog box, two of which are disabled. These are

- **Continue.** A few errors permit program execution to be continued, in which case this button is enabled; however, most errors do not permit this.
- **End.** This button terminates the program.
- **Debug.** If the program is being run in the VBA Editor, this button lets you pause the program and highlight the line of code on which the error occurred. If the project is locked with a password, however (as applications you distribute almost always will be), the Debug option is not available.
- **Help.** This button displays information about the error that occurred, including possible causes.

You can see that for an end user, the only response to an unhandled error is ending the program. This is not good! In fact, there is no excuse for it.

The Causes of Errors

Some errors are caused by mistakes in your code. Trying to access a nonexistent array element is one common example. For example:

```
Dim MyArray(100) As Single
...
MyArray(150) = 1.2  ' Causes an error!
```

Another common code-related error occurs when you try to use an object variable that has not been initialized — that is, the object has not been instantiated. In this example, r is a variable that *can* hold reference to a Range object, but it has not yet been initialized to reference an actual range, so the second line causes an error.

```
Dim r As Range
r.Value = "Data"
```

Other errors are caused by hardware problems. File operations are a common cause of errors, such as when a program tries to write to a disk that is full or tries to write to a removable media drive when there is no media inserted. While good programming practices can help prevent errors that are caused by code, some errors are clearly out of the programmer's control. This is one reason why VBA programs should always include error handling.

Errors and the Excel Object Model

Some Excel objects have their own error handling built in. This means that the object intercepts the error before it reaches your program. One example is the Workbook object. If you try to open a workbook that does not exist on disk, or if you try to save a workbook to a disk that does not exist, the Workbook object catches the error and displays its own dialog box (as shown in Figure 27-2). Error trapping in your program is never activated.

Unfortunately, Microsoft has not made any information available as to which errors are caught internally by objects and which ones are passed up to VBA to handle. All you can do is experiment to see which errors should be trapped by your code and which can be safely ignored because they are handled by Excel objects.

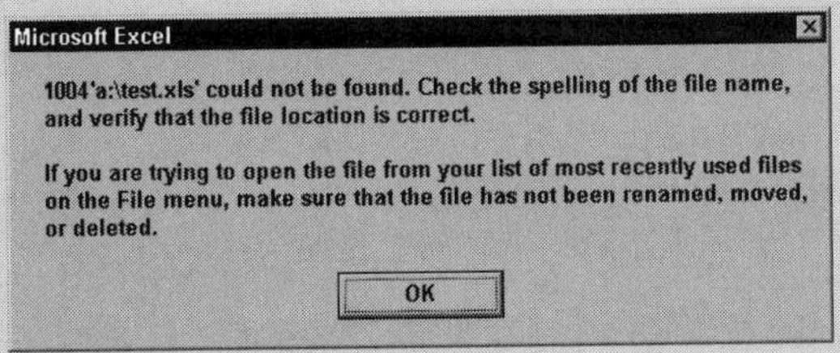

Figure 27-2 *Some Excel objects deal with errors internally and display their own dialog box.*

Preventing Errors

There are some good programming practices that can help prevent errors in your programs. These are similar to the practices that were suggested in Session 25 for preventing bugs, but they are worth repeating:

- Always use Option Explicit. By requiring variable declaration, you avoid the many errors that can result from misspelled variable names.
- Avoid use of the Object data type and the Variant data type to hold object references. Use of these data types for object references (as opposed to using the specific object type) makes it impossible for VBA to know ahead of time what the object's methods and properties are, opening the way for various kinds of errors.
- Whenever there's a chance that an array index may be out of bounds, use LBound and UBound to check the index value before trying to assign to or read from the array.
- Always validate user-entered data. A common cause of errors is the user entering data incorrectly, such as entering a string when a number is required. By validating the data on entry, you can avoid this kind of error.

Trapping Errors

Errors in VBA are handled by *trapping* them. When you trap an error, you tell VBA, "When an error occurs, do not display the default dialog box and halt the program, but rather route execution to a special section of code called an *error handler*." Then, code in the error handler deals with — that is, handles — the error. You trap errors with an On Error Goto statement. The syntax is:

```
On Error Goto label
```

Label is a program label (a name followed by a colon) that identifies the location of the error-handling code. The On Error Goto statement and the error-handling code must always be in the same procedure. The structure of a procedure with error handling would therefore look something like this:

```
Public SomeProcedure()

' Variable declarations go here.

On Error Goto ErrorHandler

' Procedure code goes here.

Exit Sub

ErrorHandler:

' Error handling code goes here.

End Sub
```

Note two things about this sample:

- The label for the error-handling code does not have to be ErrorHandler; it can be any legal VBA label name.
- The Exit Sub statement is used to prevent execution from falling into the error-handling code. This ensures that the error-handling code is executed only when an error occurs.

Before getting to the details of writing error-handling code, you need to know about the Err object, which is covered in the next section.

Because the contents of VBA procedures are independent of each other, you can use the same label for the error-handling code in multiple procedures.

Procedures and Error Handling

All error handling is done at the procedure level, which is unavoidable because the error-trapping statement and its error-handling code must always be in the same procedure. This arrangement works well because the error-handling code in a given procedure can be tailored to the specific errors that might occur in that procedure. A procedure that performs mathematical calculations should be concerned with overflow and divide-by-zero errors, but the procedure can ignore file-related errors because they cannot occur while that procedure is executing.

In a VBA program, procedures often call other procedures. If one procedure does not have error trapping enabled, any errors that occur while it is executing are passed up to the procedure that called it; therefore, if Proc1 calls Proc2, and Proc2 does not have error trapping, errors in Proc2 are passed up to Proc1 and handled there. If Proc1 does not have error trapping, errors are passed up to the next level. Only when an error reaches the top level — a procedure that was not called by another procedure — will VBA's default error mechanism be triggered.

It can be tempting to use this "bubble up" feature of VBA errors to centralize some error handling in one or a few procedures. I recommend that you avoid this practice, and give each and every procedure its own error-handling code.

Error handling works the same way for all VBA procedures, including functions and class methods.

The Err Object

The Err object is an integral part of VBA and is always available to your program. At any time, the Err object contains information about the most recent error that has occurred. The Err object has the following properties and methods:

- **Number.** The number of the most recent error, or 0 if no error has occurred.
- **Description.** A brief description of the most recent error, or a blank if no error has occurred.
- **Clear.** Erases the error information from the object.

Refer to VBA's online help for a complete list of runtime errors and their numeric codes (search for Trappable Errors).

When an error occurs, use the `Err` object to get information about the error. The `Number` property identifies the error, and the `Description` property provides information that you can, if desired, display to the user. Call the `Clear` method to be sure that the `Err` object does not retain information from a previous error.

> **The** `Description` **property of the** `Err` **object provides the same error description that is displayed in VBA's default error dialog box. Also** `Number` **is the default property of the** `Err` **object. Thus, writing** `If Err = 0` **is equivalent to** `If Err.Number = 0`.

Error-Handling Code

The task of error-handling code is to

1. Identify the error (using the `Err` object).
2. Take appropriate action, such as displaying a message to the user.
3. Resume program execution.

To identify the error, you must have some awareness of which errors are likely to occur in this specific procedure. You then test the `Err.Number` property against the code for each of these potential errors. When you find a match, take action appropriate for that error. For example, suppose your program is trying to open a workbook file that is located on a shared network drive. There are several errors that can occur:

- Error 53, file not found
- Error 76, path not found
- Error 68, device not available
- Error 75, path/file access error

Depending on which error has occurred, you might want to prompt the user to try again, contact the network administrator, or take some other action. There's no magic bullet when it comes to handling errors. You need to be aware of the errors that can occur, what — if anything — can be done to correct them, and what the error means in the context of your program.

For some errors there is no recourse but to notify the user and then end the program. For many errors, however, the program can be resumed. This means that part of the error-handling code is an instruction to resume program execution. There are three options:

- `Resume`. Resume execution by retrying the statement that caused the error. Use `Resume` when the error may have been corrected, such as inserting a diskette in the A: drive.
- `Resume Next`. Resume execution with the statement following the one that caused the error. Use `Resume Next` when the error condition cannot be fixed but the remainder of the procedure code can still be executed.

- Resume *label.* Resume execution with the statement identified by label (which must be in the same procedure). Use the Resume *label* statement when neither Resume nor Resume Next is appropriate.

> **Executing any of the** Resume **statements automatically clears the** Err **object of existing error information, as if the** Err.Clear **method had been called. The** Err **object is also cleared whenever execution exits a procedure.**

Deferring Error Handling

10 Min. To Go

Another error-handling technique is to defer the handling of the error. In other words, VBA does not trap the error but instead ignores it. Your code can then examine the Err object to see the type of error, if any, has occurred. To defer error handling, use the On Error Resume Next statement. Any subsequent error (within the procedure) is ignored, and information about the error is placed in the Err object. Your code can use this information to determine if an error occurred and, if so, what action to take. Here's how you would structure your code:

```
On Error Resume Next

' Code that might cause an error goes here.

' If no error occurred, Err.Number is 0.
If Err.Number > 0 Then
' Code to check the error number and
' respond appropriately goes here.
End If
```

This technique can be used only with some errors, specifically those errors whose handling can be deferred. The technique is not suitable for errors that cannot be ignored even temporarily. There is no way to define exactly what errors fall into this category — an error that is serious and must be trapped in one program may be acceptable in another program. Again, it is the programmer's responsibility to become familiar with the errors that can occur and how they can relate to a specific program.

> **You cannot use any of the** Resume **statements in responding to an error when** On Error Resume Next **is in effect. The** Resume **statements are permitted only in error handlers that are associated with the** On Error Goto **statement.**

Some Error-Handling Examples

When dealing with VBA error handling, a little bit of experience is valuable To provide you with some experience dealing with errors, this section presents a few examples of using VBA's error-handling capabilities.

Ignoring an Error

Excel's SpecialCells method enables you to obtain a reference to cells within a range that meet certain criteria, such as cells that contain a formula or cells that contain a comment. If no matching cells are found, an error is generated. In many situations this error can simply be ignored because it does not impact program operation.

The SpecialCells **method is covered in Session 11.**

Listing 27-1 shows a procedure that selects all cells within the current selection that contain comments. If there are no comment cells in the selection, the resulting error is ignored by using the On Error Resume Next statement, and the selection is unchanged. If there is no error, the comment-containing cells are selected.

Listing 27-1   *Using On Error Resume Next to ignore an error*

```
Public Sub SelectCellsWithComments()

Dim r As Range
On Error Resume Next
Set r = Selection.SpecialCells(xlCellTypeComments)
If Err = 0 Then r.Select

End Sub
```

Notifying the User of an Error

Continuing with the example from the previous section, you might want to notify the user if the procedure did not find any cells containing comments. The code can be modified to use On Error Goto to provide such a notification, as shown in Listing 27-2.

Listing 27-2   *Using On Error Goto to notify the user of an error*

```
Public Sub SelectCellsWithComments()

Dim r As Range
On Error Goto ErrorHandler
Set r = Selection.SpecialCells(xlCellTypeComments)
Exit Sub

ErrorHandler:
MsgBox "No cells with comments were found in the selection."

End Sub
```

Using an Error as a Programming Tool

VBA's error-trapping capability can be used as a programming tool is some situations. An error can alert you that a certain condition exists, and your program can take action accordingly.

As an example, consider the following code:

```
Dim wb As Workbook
Set wb = Workbooks("SalesData")
```

If the workbook named SalesData is open, this code works fine. If it is not open, however, an error occurs. A program can use this in situations where you cannot know ahead of time whether a specific workbook is open. Listing 27-3 illustrates a function that returns a reference to a workbook if it is open or returns Nothing if it is not open. A program can call this function and test its return value. If this value is Nothing, the program can take steps to open the workbook.

Listing 27-3   *Using an error as a programming tool*

```
Public Function GetReferenceToWorkbook(wbName As String) As Workbook

Dim wb As Workbook

On Error Resume Next
Set wb = Workbooks(wbName)

If Err = 0 Then ' wbName is open.
    Set GetReferenceToWorkbook = wb
Else    ' wbName is not open, so return Nothing.
    Set GetReferenceToWorkbook = Nothing
End If

End Function
```

Done!

REVIEW

In this session you learned how to use VBA's error-handling tools to deal with runtime errors.

- An unhandled error stops the program and may result in data loss.
- You enable VBA's error trapping by executing one of the On Error statements.
- All VBA error handing occurs at the procedure level.
- When an error has occurred, the Err object provides information about the error.
- You can postpone error handling with the On Error Resume Next statement.
- Errors can sometimes be used as a programming tool.

QUIZ YOURSELF

1. When is it acceptable to let errors occur without being handled? (See the "What's a Runtime Error?" section.)

2. Explain if all potential causes of errors are under the programmer's control. (See the "The Causes of Errors" section.)

3. Can you place the On Error Goto *label* statement in one procedure and the error-handling code in another procedure? (See the "Trapping Errors" section.)

4. What value does the Err.Number property have when no error has occurred? (See the "The Err Object" section.)

5. In error-handling code, how do you resume program execution with the statement that caused the error? (See the "Error-Handling Code" section.)

Database Tasks

**30 Min.
To Go**

While Excel is designed as a spreadsheet application, it also provides tools that offer database functionality. This session explains what a database application is and how you can use Excel for database tasks.

Databases and Excel

Database programs are undoubtedly the most widely used type of computer application. They are common everywhere information is managed, even though most people are not aware of it.

- When you use your library's online catalog to look up a book, you use a database application.

- When you place a phone order for clothing, software, or electronics, the sales rep with whom you speak is using a database application to check stock and enter your order.

- When you use Quicken or another home finance program to balance your check-book, that, too, is a database program.

Most database applications are highly specialized for database tasks and can do nothing else. Being a spreadsheet program, Excel does not have the database capabilities of these specialized programs, and there are many database tasks that are simply beyond Excel's capabilities. Even so, Excel's database tools provide a good deal of functionality and are more than adequate for simpler database tasks. As a side benefit, because Excel's database capabilities are limited, they are relatively simple to learn and use.

Database Fundamentals

The term *database* refers to a special way of organizing information. It's a common-sense approach, and almost everyone has used it in one way or another even if they have never used a computer. Do you have an address book? That's a database, albeit a manual one as opposed to a computerized one.

A database is based on the concepts of records and fields:

- A record contains the information for one of whatever it is the database is keeping track. In an address list, a record corresponds to one person. In an auto parts inventory, a record corresponds to one part.
- A field contains one piece of information for a record. An address list database would contain fields for First Name, Last Name, Address, Phone Number, and so on.

An essential aspect of databases is that each record contains the same fields as every other record. Of course, the data in the fields are different from record to record, but the fields are the same.

It may have occurred to you that the structure of a database and the structure of an Excel workbook seem to be made for each other. By treating a worksheet row as a database record and each column as a database field, it is a simple matter to put database data into a spreadsheet. The top row is used for the field names, and all the rows below that for the actual data. Figure 28-1 shows an example. In this worksheet the field names are in bold-face, but that's just for appearance.

At this point some readers may be thinking "so what?" The ability to create a list of data in a worksheet is hardly new or exciting. This is true enough, but what's interesting is the special tools that Excel provides for working with data in this record and field format.

The term *table* is sometimes used to refer to data that is organized as a database, in records and fields. Sometimes a database will contain more than one table. Excel sometimes uses the term *list* in the same way.

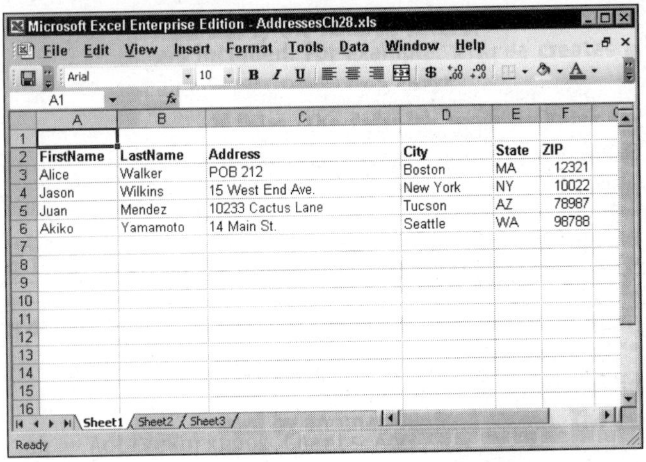

Figure 28-1 *The records and fields of a database table are a good match for Excel's row and column structure.*

Sorting Data

**20 Min.
To Go**

The data in a table can be sorted based on the data in one or more fields. For example, a list of names can be sorted alphabetically by the LastName field. To perform a sort in Excel, place the cursor anywhere in the table and then select Data ⇨ Sort. Excel automatically selects the table of data and displays the Sort dialog box (see Figure 28-2).

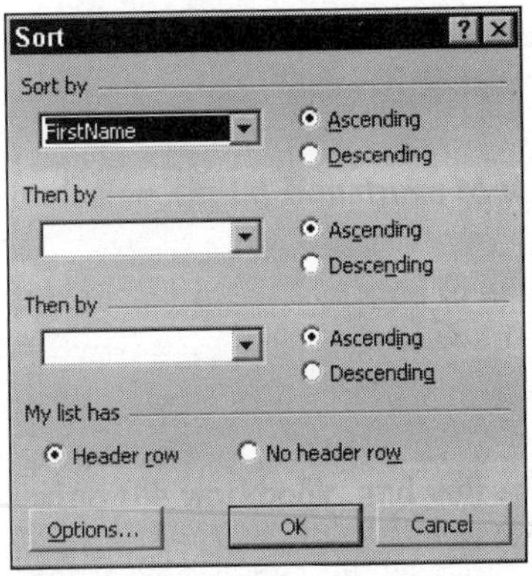

Figure 28-2 *Using Excel's Sort command to sort a table of data*

If your table has field names at the top of each column, as it should, each of the three drop-down lists in this dialog box will list all of the field names. In the Sort by list, select the field on which the data should be sorted. For additional sorting, use the Then by lists to select other sort fields. These will be used to sort the records if there is a tie (identical data) in the first field.

To sort data in VBA code, use the Range object's Sort method. The syntax is:

```
SomeRange.Sort Key1, Order1, Key2, Order2, Header
```

The arguments for this method are as follows:

- **SomeRange.** A Range object identifying the range to be sorted. It can reference the entire range or any single cell in the range (in which case Excel automatically selects the entire range that contains data).
- **Key1.** A Range object indicating the column on which the sort is based. This range can refer to any cell in the column.
- **Order1.** An optional constant indicating the sort order. Set to xlAscending (A-Z, the default) or xlDescending.
- **Key2.** An optional Range object indicating the secondary sort column (as Key1).
- **Order2.** An optional argument that indicates the secondary sort order (as Order1).
- **Header.** An optional constant indicating whether the table has a header row of field names. Set to xlYes, xlNo, or xlGuess (the default). If you use xlGuess, Excel examines the data to determine whether there is a header row.

In the syntax for the Sort method, I have omitted several optional arguments that are beyond the scope of this book. For this reason you should always use named arguments when calling this method.

Here's an example of using the Sort method to sort a table. Assume that the worksheet contains a table that has a header row, and that cell A2 is within the table. This code sorts the order by the field in column B with a secondary sort on column D.

```
Worksheets("SalesData").Range(A2").Sort Key1:= _
    Worksheets("SalesData").Range("B2"), Key2:= _
    Worksheets("SalesData").Range("D2"), Header:=xlYes
```

Filtering Data

The term *filtering* means to select certain data from a table. For example, with an address database, selecting all people who live in California is a type of filter. When working in Excel, you can apply what is called an *auto filter*. Your table should have a header row of field names to use this feature. Here's how:

1. Place the Excel cursor anywhere in the data table.
2. Select Data ➪ Filter ➪ AutoFilter. Excel displays a down arrow next to each field name.

3. Click the arrow next to the name of the field on which you want to filter. Excel displays a list of available filters (see Figure 28-3). These include

- **w(All):** Removes a previously applied filter and display all records.
- **(Top10):** Filters on the ten most frequent values in this field.
- **Specific value:** Filters on that value (for example, Mendez in the figure).

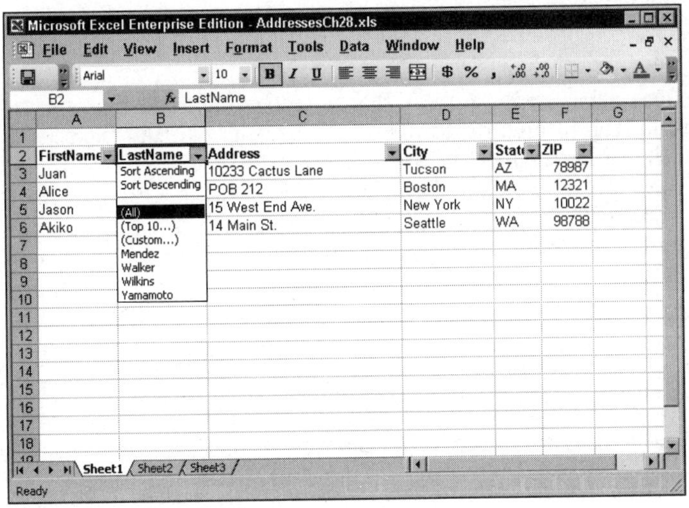

Figure 28-3   Using the auto filter feature

4. To remove the auto filter and display all records, select Data ⇨ Filter ⇨ AutoFilter again.

> **Each auto filter drop-down list includes Sort Ascending and Sort Descending commands. This is a quick way to sort a table when the auto filter is displayed.**

> **When you filter a table, some records seem to disappear. Don't worry; they are still there — just hidden temporarily.**

To apply a filter in code, use the AutoFilter method. The syntax is

```
SomeRange.AutoFilter(Field, Criteria1, Operator, Criteria2,
VisibleDropDown)
```

- `SomeRange`. A Range object identifying the range to be sorted. It can reference the entire range or any single cell in the range (in which case Excel automatically selects the entire range that contains data).
- `Field`. An optional numerical value identifying the field on which to filter. The value is an index into the fields, with the leftmost field being 1.
- `Criteria1`. Optional criterion for the filter. If omitted, all records are selected.
- `Operator`. An optional constant specifying how `Criteria1` (and sometimes `Criteria2`) are interpreted. See Table 28-1 for details.
- `Criteria2`. Optional secondary criterion for the filter.
- `VisibleDropDown`. Optional True/False value. If True (the default), Excel displays the drop-down arrow for the filtered field in the worksheet, permitting the user to manually work with the filter. If False, the arrow is not displayed.

Table 28-1　*Constants for the AutoFilter Method's Operator Argument*

Constant	Meaning
`xlAnd`	`Criteria1` and `Criteria2` must be met (this is the default).
`xlOr`	Either `Criteria1` or `Criteria2` (or both) must be met.
`xlBottom10Items`	The least frequent ten items are selected.
`xlBottom10Percent`	The least frequent 10 percent of items are selected.
`xlTop10Items`	The most frequent ten items are selected.
`xlTop10Percent`	The most frequent 10 percent of items are selected.

If you call the `AutoFilter` method with no arguments, its effect is to toggle the display of the auto filter drop-down arrows in the specified range. When an auto filter is applied, the drop-down button in the field that the table is filtered on is displayed in blue instead of the usual black.

The criteria for the `AutoFilter` method is a string specifying the value to filter on. For example, setting `Criteria1` to "NY" and filtering on the State field selects all records where state is NY. There are two special values you can use for a criteria:

- `=`. Selects records where the field is blank.
- `<>`. Selects records where the field is not blank.

The `Operator` argument controls the filter as explained in Table 28-1. The `xlAnd` and `xlOr` settings are used to filter on two fields, specified by `Criteria1` and `Criteria2`. The other settings are used for special filters where the criteria arguments are omitted.

The following examples use the database table shown in Figure 28-1, assuming that there would be a lot more records in the table. All examples assume that the active cell is within the table. This code filters the table to show only records for people in the city New York:

```
Selection.AutoFilter Field:=4, Criteria1:="New York"
```

This code filters for people in the ten states with fewest records:

```
Selection.AutoFilter Field:=5, Operator:=xlBottom10Items
```

This code filters for people with last name Smith or Jones:

```
Selection.AutoFilter Field:=2, Criteria1:="Smith", _
    Criteria2:="Jones", Operator:=xlOr
```

Data Entry Forms

**10 Min.
To Go**

When you are working with a database table, entering and editing data directly in the worksheet is not always the best approach. It is much better to have a custom form that displays the data, one record at a time, in a format that is easier to read and use. For more complex database application, you may want to design a user form (covered in Sessions 19 through 22) that provides you with complete flexibility in designing the appearance of the form, and also lets you include data validation.

For simpler tasks you may be able to make do with a form that Excel can generate automatically. With the Excel cursor in a database table, select Data ⇨ Form, and Excel automatically creates and displays a form based on the fields in your table. An example is shown in Figure 28-4.

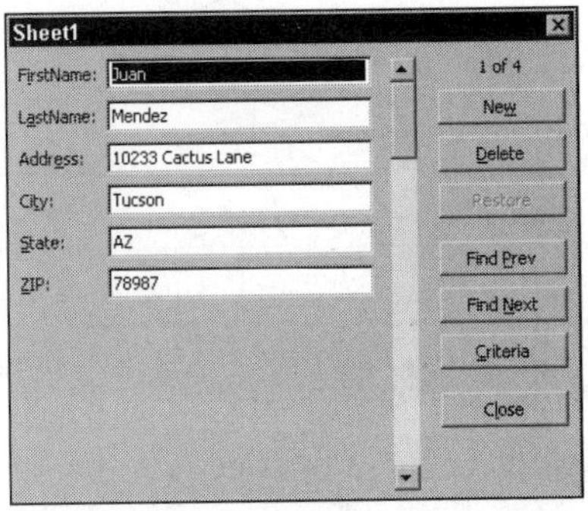

Figure 28-4   *The data form generated by Excel for the Addresses database table*

The buttons on this form let the user perform the following actions:

- **New.** Enter data for a new record (inserted at the bottom of the table).
- **Delete.** Deletes the current record.
- **Restore.** Undoes the most recent Delete command.
- **Find Prev.** Moves to the previous record (if any).
- **Find Next.** Moves to the next record (if any).
- **Criteria.** Enter criteria for filtering the table.
- **Close.** Closes the form.

To display the automatic data form from a VBA program, call the Worksheet object's ShowDataForm method. For example:

```
ActiveSheet.ShowDataForm
```

When this method is called, the macro pauses until the user closes the form. Only then are subsequent statements in the macro executed.

Database Functions

Excel provides a number of built-in functions designed specifically for working with data in a table. Called the *database statistical functions*, they all have names beginning with D to mark them as being database functions. Each of the database functions has a counterpart that performs the same task outside of a database table. For example, the database function DSUM has the counterpart SUM, DAVERAGE has AVERAGE, and so on. The database functions are described in Table 28-2.

Table 28-2 *Excel's Database Statistical Functions*

Function	Description
DAVERAGE	Calculates the average
DCOUNT	Counts records
DMAX	Finds the maximum value
DMIN	Finds the minimum value
DSTDEV	Calculates the standard deviation
DSUM	Calculates the sum
DVAR	Calculates the variance

The database functions all have the following syntax:

```
FunctionName(database, field, criteria)
```

The arguments for this method are as follows:

- **Database.** The range containing the database table; for example, A6:F30.
- **Field.** The database field on which to perform the calculation. This can be a string containing the field name or a number giving the field offset from the left edge of the table (first column = 1).
- **Criteria.** The range containing the criterion; for example, A1:A2.

The criterion is perhaps the trickiest part of using the database functions. You specify the criterion in a range of two worksheet cells, one above the other:

- The top cell contains the name of the field that the criterion is to be applied to.
- The bottom cell contains the criterion itself, using VBA's comparison operator.

Suppose your database table contains a field named Age, and you want to create a criterion that selects only those records where Age is greater than 40. The top cell of the criterion range should contain Age and the lower cell should contain >40.

The following example of using the database statistical functions are based on the database table shown in Figure 28-5.

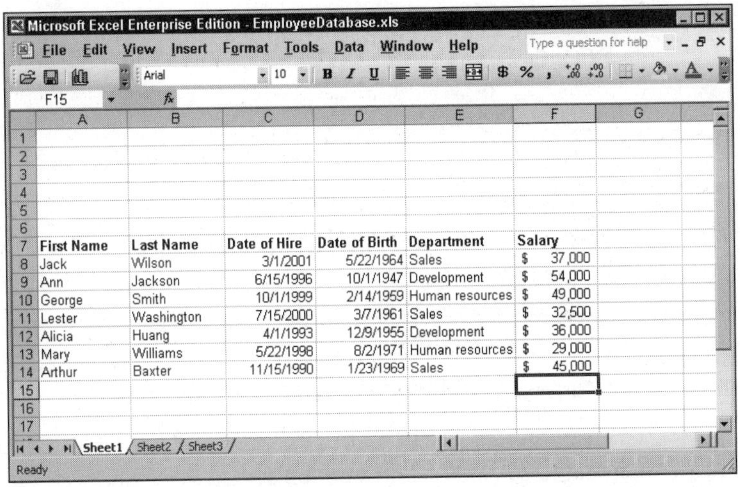

First Name	Last Name	Date of Hire	Date of Birth	Department	Salary
Jack	Wilson	3/1/2001	5/22/1964	Sales	$ 37,000
Ann	Jackson	6/15/1996	10/1/1947	Development	$ 54,000
George	Smith	10/1/1999	2/14/1959	Human resources	$ 49,000
Lester	Washington	7/15/2000	3/7/1961	Sales	$ 32,500
Alicia	Huang	4/1/1993	12/9/1955	Development	$ 36,000
Mary	Williams	5/22/1998	8/2/1971	Human resources	$ 29,000
Arthur	Baxter	11/15/1990	1/23/1969	Sales	$ 45,000

***Figure 28-5** The database table used in the database function examples*

Suppose you want to determine the number of people in the Sales department and their average salary. Here are the steps to follow.

1. Use cells A1:A2 for the criterion. Enter Department in cell A1 to indicate that the criterion will apply to the Department field.
2. Enter Sales in cell A2.
3. Enter Total employees in Sales in cell C3.
4. Enter Average salary in cell C4.
5. Enter =DCOUNT(A7:F15, "Salary", A1:A2) in cell E2.
6. Enter =DAVERAGE(A7:F15, "Salary", A1:A2) in cell E3.
7. Click the Currency Style button (the one with a $) on the toolbar to apply Currency format to cell E3.

The resulting worksheet is shown in Figure 28-6. You can see that the database formulas that you entered display their results. If the data in the table was supposed to change, the results would automatically update as needed. Note, however, that if one or more new records were added to the table, the formulas would not take this into account. This is because the range that contains the table is hard-coded into the formula. You'll have to edit the formula as needed.

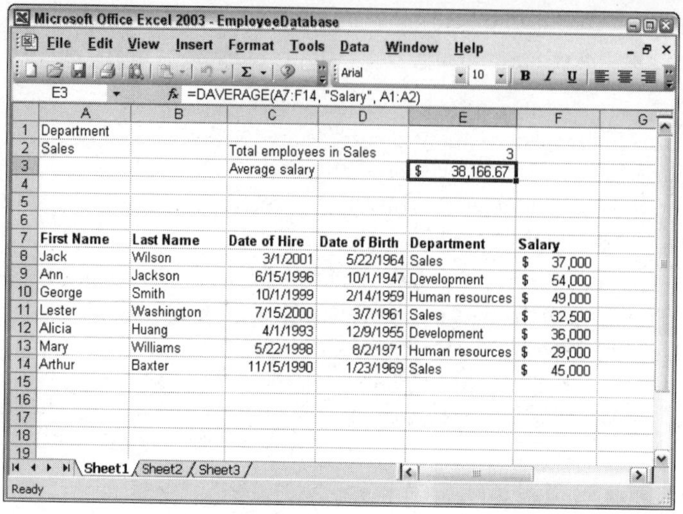

	A	B	C	D	E	F	G
1	Department						
2	Sales		Total employees in Sales		3		
3			Average salary		$ 38,166.67		
4							
5							
6							
7	First Name	Last Name	Date of Hire	Date of Birth	Department	Salary	
8	Jack	Wilson	3/1/2001	5/22/1964	Sales	$ 37,000	
9	Ann	Jackson	6/15/1996	10/1/1947	Development	$ 54,000	
10	George	Smith	10/1/1999	2/14/1959	Human resources	$ 49,000	
11	Lester	Washington	7/15/2000	3/7/1961	Sales	$ 32,500	
12	Alicia	Huang	4/1/1993	12/9/1955	Development	$ 36,000	
13	Mary	Williams	5/22/1998	8/2/1971	Human resources	$ 29,000	
14	Arthur	Baxter	11/15/1990	1/23/1969	Sales	$ 45,000	
15							
16							
17							
18							
19							

Figure 28-6 *The completed worksheet showing the results of the database functions*

Done!

REVIEW

This session showed you how to use Excel and VBA to work with database data.

- A database organizes data into records and fields.
- In Excel, records are represented by rows; fields are represented by columns.
- To sort the records in a table, use the `Range.Sort` method.
- To filter the records in a table, use the `AutoFilter` method.
- The database statistical functions are used to extract summary information from a table.

QUIZ YOURSELF

1. What should be at the top of each column in a database table? (See the "Database Fundamentals" section.)
2. What is the purpose of a secondary sort key? (See the "Sorting Data" section.)
3. What method is used in VBA code to filter a database table? (See the "Filtering Data" section.)
4. Suppose you do not want to design a user form for use with a database table. Do you have any other options? If so, what? (See the "Data Entry Forms" section.)
5. How is a criterion created for use with a database statistical function? (See the "Database Functions" section.)

Creating Add-Ins

**30 Min.
To Go**

Most Excel applications are distributed as workbooks, as you learned in Session 25; however, there's another way to distribute an application — as an add-in, which is preferred in certain circumstances. This session explains how to create and use Excel add-ins.

Add-Ins versus Workbooks

When deciding whether to create your application as a workbook or as an add-in, you need to know how the two approaches differ. There are more similarities than differences between workbooks and add-ins. In fact, an add-in starts out as a workbook and can contain worksheets with data as well as VBA code. It is converted to an add-in when you decide how to distribute it.

Excel comes with several add-ins that provide tools for specialized tasks, such as the Analysis Toolpak and Euro Currency Tools.

An add-in differs from a workbook in several ways:

- The workbook window is hidden and cannot be unhidden. This means that data in a worksheet that is part of an add-in cannot be displayed to the user unless it is copied to a visible worksheet.
- The programs (macros) in an add-in are not displayed in Excel's Macros dialog box.
- An add-in is not installed using the usual File ⇨ Open command, but rather using the Add-In Manager (covered later in this session).
- The IsAddIn property of the ThisWorkbook object is True.

You can use an add-in for anything you could use a workbook for except displaying data and charts. However, an add-in can contain user forms. The three most common reasons you might use an add-in are:

- To provide VBA programs (macros) for the user to run. For example, an add-in could contain a collection of VBA procedures to apply special formatting to the user's worksheets.
- To provide functions for use in worksheets. Your add-in could contain an assortment of specialized accounting functions that the user can use in his own worksheet, similar to Excel's built-in worksheet functions.
- To provide data the application needs access to but that the user does not need to see. An add-in could, for example, contain a worksheet with several tables of interest rate or depreciation information that is used by the application.

 Even though an add-in's macros are not displayed in the Macros dialog box, you can run them by entering the macro name in the Macro Name field of the dialog box. This is not recommended as a way to have your end-users run your macros, however. You should provide toolbar buttons for this purpose.

When would you want to distribute an application as an add-in instead of as a regular workbook? If your application does not contain worksheet data or charts that the user needs to see, an add-in is almost always preferred over a workbook. There are several potential advantages:

- Less chance for confusion. Because add-in worksheets are always hidden, there is less chance for a user to confuse your application's worksheets with her own workbook's worksheets.
- Easier access to the application. After it's installed on the user's system, an add-in is always available through the Excel Add-In Manager. An add-in can also be loaded automatically when Excel starts.
- Easier access to custom functions. A function in an add-in can be accessed without qualifying the function name with the workbook name.

It's important to remember that the add-in-versus-workbook choice is not always clear cut. Many custom applications could be distributed either way, so there's not always one correct choice.

Creating an Add-In

The steps for creating an add-in are simple. The development of the application itself is essentially the same regardless of whether you are distributing it as a workbook or as an add-in. If the application contains macros, you must provide a way to execute them because, as mentioned earlier in this session, they are not accessible from the Excel Macros dialog box. Most often this is done by creating a custom toolbar, as covered in Session 16.

Be sure to test the application when another workbook is active because this is the way an add-in must be used (an add-in is never the active workbook). After the testing is completed, use the techniques covered in Session 24 to lock the project's code against viewing and manipulation.

A workbook that is going to be saved as an add-in must contain at least one worksheet, even if it is empty.

By convention, add-in files have the .xla extension. This is not required, and you can use another extension if you want to, but I recommend staying with the usual extension to avoid confusion.

To create the add-in, perform the following steps:

1. In Excel, select File ⇨ Properties to display the Properties dialog box for the workbook. Select the Summary tab (see Figure 29-1).

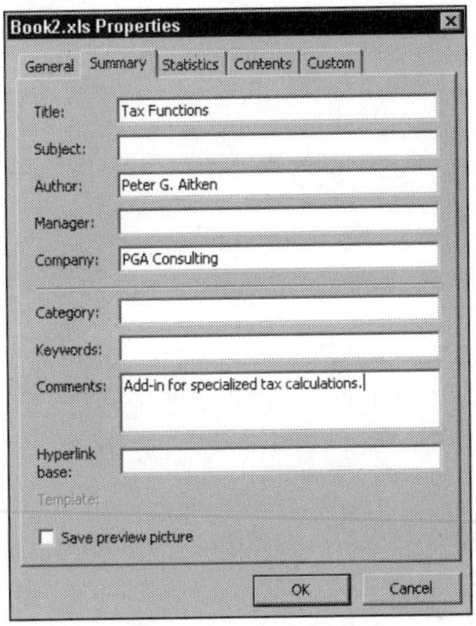

Figure 29-1   Entering property information for an add-in

2. Enter a title for the add-in in the Title field and a description in the Comments field. This information is displayed in the Add-In Manager and can be helpful to the end user. Click OK to close the Properties dialog box.

3. Select File ⇨ Save As.
4. From the Save As Type list, select Microsoft Excel Add-In (*.xla).
5. Select a folder for the file, if necessary, and enter a name in the File Name field.
6. Click Save.

20 Min. To Go

Distributing an Add-In

There's nothing more to distributing an add-in than giving your users a copy of the .xla file that you created. The file can be placed in any location on the disk as long as this location is remembered because the user has to locate the file to use it in Excel (this is explained in the next section).

Using Excel's Add-In Manager

The Add-In Manager lets the user locate and install add-ins. To open the Add-in Manager, select Tools ⇨ Add-Ins from the Excel menu. The Add-Ins dialog box, shown in Figure 29-2, lists the currently available add-ins. Any add-ins that are installed display a check mark in the adjacent box.

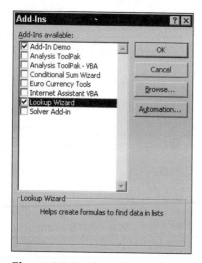

Figure 29-2 *The Add-Ins dialog box lists available add-ins, with installed ones checked.*

Excel automatically detects add-ins located in the Library default folder, which is usually `c:\program files\Microsoft Office\Office11\Library`. To let Excel know about add-ins located elsewhere, do the following:

1. Click the Browse button to open the Browse dialog box.
2. Navigate to the folder containing the add-in file.
3. Select the add-in file and then click OK.

Opening Add-Ins with File ⇨ Open

An add-in can be opened in Excel using the File ⇨ Open command. This opens the add-in as a regular workbook, and its worksheets are then visible. However, it is not considered installed. Because you usually do not want your users opening add-ins in this way, it is a good idea to keep add-in files in a different location from workbook files.

After Excel knows about an add-in, its title (the same title that was entered in the Properties dialog box when the add-in was created, as described earlier in this session) is included in the list in the Add-Ins dialog box. To install the add-in, which makes its commands and functions available in the workbook, put a check mark next to its name in the Add-Ins dialog box. Remove this check mark to uninstall the add-in and free up memory.

 If you load an add-in, it is automatically loaded the next time you start Excel. You must explicitly unload it if you do not want it available.

Events in Add-Ins

There are two workbook events particularly important for add-ins (although they are used in regular workbooks as well). These are Workbook_Open and Workbook_BeforeClose. Recall from earlier in this session that the macros in an add-in are not listed in Excel's Macro dialog box. This means you must provide some way for the user to run the macros (assuming the add-in has macros, which not all do). You usually do this by creating a custom toolbar that has buttons associated with the macros. The Workbook_Open event procedure is the place to put the code to create and display this toolbar, and the Workbook_BeforeClose event procedure is the place to hide it (when the add-in is being unloaded). An example of this is shown in the add-in demo later in this session.

Functions in Add-Ins

One common way that add-ins are used is to provide custom functions for use in the worksheet. You could, for example, create an add-in with a collection of specialized tax functions. When the add-in is installed, these functions are available for use in worksheet formulas, similar to Excel's built-in functions.

To be available in a worksheet, an add-in function must follow these rules:

- It must be located in a code module within the add-in and not in a module associated with a specific worksheet or in the ThisWorkbook module.
- It must be declared with the Public keyword (which is VBA's default).
- It must be a function procedure — that is, it must return a value.

When an add-in is loaded, any public functions it contains in code modules are listed in Excel's Insert Function dialog box in the User-Defined category. This is true of all public functions, not just those in add-ins. Look at Figure 29-3, for example. The Insert Function dialog box lists four functions in the User Defined category. Three of these functions are defined in the PERSONAL.XLS workbook; the fourth, called OneHalfOf, is defined in an installed add-in. Note that there's no way to tell if a function is defined in an add-in or in the current workbook because the function name is not qualified by a workbook name in either case. This makes no practical difference, however, because the functions are used the same way.

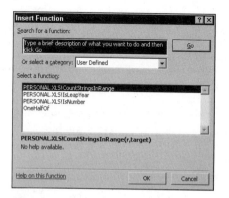

Figure 29-3   *Add-in functions are listed in the Insert Function dialog box.*

 An add-in may well contain functions that are intended only for internal use in the add-in itself, not for use in a worksheet. To prevent these functions from appearing in the Insert Function dialog box, declare them with the `Private` keyword instead of `Public`.

 If a worksheet uses a function that is defined in an add-in but the add-in is not installed, that worksheet cell displays `#NAME?`.

Using VBA to Manipulate Add-Ins

The `Application` object's `AddIns` collection contains all of the add-ins that Excel knows about (those listed in the Add-Ins dialog box). You can add an add-in to this collection using its Add method. This has the same effect as browsing for the add-in from the Add-Ins dialog box, covered earlier in this session. The syntax is

```
Add Filename, Copy
```

Filename is the name of the add-in file, including path information, and *Copy* is an optional True/False argument that specifies whether the add-in file should be copied to Excel's Library folder. The default is False. You should always set Copy to True if the add-in file resides on a removable disk, and you may want to do so at other times as well.

There is no direct way to remove an add-in from the `AddIns` **collection. To do so, you must set the** `Installed` **property to False in code.**

To use an add-in, it must be installed. This is done by setting the add-in's `Installed` property to True. You access members of the `AddIns` collection by the add-in's `Name` property, which is the same as the title displayed in the Add-Ins dialog box. For example, this code installs the add-in with the title "Analysis Toolpak":

```
Application.AddIns("Analysis Tookpak").Installed = True
```

If the specified add-in is not available (that is, not in the `AddIns` collection), a Subscript Out of Range error occurs (error code = 9). It is therefore advisable to use error trapping to deal with this possibility. Listing 29-1 shows a procedure that installs an add-in and displays a message to the user if the add-in is not available.

Listing 29-1 *A procedure to install an add-in*

```
Public Sub InstallAddIn(AddInName As String)

On Error Resume Next
AddIns(AddInName).Installed = True
If Err = 9 Then
    MsgBox "The add-in " & AddInName & " is not available."
End If

End Sub
```

VBA's error-trapping tools are covered in Session 27.

If an add-in is already installed, setting its `Installed` **property to True has no effect.**

An Add-In Demonstration

**10 Min.
To Go**

To complete this session, you will now walk through all the steps required to create and use an Excel add-in. To keep things simple, the add-in contains only two elements: a function that can be used in the worksheet and a short program that can be called to format part of the worksheet. When installed, the add-in displays a toolbar that enables the user to call the program.

The first step is to start Excel. Use the new, blank workbook that is created when Excel starts up. This add-in does not require any worksheets, but remember that an add-in must have at least one worksheet. To reduce the size of the add-in file, delete Sheet2 and Sheet3 as follows:

1. Make the worksheet active.
2. Select Edit ⇨ Delete Sheet.
3. If prompted, select Delete.
4. Repeat for the other worksheet.

Before continuing, use the File ⇨ Save command to save the workbook as AddInDemo.wks.

Code the Function

The function in this add-in calculates one-half of a value and can be used in the worksheet like other Excel functions. This is not something for which you would write a real add-in function, but remember this demo is to illustrate how to create an add-in. Here are the required steps:

1. Press Alt+F11 to open the VBA editor.
2. In the project window, right-click the project VBAProject (AddInDemo.xls) and then select Properties from the pop-up menu to display the Project Properties dialog box (see Figure 29-4).

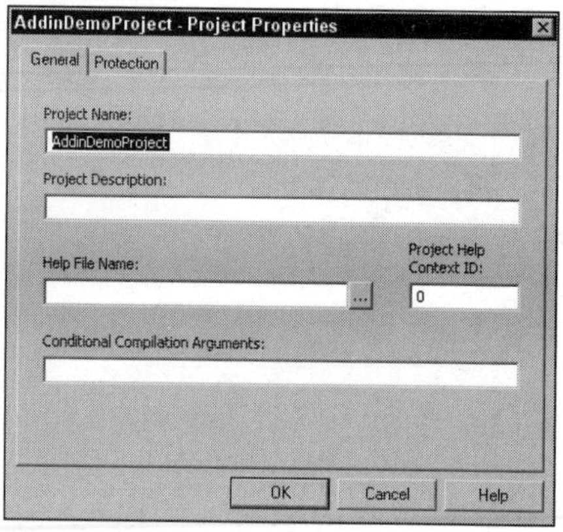

Figure 29-4   *Changing the project name for the add-in project*

3. Change the Project Name to AddInDemoProject; then click OK.
4. Select Insert ⇨ Module to add a new code module to the project.
5. Use the Insert ⇨ Procedure to add a function named OneHalfOf to the module.
6. Edit the function as shown in Listing 29-2.

Listing 29-2 *The OneHalfOf function*

```
Public Function OneHalfOf(value)

OneHalfOf = value / 2

End Function
```

Code the Program

The program, or macro, in the add-in is also simple. It formats the current region as bold-face (this is the area of cells containing data around the active cell). To create this macro, use the Insert ⇨ Procedure command to add a sub procedure named FormatBoldFace to the code module; then edit the procedure as shown in Listing 29-3.

Listing 29-3 *The FormatBoldFace procedure*

```
Public Sub FormatBoldFace()

Dim r As Range

Set r = Selection.CurrentRegion
r.Font.Bold = True

End Sub
```

Create the Toolbar

The user needs some way to run the FormatBoldFace macro. The following steps provide a custom toolbar with a button for that purpose.

1. Select View ⇨ Toolbars ⇨ Customize to display the Customize dialog box.
2. Click the Toolbars tab.
3. Click the New button; Excel prompts you for a name for the new toolbar.
4. Enter MyToolbar and then click OK.

At this point the new toolbar is displayed in Excel, and the Toolbars pane of the Customize dialog box is still open (you may need to move the Customize dialog box to see the new toolbar). The next steps add a button to the new toolbar and link that button with the FormatBoldFace macro.

1. In the Customize dialog box, click the Commands tab.
2. In the categories list, select Macros (see Figure 29-5).

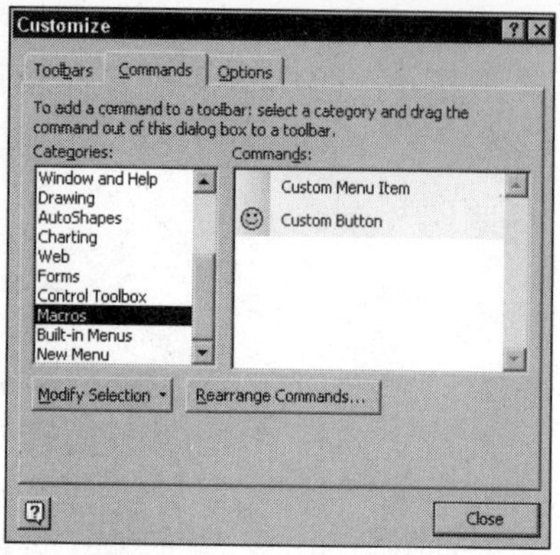

Figure 29-5   *Adding a custom button to the add-in toolbar*

3. From the Commands list, drag the Custom Button item (the one with the smiley face), and drop it on the new toolbar.

4. Right-click the button that you just added to the toolbar and then select Assign macro from the pop-up menu.

5. In the Assign Macro dialog box that displays, select FormatBoldFace from the list of macros; then click OK.

6. In the Customize dialog box, click the Toolbars tab.

7. Remove the check mark next to MyToolbar so it will not be displayed by default.

8. Click Close.

> **Note**
>
> **For this project the custom toolbar button retains its default smiley face icon. Please refer to Session 16 for information on how to change a toolbar button's icon.**

At this point the required toolbar has been created. You now need to create the code that displays the toolbar when the add-in is installed, and hide it if the add-in is uninstalled.

1. In the VBA Editor, double-click the ThisWorkbook item in AddInDemoProject.

2. In the editing window, select Workbook in the object list at the upper left. VBA automatically enters the outline of the Workbook_Open event procedure.

3. Enter the following line of code in the event procedure:

   ```
   Toolbars("MyToolbar").Visible = True
   ```

4. From the event list at the upper right of the editing window, select BeforeClose. VBS enters the outline of the Workbook_BeforeClose event procedure.

5. Enter the following line of code in the procedure:

   ```
   Toolbars("MyToolbar").Visible = False
   ```

Securing the Code and Saving the Add-In

As mentioned earlier in this session, you should always lock the VBA code in an add-in to prevent the user from viewing or changing it, by performing the following steps:

1. Right-click the AddInDemoProject item in the Project window, and select Properties from the pop-up menu.
2. In the Properties dialog box, click the Protection tab.
3. Select the Lock Project for Viewing option.
4. Enter a password twice, as directed.
5. Click OK.

The final step is to save the workbook as an add-in:

1. From the Excel menu, select File ⇨ Save As.
2. Select Microsoft Excel Add-in in the Save As Type list.
3. If desired, navigate to a different drive and/or folder.
4. Accept the default name, which is AddInDemo.xla (because the workbook had been saved as AddInDemo.wks).
5. Click OK.

Your add-in is complete and ready for testing.

Testing the Add-In

To test the add-in, be sure to close the AddInDemo workbook; alternatively, you can quit Excel and start it again; then:

1. Select Tools ⇨ Add-Ins to display the Add-Ins dialog box.
2. If you saved the add-in file to Excel's default add-in folder, AddInDemo is already listed, and you can proceed to step 5; otherwise, continue with step 3.
3. Click the Browse button, and navigate to the location of the AddInDemo.xla file.
4. Select the file and then click OK. AddInDemo is now listed in the Add-Ins dialog box.
5. Click the add-in name to place a check next to it.
6. Click OK to close the Add-Ins dialog box.

Your custom toolbar is displayed. Test it by entering data in a block of worksheet cells; then, with the cell pointer in the block, click the toolbar button. All the cells are now formatted in boldface.

To test the function, use it as a worksheet cell. The OneHalfOf function is also listed in the Insert Function dialog box.

To complete your testing, select Tools ⇨ Add-Ins to again display the Add-Ins dialog box, and remove the check mark from the AddInDemo entry. The custom toolbar is no longer displayed.

Done!

REVIEW

This session showed you how to create Excel add-ins and explained why you should distribute some applications as add-ins rather than as workbooks.

- An add-in differs from a workbook primarily in that an add-in's worksheets cannot be viewed.

- To create an add-in from a workbook, use the Save As command to save it as an Excel Add-In.

- An add-in is loaded into Excel using the Tools ➪ Add-Ins command.

- Public functions defined in an add-in can be used similar to Excel's built-in functions.

- You should always lock an add-in's VBA code to prevent unauthorized viewing and modifications.

QUIZ YOURSELF

1. Your application includes a chart sheet for the user to view. Should you distribute this application as an add-in? Please explain. (See the "Add-Ins versus Workbooks" section.)

2. You want to write an add-in function that will be available for use in a worksheet. In what VBA module should the code be placed? (See the "Functions in Add-Ins" section.)

3. How does the end user run a program, or macro, that is defined in an add-in? (See the "Add-Ins versus Workbooks" section.)

4. How would you write a VBA function in an add-in that you do not want available for use in the worksheet? (See the "Functions in Add-Ins" section.)

5. What event is triggered when an add-in is installed? (See the "Events in Add-Ins" section.)

Adding Online Help to Your Application

**30 Min.
To Go**

Almost every computer application comes with some form of online help, and there's no reason your custom Excel applications should be any different. Though you might not need help for simple applications, you have several options in the event you do.

Online Help for Excel

The term *online help* means that help information is available to the user on his computer while he is using the application — there is no need to locate and thumb through a printed manual. In many cases, online help provides some elements of context sensitivity; that is, the help information displayed at a given moment is related to what the user is doing. When your application grows to the point where its use is not intuitive, you should consider including online help in the application.

There are several ways to provide help for your Excel applications. Some use only Excel and its components; others use external components that are part of the Windows operating system. Take a look at these in turn.

Using Excel Components for Help

Given the power and flexibility of Excel, it is not surprising that you can provide help for your applications without having to use another application. Excel provides several methods for creating help for your users.

Putting Help in the Worksheet

One of the simplest help approaches is to include help information directly in the worksheet. If you need to explain to the user what value should be entered into a worksheet cell, put the information in an adjacent cell. It's always visible, and there's no need for the user to go looking for it. It does place limitations on your worksheet layout, however, and cannot hold too much text without taking up a lot of room on-screen.

Another simple approach is to place help text in comments associated with the cell (select the cell; then select Insert ➪ Comment). When the mouse pointer hovers over a cell with a comment, the comment displays automatically. At other times, the cell displays a small red triangle in its upper right corner to indicate that it contains a comment. (In your general instructions, you can inform users that help information is located in cell comments.) In addition to taking up little of the valuable space in the worksheet, the advantage here is that each piece of help information is directly associated with the relevant cell. Figure 30-1 shows the Loan Calculator worksheet with a comment containing help information.

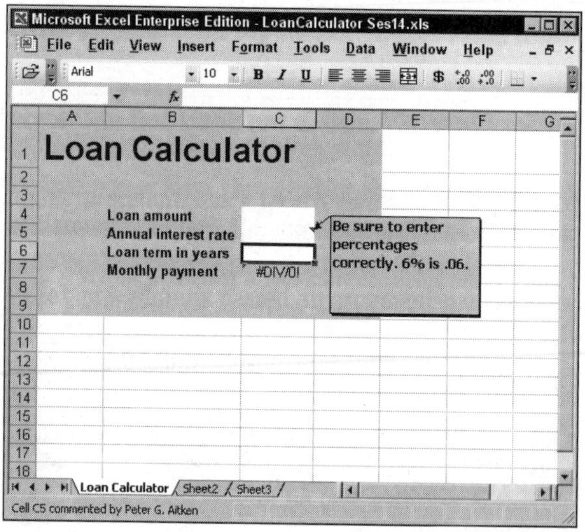

Figure 30-1   *Putting help information in cell comments*

Putting Help in a Separate Worksheet

Instead of putting help information in a worksheet along with other worksheet components, you can devote one or more entire worksheets to help. By assigning the worksheet an appropriate name, such as Application Help, it will be clear to users where to find this information.

Using a worksheet for help information provides a lot more flexibility than you might think. You are not limited to the row-and-column grid arrangement that is the default for worksheets. For example, you can merge two or more cells to create attractive tabular layouts. You can also use Excel's Control Toolbox toolbar to place other elements on the worksheet, such as graphics (using the Image control) and scrolling text boxes (using the TextBox control). The Drawing toolbar can be used to add various graphical elements, such as organizational charts and clip art.

Using the Drawing and Control Toolbox toolbars is beyond the scope of this book. You can find information in Excel's online help.

To merge two or more cells, select the cells, press Ctrl+1 to display the Format Cells dialog box, and then select the Merge Cells option on the Alignment tab.

Putting help information in a worksheet does not work if you are going to distribute your application as an add-in, because an add-in's worksheets are never visible. You have to use one of the other techniques presented in this session.

When help information is located in a separate worksheet, you are not limited to letting the user display the help worksheet manually (by clicking its tab). You can use a CommandButton control in the main worksheet to display the help worksheet. This option opens up a lot of possibilities. For example, you could create several help worksheets, each with help information relevant to a different part of the application. Then, by placing Command Button controls at strategic locations in the application's worksheets, you could let the user display the relevant help information.

To demonstrate this technique of using CommandButton controls to display help, you are going to add help information to the Loan Calculator application from an earlier session. There's only one button and one help worksheet in this demo, but the techniques are exactly the same to create multiple help worksheets.

To begin, start Excel and open the Loan Calculator workbook that you last modified in Session 24. Then:

**20 Min.
To Go**

1. Activate Sheet3, and then select Edit ➪ Delete Sheet to delete the worksheet. The application does not need this worksheet, and deleting it reduces clutter in the application.

2. Activate Sheet2 and change its name to "Help," by double-clicking the sheet's tab and entering the new name.

3. Enter whatever help information you want in this worksheet, formatting it as desired.

4. Activate the Loan Calculator worksheet.

5. Select Tools ⇨ Protection ⇨ Unprotect Sheet, then enter your password. This is necessary because you cannot add controls to a locked worksheet.

6. Select View ⇨ Toolbars ⇨ Control Toolbox to display the Control Toolbox, as shown in Figure 30-2.

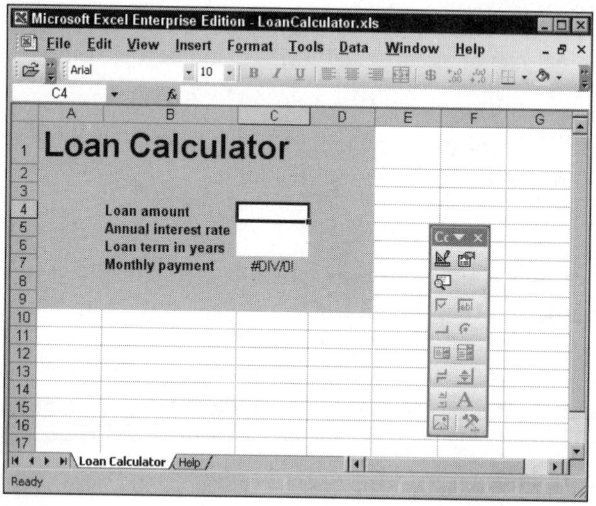

Figure 30-2 *Adding a button control to the Loan Calculator worksheet*

7. Click the Command Button icon in the Control Toolbox, then drag on the worksheet to place the button.

8. Right-click the button and select Properties from the popup menu. Excel displays the Properties window for the control (see Figure 30-3).

9. Change the Caption property to "Help."

10. Click the X button at the top right of the Properties window to close it.

11. Double-click the button to open the code-editing window in the VBA Editor. The Click event procedure is displayed (this is the default event for a Command Button control).

12. Enter the following line of code in the Click event procedure:

```
Worksheets("Help").Activate
```

Properties		☒
CommandButton1 CommandButton		▾

Alphabetic | Categorized |

(Name)	CommandButton1	
Accelerator		
AutoLoad	False	
AutoSize	False	▾
BackColor	☐ &H8000000F&	
BackStyle	1 - fmBackStyleOpaque	
Caption	CommandButton1	
Enabled	True	
Font	Arial	
ForeColor	■ &H80000012&	
Height	20.25	
Left	145.5	
Locked	True	
MouseIcon	(None)	
MousePointer	0 - fmMousePointerDefault	
Picture	(None)	
PicturePosition	7 - fmPicturePositionAboveCenter	
Placement	2	
PrintObject	True	
Shadow	False	
TakeFocusOnClick	True	
Top	29.25	
Visible	True	
Width	87	
WordWrap	False	

Figure 30-3   *The Command Button control's Properties window*

13. Switch back to the Excel application.

14. Click the Exit Design Mode button in the Control Toolbox (the top left button). This switches Excel from design mode, in which you can place and move controls, and activates the button so clicking it runs its Click event procedure.

15. Click the X button at the top right of the Control Toolbox to close it.

16. Select Tools ⇨ Protection ⇨ Protect Sheet to turn protection back on (enter your password as prompted).

17. Select File ⇨ Save to save the modified workbook.

 You can tell if you are in design mode by the appearance of the Design Mode button on the Control Toolbox. When in design mode, the button appears depressed; when not in design mode, it does not appear depressed.

The workbook is complete and should look something like Figure 30-4. You can try it out — click the Help button and the Help worksheet is activated.

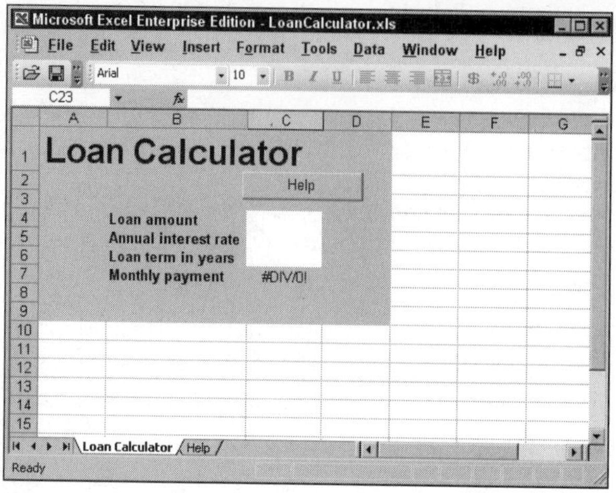

Figure 30-4 The completed worksheet with its Help button

It would be a simple matter to add another CommandButton control (on the Help worksheet) to hide Help and return to the main Loan Calculator worksheet.

Putting Help in a User Form

The final way to provide help using Excel components is by means of a user form. This technique has the advantage that the help information is in a separate window from the worksheet, so you can arrange both on the screen to view at the same time. By displaying the user form as a modeless form, the user is able to leave the help information on the screen while switching back to Excel. You can set up the application to display a user form with a toolbar button, a key combination, or a command button.

User forms were covered in Sessions 19 through 22.

Using External Components for Help

10 Min.
To Go

You may want to go beyond Excel's capabilities to provide online help for some applications. Two of the most popular ways to do this are covered in this section.

HTML Help

HTML Help is the current standard for providing help for Windows applications. It is called HTML Help because the information is organized in one or more HTML (hypertext markup language) files. Before the help is distributed, the HTML files and related information, such as an index and table of contents, are compiled into a single compressed help file that has the .chm extension. The help is viewed using the HTML Help Viewer, a component that is part of the Windows operating system and is therefore available to all applications. Most applications that you use under Windows use HTML Help for their online help system.

One nice feature of HTML help is that you can associate a numerical identifier, called a *help context ID*, with specific information in the help file. Then your application can display this particular part of help by using this ID. Since an explanation of designing and creating help with HTML Help is beyond the scope of this book, you can find detailed information and downloads at the Microsoft Web site (go to www.msdn.microsoft.com and search for "HTML Help").

Several specialized HTML Help–authoring applications are available, which can simplify an otherwise complex task. The HTML Help Workshop, available free from Microsoft, is a good place to start. Commercial products provide more power at a price.

Once you have created your HTML Help, you need to associate it with your application. You can do this by setting a project property, as follows:

1. Right-click the VBA project name in the Project window and select Properties from the popup menu.

2. On the General tab (see Figure 30-5), enter the name of the compiled help file in the Help File Name field. Include the path where the help file will be installed (unless it is in the same folder as the application itself, in which case no path is needed).

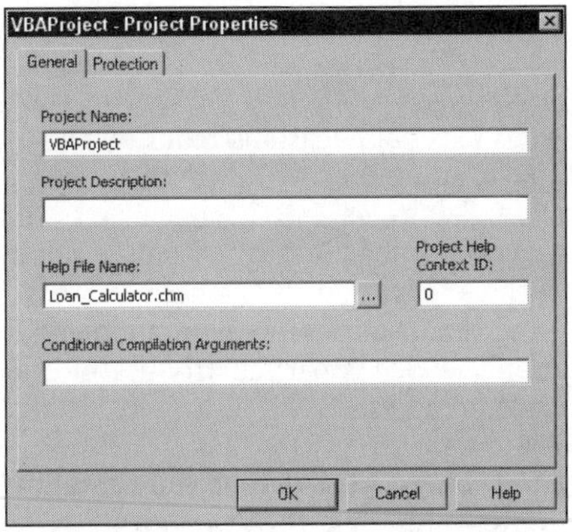

Figure 30-5   Associating a help file with an Excel application

3. Click OK.

You can achieve the same result in VBA code by setting the project's `HelpFile` property in code. This code could be placed in the `Workbook_Open` event procedure:

```
ThisWorkbook.VBProject.HelpFile = ThisWorkbook.Path & _
    "\HelpFileName.chm"
```

Note how this code uses the `Path` property to determine the location where the application is installed. This assumes that the help file is installed to the same folder, which is always a good idea.

To display HTML help from your application, call the `Help` method from VBA code. The syntax is:

```
Application.Help HelpFile, HelpContextID
```

`HelpFile` is the name of the compiled help file. This argument is optional, but if omitted, the call to the `Help` method brings up Excel's own help. HelpContextID is the ID number of the help topic to be displayed. If omitted, the help file's default topic (as defined when you created the help file) is displayed.

The F1 key is traditionally associated with online help. In Excel, this key is associated with Excel's own help file.

You have several options for displaying your application's online help using the `Help` method. Any technique for executing VBA code is usable. This includes:

- A VBA macro associated with a custom toolbar button.
- VBA code executed from a control, such as a Command Button, that is placed in a worksheet.
- VBA code executed from a control on a user form.
- A macro associated with a key combination.

Web-Based Help

The final technique for providing online help in your Excel applications relies on the Internet and the fact that you can insert hyperlinks in a worksheet. To use this technique, the help information must be created as one or more Web pages — HTML documents that are available locally or on a Web server. If the help pages are linked locally — that is, not over the Web — they have to be distributed along with the application. If they are Web-based, your end-users need Web access to use this help, and this is becoming more and more common. The technique of providing application help on the Web is particularly useful in organizations that have an intranet because you can control access.

One significant advantage of using Web-based help is that you can update the help material without having to distribute new files to your users. A disadvantage is that users must be online to access help.

The details of authoring Web pages and publishing them to the Web are beyond the scope of this book. To follow the techniques presented here, you must know the URL (Web address) of the page(s) that contain the help information (for Web links). Then do the following:

1. Select the worksheet cell where you want the help link displayed.
2. Select Insert ⇨ Hyperlink to display the Insert Hyperlink dialog box (see Figure 30-6).

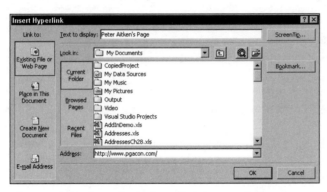

Figure 30-6   *Inserting a hyperlink in a worksheet*

3. In the Link To section, select Existing File or Web Page.
4. Enter the text to be displayed in the worksheet in the Text to Display field.
5. For a Web link, enter the complete URL of the target file in the Address field (for example, `http://www.mycompany.com/help/finance.html`). For a local link, enter the complete path to the file (for example, `c:\documents\help\finance.htm`). You can also use the tools in the center of the dialog box to browse for the file.
6. Click OK.

If you enter a local address for a file, the help file must be installed to the same path on the user's system.

A hyperlink in a worksheet is displayed as underlined in a special color, blue by default. When the mouse pointer is over a hyperlink, it changes to a pointing hand. Clicking the hyperlink opens the target file in the browser, which is usually Microsoft Internet Explorer on most systems. This is a separate window from Excel, so the user can keep the help information displayed while working in the workbook.

You cannot select a cell containing a hyperlink by simply clicking it because that activates the link. You must hold the mouse button down for a few seconds, until the mouse pointer changes from a pointing hand to a cross.

Done!

REVIEW

This session showed you several techniques for providing online help in your Excel applications.

- Online help provides information on the computer screen so the user does not have to use a book or other printed material.

- Help information can be placed directly in a worksheet, either as cell comments or cell text.

- One or more custom user forms can be used to display help information.

- You can display help using a toolbar button or a command button placed directly in the worksheet.

- The Windows standard help format, HTML help, can be used with an Excel project.

- By placing hyperlinks in a worksheet, you can link your application to help information located on the Web.

QUIZ YOURSELF

1. Name one advantage of using cell comments for help information. (See the "Putting Help in the Worksheet" section.)

2. What help techniques are not appropriate for applications that will be distributed as add-ins? Please explain. (See the "Putting Help in a Separate Worksheet" section.)

3. Name an advantage of putting help in a user form instead of in a worksheet. (See the "Putting Help in a User Form" section.)

4. How does an Excel application display a topic in HTML help? (See the "HTML Help" section.)

1. What happens when an untrapped runtime error occurs in a VBA program?
2. Where should you place error-handling code?
3. In the following procedure with error handling, what's missing?

```
Public SomeProcedure()

' Variable declarations go here.

On Error Goto ErrorHandler

' Procedure code goes here.

ErrorHandler:

' Error handling code goes here.

End Sub
```

4. Procedure A has error-handling code, but procedure B does not. When procedure A calls Procedure B and a runtime error occurs in procedure B, what happens?
5. What does it mean if `Err.Number` is 0?
6. How is data organized in a database?
7. When using the `Range.Sort` method to sort data, how many sort keys can you use?
8. What does the term *filtering* mean when referring to a database?
9. How can you automatically create a data entry form for a database table?
10. True or False: You should delete all empty worksheets from a workbook that will be distributed as an add-in.
11. True or False: You can create HTML from within Excel.

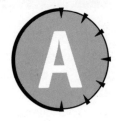
Answers to Part Reviews

Following are the answers to the Reviews at the end of each part of the book.

Friday Evening Review Answers

1. A series of instructions to the computer.
2. Press Alt+F11, or select Tools ⇨ Macro ⇨ Visual Basic Editor.
3. Select Insert ⇨ Module from the VBA Editor menu.
4. Export the module from the first project; then import it into the second project.
5. A piece of information that identifies or controls some aspects of an object's appearance or behavior.
6. By placing a dollar sign ($) in front of the column letter and the row number.
7. A property is a piece of information associated with the object; a method carries out an action.
8. No. By using named arguments, you can include them in any order.
9. The For Each...Next statement.
10. Never. The Application object is always available as an implicit reference.
11. Call the Workbook object's SaveCopyAs method.
12. The Workbook.PrintOut method.
13. Use the Workbook.ActiveSheet method.
14. Set the Worksheet object's Name property.
15. Set the DisplayAlerts property to False.
16. Nothing is the value of an object reference that does not reference any object.
17. Use the Worksheets.Count property.
18. If this property is True, a backup copy is created each time the workbook is saved.

19. By reading the `Workbook.FullName` property.

20. Call its `Activate` method.

21. If the `Workbook` object's `Saved` property is True.

22. You can use the line continuation character anywhere except within quoted text.

23. Trick question — there are no rules. You can use indentation to improve readability, but it does not affect how the program runs.

24. As the number of days since December 30, 1899.

25. 101, elements 0 through 100.

26. By using the `UBound` and `LBound` functions.

27. Variable scope refers to the parts of a program in which a variable is visible.

28. You would do it at the module level using the `Public` keyword.

Saturday Morning Review Answers

1. 2. Eleven divided by 3 gives 3 with 2 left over, hence the answer is 2.

2. True.

3. It depends. By default, it evaluates to False, but if the `Option Compare Text` statement is in effect, it evaluates to True.

4. With the `Is` operator: `Obj1 Is Obj2`.

5. No. `4 + 2 * 8` evaluates to 20 because of operator precedence that performs the multiplication first and the addition next. `(4 + 2) * 8` evaluates to 48 because the parentheses force the addition to be performed first.

6. No. Unless there is an `Else` clause, it is possible that no statements in the `If...End If` will be executed.

7. The `Else` part can be omitted if there is no code to be executed when none of the `Case` statements match.

8. The `Iif` function evaluates a condition and returns one value if it is True and another value if it is False.

9. The statements are guaranteed to be executed at least once only when the condition is placed at the end of the loop.

10. Never. While still supported, `While...Wend` has been supplanted by the more flexible `Do...Loop` statement.

11. There is no limit.

12. A function returns a value to the program while a sub procedure does not.

13. There is no limit, but good programming practice dictates that procedures should not be very long. A maximum of 30 to 40 lines of code is a reasonable target to shoot for.

14. The array name should be followed by empty parentheses.

15. By assigning the value to the function's name.

16. Yes, by declaring the variable with the `Static` keyword.

17. By enclosing it in # characters.

18. The DateAdd function.
19. InStr and InStrRev.
20. Call the StrConv function with the vbProperCase argument.
21. No. Upper- and lowercase versions of the same letter have different ASCII values.
22. Use the Left function.
23. The Range object.
24. The Range object's Value property returns a blank string.
25. The smallest range that contains all of the used cells in the worksheet.
26. Obtain a Range object that references the cell; then call the AddComment method.
27. Only one.
28. For single-cell ranges, they are the same. For multiple-cell ranges, Activate selects the one cell at the upper left corner of the range, while Select selects the entire range.

Saturday Afternoon Review Answers

1. Use the Range.Rows.Count and the Range.Columns.Count properties.
2. Columns in the active worksheet.
3. It moves over to the right to become column C.
4. Cell B2. The Cells property, when used with a single numeric argument, counts cells across and then down.
5. All cells in the SalesData worksheet.
6. Use the Range.SpecialCells method with the xlCellTypeBlanks argument.
7. It does not change at all because the formula uses absolute cell references.
8. The column reference is adjusted to reflect the destination, but the row reference remains unchanged.
9. By using the syntax sheetname!CellReference.
10. All formulas begin with the = character.
11. When a formula in one cell references another cell that directly or indirectly references the first cell.
12. The PMT function.
13. The DOLLAR function.
14. Yes, by using the WorksheetFunction object.
15. Set the Range.NumberFormat property.
16. Red, green, and blue.
17. The Range.Interior.Color property.
18. The width of one character in the default font.
19. The AutoFit method.

20. You would actually call two methods: Find to locate the first instance; then FindNext to find other instances.

21. Nothing.

22. Select View ⇨ Toolbars and then select the toolbar(s) to display or hide.

23. There are no buttons; new toolbars start out empty.

24. With the Customize dialog box displayed, right-click the button and then select Assign macro from the pop-up menu.

25. No. You must use the Attach command to associate a custom toolbar with a particular workbook.

26. A toolbar can be floating or docked.

Saturday Evening Review Answers

1. An embedded chart is on a regular worksheet along with data and other charts. A chart sheet is a single chart on a worksheet with no data or other elements.

2. You don't. Its position and size are determined by the sheet.

3. Call the Charts collection's Add method.

4. Call the Chart object's SetSourceData method.

5. Ch.ChartTitle.Font.Italics = True.

6. Charts("Sales Summary").PrintOut.

7. Call the Chart object's Protect method.

8. Call the ChartObject.BringToFront method.

9. A scatter chart plots values on the horizontal axis rather than categories.

10. Call the PrintOut method on the workbook's Charts collection.

11. Set the ChartObject.PrintObject property to False.

12. The form itself, the controls on the form, and the VBA code associated with the form.

13. By setting the UserForm.StartupPosition property to CenterScreen.

14. Call the UserForm.Hide method.

15. Only one OptionButton in a group can be on. This restriction does not apply to the CheckBox control.

16. By placing the OptionButton controls on a Frame control.

17. By double-clicking the control.

18. Set the CommandButton control's Default property to True.

19. The RefEdit control.

20. The CheckBox control.

21. The Enabled property.

Sunday Morning Review Answers

1. Just before the control loses the focus.
2. It can't. The double-click interval is a Windows operating system settings.
3. False. The Keycode argument identifies only the key. You must use the Shift argument to determine if the Shift key was pressed.
4. By setting the KeyCode argument to 0.
5. By using the Align commands on the Format menu.
6. Call the hidden control's ZOrder method with the fmTop argument.
7. Set the control's TabStop property to False.
8. By using the object name followed by an underscore and the event name.
9. Events on user forms.
10. The Workbook.SheetChange event.
11. By holding down the Shift key.
12. Data validation is the process of ensuring that the user does not enter invalid data, such as text when a number is expected.
13. In the ThisWorkbook module.
14. With the OnTime event.
15. By assigning a "modify" password from the Tools menu in the Save As dialog box.
16. False. A VBA project must be locked separately from any password assigned to the workbook, using the Protection tab in the Project Properties dialog box.
17. False. A bug prevents a program from operating properly but does not prevent it from running.
18. Always. Option Explicit is an important way to avoid bugs and errors.
19. A breakpoint causes program execution to pause on a specified line of code.
20. Step Over executes all code in a procedure and pauses when execution exits the procedure. Step Into executes the next line of code regardless of where it is located and then pauses.
21. Hover the mouse pointer over the variable name.
22. False. Watch values are updated only when the program enters break mode.
23. It doesn't. There's no way to find bugs other than by testing the program.
24. True. There is no way to run an Excel application without the Excel program.
25. In a class module.
26. False. Custom VBA classes can have no visual elements.
27. By deleting its Property Let procedure.
28. True.
29. By placing code in the Property Let procedure to check the new property value and accept it only if it is correct.

30. By using the standard `ObjectName.PropertyName` syntax.

31. Other than being in a class module, it is no different.

32. A method that is intended to be called only from within the class and not from code outside the class.

33. The `Terminate` event.

Sunday Afternoon Review Answers

1. A dialog box is displayed with information about the error, and the program terminates.

2. In the procedure where the error may occur.

3. The code needs an `Exit Sub` statement just before the `ErrorHandler:` label to prevent execution from entering the error handler when there has not been an error.

4. The error is passed up from procedure B to procedure A and is handled there.

5. No error has occurred.

6. Each entry is a record, and each record has the same fields.

7. A maximum of two.

8. To display only those records that meet certain criteria.

9. Put the cursor anywhere in the table and then select Data ⇨ Form.

10. False. To be distributed as an add-in, a workbook must contain at least one worksheet even if it is empty.

11. False. You need a separate application to create HTML help.

APPENDIX

What's on the Web Site

This appendix provides you with information on the contents of the companion Web site for this book, which you can find at www.wiley.com/compbooks/aitken. Here is what you will find:

- The self-assessment test
- Downloadable examples from the exercises in the book

The Self-Assessment Test

If you want to find out where you stand with your Excel programming knowledge before or after the course, you can take the self-assessment test, which consists of 83 multiple-choice and true or false questions. The test is divided by topics and is self-scoring for your convenience.

Downloadable Examples from the Exercises in the Book

All code listings of sample programs from the book are on the Web site.

Troubleshooting

If you have trouble with the Web site, please call the Customer Care phone number: (800) 762-2974. Outside the United States, call 1 (317) 572-3994. You can also contact Customer Service by e-mail at techsupdum@wiley.com. Wiley Publishing, Inc. will provide technical support only for installation and other general quality control items; for technical support on the applications themselves, consult the program's vendor or author.

Index

Symbols & Numbers

Continued

Continued

Continued

Continued

Continued

Continued

Continued